THE ULTIMATE BOOK OF

DOING UP **OLD JUNK**

THE ULTIMATE BOOK OF

DOING UP OLD JUNK

MEREHURST

First published in1999 by Merehurst Limited
Ferry House, 51–57 Lacy Road, Putney, London, SW15 1PR

ISBN 1 85391 870 9

A catalogue record of this book is available from the British Library.

Editor: Jackie Griffin
Project Editor: Angela Newton
Commissioning Editor: Anna Sanderson
Design Concept & Art Direction: Laura Jackson
Design & Editorial Assistance:
Axis Design, Sarah Wilde, Susan Cawthorne
Publishing Manager: Fia Fornari
Production Manager: Lucy Byrne
CEO & Publisher: Anne Wilson
UK Marketing & Sales Manager: Kathryn Harvey
International Sales Director: Mark Newman

Colour separation by Colourscan in Singapore
Printed in Singapore by Tien Wah Press

SAFETY GUIDELINES

Children's rooms

When working on projects for children's rooms, make sure that all materials, especially paints and varnishes, are non-toxic, and do not put anything that has small or loose parts within the reach of a baby. Always keep DIY equipment and materials, together with any unfinished projects, in a locked cupboard and out of the reach of children.

Cutting equipment

When working with a scalpel or craft knife, use a cutting mat or piece of thick card to protect the work surface. Always cut away from your body in case the knife slips, and do not place your other hand in the path of the scalpel blade.

Protective gloves

Wear protective gloves when using paint and varnish strippers, because both are caustic and should not be allowed in contact with the skin. If you find ordinary household rubber gloves cumbersome, try lightweight surgical gloves. However, do not wear rubber gloves when working with a heat source.

Step ladders

When using a step ladder, make sure that the base is secure and stable so that it will not slide or move when you are on it. Never stand on the top platform. Rather than leaning or stretching to reach difficult areas, adjust the ladder. Remove any paint or tools from the platform before moving the ladder.

Heat strippers

When using a hot air paint stripper protect your eyes with safety goggles and consider using cotton gloves. Do not wear loose fitting clothing which could get in the way of the heat source, and tie back long hair. Make sure that the work area is clear of anything which could catch alight, such as bedding or curtains, and never cover the floor with newspaper. Protect glass and plastic with a deflector when working near them with a heat stripper.

Ventilation

When using oil- and solvent-based adhesives, paints and varnishes, work in a well-ventilated area and do not allow naked flames or cigarettes nearby. Always wear a face mask to protect you from fumes and dust, even when working outdoors.

Safety goggles

Always wear safety goggles when you are doing any job that could produce dust or flying debris, such as paint stripping, sanding, sawing or hammering.

Electricity

If you have problems with an electrical tool, always unplug it before making any investigations or attempting to fix it. Keep power tools away from water. Before working on an electrical fitting or appliance, cut off the electricity supply either by unplugging the appliance or cutting off the power at the main fuse box.

CONVERSION CHARTS

UK	Australian
eggshell paint	semi-gloss enamel paint
emulsion glaze	acrylic clear varnish
emulsion paint	acrylic paint
gilt wax cream	gold wax
mutton cloth	(none, use a soft cotton cloth)
oil stencil stick	oil-based art and stencil crayons
paint kettle	(none, use a plastic container)
silk finish paint	low sheen paint
silk sheen paint	low sheen paint
tile primer	none
acrylic varnish	acrylic clear
vinyl matt paint	flat acrylic paint
vinyl paint	acrylic paint

UK	Australian
vinyl silk paint	low sheen acrylic paint
white spirit	mineral turpentine
wire wool	steel wool
yacht varnish	marine varnish

Metric	Imperial (approx)
1m	3ft
2.5cm	1in
6.5sq cm	1sq in
1litre	35fl oz
100g	3½oz

Contents

Introduction

COLLECTING AND DOING UP old pieces of junk is becoming a popular pastime. No longer an activity for simply the eccentric or short-of-cash, junk restoration is now big business, attracting interior designers, antiques dealers and anybody with an eye for something unique.

People start doing up junk for a variety of reasons. Many get given old family furniture that they just can't bear to throw away, others find that when clearing that bulging attic, they do own a spare chair (albeit in need of repair), afterall. Others simply admire the handiwork of their neighbours and friends, wishing that they too, could create a perfect style for their homes.

Whatever the reason, it's more than likely that what started as a money-saving mission becomes a passionate hobby. Once all of the old household junk has been used up, enthusiasts move on to different sources, checking out local sales, junk shops and even their neighbours' rubbish tips. Many end up with 'useful' bits that they don't actually need – although a little imagination can often turn one person's cast-off into another person's ideal gift.

Part of the appeal of doing up junk is the individuality involved. Any piece of junk could take on a whole host of different effects – the chosen look reflects the character of the person who uses the piece. Like the shade of paint covering the walls of your home, the furniture and accessories you use also reflect your personality. In fact, doing up old junk is the perfect solution to getting the piece of furniture that is just right for you. After endless, fruitless visits to expensive retailers, knowing exactly what you want but being unable to find it, transforming a piece of junk can provide the vital answer. Turning ugly, budget range furniture into something special saves money, frustration and unnecessary waste. In fact, recycling old junk is as good for the planet as it is for your pocket.

One of the main hurdles to overcome when doing up old junk is a lack of confidence. All too often, people jealously admire a friend's decorated furniture, adamant in the belief that they have neither the skills nor patience to achieve a similar effect. In fact, many experts willingly encourage people to think that decorative techniques take resources, skill and training, keeping an air of secrecy around their trade.

However, this book sets out to show that even the most elaborate, decorative finish can be achieved with a little patience and practice. Offering advice on all aspects of doing up old junk, and providing great ideas for both the beginner and more accomplished enthusiast, it should provide inspiration to go on and achieve your own individual style. With a few simple pieces of equipment, a little practice and a lot of enthusiasm, it's easy to see how one person's rubbish can become another person's gold.

Sourcing Junk

BY FAR, THE CHEAPEST and most resourceful place to find spare items of junk is your own home. Many people have old bits of furniture lying around in the attic or loft, not to mention unused items which are 'temporarily' stored in the garage or shed that tend to get forgotten and left to collect dust for months or even years. Many of these pieces tend to be useful 'hand-me-downs' offered by good-natured friends or family, which have now passed their useful life as newer, or more appropriate pieces of furniture are acquired for the home.

IT'S AMAZING HOW EVEN the most ugly piece of junk can be transformed so never dismiss a potential resource. In fact, even once you've used all the objects lying around your home, there's a good chance that friends or family would also be happy to hand over bits of junk; items that they have no real use for but just can't bear to throw away. Offering a good home to these objects – or even offering to restore and decorate them as a favour – can be just as much fun as renovating your own old pieces of junk.

Sales

Once you've used all of your immediate resources, or even if you can't quite find the piece you're looking for, begin to seek junk from further afield. House clearance sales, garage sales and local charity jumble sales can have great bargains – even if some cleaning and preparation work are going to be needed.

A whole range of large and small items tend to go on offer at an extremely good price. Tools and equipment, spare hinges and door handles are commonly available too, so if you

Children's furniture which has outlived its usefulness such as this simple doll's cradle is often found at garage sales

don't find a piece of junk you would like, be on the look out for useful accessories. Also, look out for odd pieces of wood which could be useful for repairing damaged furniture, and be prepared to rummage through boxes. Try to think about what you might need for any forthcoming projects; these items help to keep the costs of repairs down. Most sales of this nature are reasonably priced but, if you feel the cost is too high, most people will accept a sensible offer. Alternatively, take a walk around the sale later in the day. Most vendors would rather sell for a low price than take the object home – but beware that there may be other potential buyers.

Dealers

Junk shops and secondhand dealers are also a good source of potential pieces. Remember, however, that the aim is to find and do up old, almost worthless junk, not find a valuable antique which will only be devalued with amateur repairs and decorative techniques.

A good time to visit junk shops is at the weekend. Dealers are often engaged in house clearances and, to clear space in their shops, may be keen to sell pieces quickly. Take time to look in the back of shops, behind cupboards and in corners, and if you are after something in particular, ask the dealer to keep an eye out on your behalf.

Once you are a regular customer, dealers are usually happy to offer a good price and even accept deposits on items that you can't yet afford but don't want to pass up. This can be useful in shops that have a high turnover of stock. Remember that it may take time to find exactly what you want.

With some work, even an old, plain desk found in a stableyard can be transformed

Left in a corner at the back of a junk shop this partially burned picnic hamper was restored using decoupage

Old church chairs turn up regularly in second-hand shops and can be cheap and useful additions to the home

Auctions

This is another good place to source junk furniture. Auctions are usually advertised in local newspapers and may even offer viewing times. Take the time to view the catalogue list before carefully examining any items that may be of interest. If a piece suits your needs, decide on the price you are prepared to pay and stick to it. There are many professional dealers at auctions who are looking to restore or sell on, so the prices they give are usually lower than a shop retail price. This means that, if you really want a piece, there is every chance that other potential buyers will drop out at a low price and you could pick up a bargain. Remember, however, that items usually have a reserve price put on them by the owner, indicating the lowest price they are willing to accept and there may be some additional charges to be paid on top of the agreed price.

If you are a novice, go to two or three auctions just to get an idea of how things operate and how bids are made, before putting in any offers. This

This commonplace glass jar could become a perfect gift

will also give you a sense of current prices, helping to identify the kind of items that are popular – and therefore more expensive – in the secondhand market. Auctions are conducted in a very rapid manner and it can be easy to lose track of the proceedings – possibly ending up with the wrong purchase – so become familiar with the procedure before attempting to place a bid.

Charity shops

Commonly overlooked, charity shops sell a variety of junk and bric-a-brac, all at very reasonable prices. Pottery, lampshades, and other small items, as well as large pieces of furniture, can all appear in such places, often donated by people who simply don't have the time to set up a garage or car boot sale stall. Most shops have a high turnover of stock with new donations arriving regularly, so be prepared to rummage in local stores at least once every few weeks.

Newspaper advertisements

Many people choose to sell off individual pieces of furniture through newspaper advertisements. Although these people will no doubt be after a good price, many are motivated by the need for more space and will accept reasonable offers. Try to get a good description of the piece before turning up and be prepared for other potential buyers to be present. Remember that specialized dealers may also use

newspapers as their main method of sales. People who clear churches, for example, will often have a vast range of chairs, pews, and possibly even pulpits, lecterns and windows in storage, and use newspapers to advertise their stock. Once you have arranged a convenient viewing time, do not feel rushed or pressurized into making any decisions, but remember that much of this stock gets sold in bulk and dealers will be seeking a fast turnover.

A bargain snapped up at a monthly antique market

Waste collections

Remember, however, that finding the perfect piece of junk needn't always involve incurring a price. One person's waste can be another person's gold, so keep an eye on neighbours' skips or even the large items of furniture they put out for council collection. Be sure, however, to check with the owner before removing any pieces. Although it may appear to be unwanted waste, it is common courtesy to check that the piece really is no longer needed.

This rather heavy bedstead was transformed by decoupage for a child's room

What to look for

Everybody defines junk differently so there is a very good chance that what one person sees as rubbish, another views as the perfect potential home accessory. Everything, from cabinets to hinges, fireplaces to glass jugs can all be transformed with the right approach. For grand fixtures and fittings, keep an eye out for large houses that are being renovated; beautiful doors, old mirrors and fireplaces are common sacrifices in modern decoration.

Light fittings can quickly become out of date, so be on the look out for discarded pieces. Examine fittings with a new eye and look for potential – a plain piece might lend itself to becoming a simulated chandelier, an old ceramic lamp can be completely transformed with painting or stencilling techniques. Ageing techniques can turn a plain old base into an imitation antique, while glass shades may be sprayed to create a frosted finish. Existing home décor, such as the design on upholstery and curtains, can be copied onto fabric shades, creating the illusion of expensive, matching furnishings.

Plain glass and chinaware can be given a new lease of life with various painting techniques. Similarly, wooden boxes, which are quite easy to find, can be painted, distressed or covered with decoupage to make useful needlework, jewellery or general storage boxes.

Small pieces are ideal for beginners' projects as they tend to involve less expense and time – producing rewarding results that can also make delightful gifts.

Remember that junk does not have to be dirty or particularly old. Even modern, cheap furniture can be given a dramatic overhaul, creating the perfect and highly original effect for a home at half the price of a genuine period or contemporary designer piece.

Check the condition

The most important points to check when sourcing old junk are the shape and condition of the piece. Generally speaking, avoid pieces with dry rot or too much woodworm, made from poor quality wood or that are badly repaired.

Similarly, rust, tears, dents and cracks can be prohibitive, although if you are prepared to carry out the basic repair work, the final piece can be transformed quite dramatically to look almost new.

Even a poor finish such as the one on this glass fronted cupboard can be disguised

When examining wooden furniture, check every part of the piece, including inside the drawers. Look for woodworm infestation, visible as small round holes, often in patches. If woodworm is active, the holes will have a newly bored appearance and there may be traces of wood dust visible. Woodworm can easily be treated with the application of specialist parasite fluid but this should be performed before the piece is taken into the house, in order to prevent the infestation from spreading further.

If the wood is dry and cracked and the grain very open, with split and warped mouldings, the furniture may have been out in the rain or kept in a damp place. If it is not too badly damaged it can be treated by applying linseed oil and allowing this to soak into the wood.

Dry rot appears in the bottom of furniture; if you touch the wood it goes powdery and breaks up. These sections will need to be cut out, the wood treated and the sections replaced with new wood. If there is extensive dry rot, leave the piece where it is, no matter how much you like it.

Older furniture is usually made using good, solid wooden drawers and bases, and tends to be very sturdy. It can normally be stripped or rubbed down and should offer more years of service. If a small part is broken or missing, check other parts, such as the backs of drawers, to see if wood can be taken from more inconspicuous areas and used for repairs.

A badly applied coat of paint needed to be stripped off this mirror

---

TO BUY OR NOT TO BUY

The most important points to check when sourcing old junk are the shape and condition of the piece. Avoid pieces which will require a lot of repair work.

Of course, the price (if there is one) and the suitability of the item will also influence your decision. If you've been seeking a certain piece of junk for a long time, be prepared to spend a little more money than you originally intended, or accept that additional repair work will be worth all the effort. Before being tempted by a bargain stop to consider carefully whether it will be a suitable item for your home, where it will go and if it will fit in with the decoration.

It is common to find something that has a certain appeal but which you are not entirely sure about. If this is the case, look at the piece carefully and consider if it

would suit your purpose, or whether it has the potential to make a suitable gift. If you like the overall look of it, think about what kind of improvements could be made and try to picture the finished product in your mind. If you are confident that you will make the time and resources available to transform the piece, and it is not too expensive, why not buy it and experiment with your ideas? Many 'favourite' items or techniques derive from cautious and tentative experimentation. However, bear in mind that if you don't really feel that strongly about a piece you will be far less willing to carry out any extensive renovation. (It is easy to pick up a 'bargain' with every intention of transforming it, only to leave the object cluttering the shed or attic for months or even years to come.)

Stripping and sanding

When buying a piece, it's important to know whether its surface can be treated in the way you wish. For example, any wood painted in a black oil gloss is not usually suitable for stripping, but it can be rubbed down and then painted. Thick primers or oil-based undercoats are often difficult to remove, but most varnished surfaces are easy to strip back and there are several good products on the market especially for this.

Many paints can be applied over existing painted surfaces, providing the piece is prepared correctly (see the 'Basic Techniques' section). If there are many irregular layers of paint or the surface is peeling, it is best to strip or sand the piece back to its original state.

Paint techniques

All broken colour techniques, using transparent oil and acrylic glazes, can be applied to great effect on almost any piece of furniture, wood and MDF (medium density fibreboard), so long as the surface has been well prepared and painted with appropriate base coats. Unlike acrylic and water-based paints, oil glaze can also be used effectively to transform melamine and other synthetic products.

New products are being launched all the time, so visit your local paint supplier or contact manufacturers for the latest range of decorating ideas and products. Most suppliers provide free

New timber was used to repair the broken lid of this otherwise serviceable trunk

leaflets, full-colour paint charts and useful tips for different products, and many are now available in environmentally friendly, non-toxic alternatives.

If you want a sheen finish when using acrylic products you will need a finishing acrylic varnish. If you intend to use a coloured varnish, furniture wax, or thin wood wash, you'll need a well-prepared surface with an attractive grain or smooth finish, as these transparent mediums will show up defects.

Stencilling has grown in popularity and there is a variety of stencil paints and sticks available, in oil, water-based, and acrylic fast-drying paints. Stencils are more effectively applied on to flat surfaces, such as wardrobes, trunks or tables. A plain table can look stunning when painted, stencilled and varnished.

Round metal tables are cheap and easy to find

Transforming furniture

Even the most basic items of furniture can be quickly and easily transformed into mock classical pieces. For example, it is possible to buy a cheap, large wardrobe with a flat top, and transform it into a masterpiece in the French armoire style of the late 18th century. Simply fit an ornate top pediment, hand paint designs and create a distressed finish. In fact, an entire bedroom suite can be transformed in this way by adding flower and bow decorations, gilding and filigree edgings. Such techniques can be used on any appropriate furniture, including bookcases, stools and screens.

The same technique can be used to re-create many other styles of furniture. For example, Scandinavian cupboards also featured pediments, although these were not as ornate as the French style. Try re-creating the German dower chests that originated with the settlers in Pennsylvania in the late 18th century, by painting favourite folk motifs on to natural pine. Similarly, use floral or animal paintings, and ornate scrolls to imitate Austrian and Swiss pieces. There are many books available with illustrations of designs from all over the world from which to find inspiration.

Good quality 1950s furniture is often a good investment because it is well made, often a nice shape and inexpensive. Create your own ageing effect on such items, or use different paint techniques, stencilling or hand-painted designs, to make the piece more suitable. Small carved scrolls, wooden decorative pieces and edges that can be added to any plain door or drawers to make a piece more eye-catching and elaborate, are available from good wood shops. There are also specialist companies that will cut your designs to order. If you are adept with a jigsaw, try your hand at creating your own pediments. If not, commission a local carpenter to do it.

Items that have been in the home for years may be crying out for a re-vamp

A cheap terracotta vase can be quickly cheered up

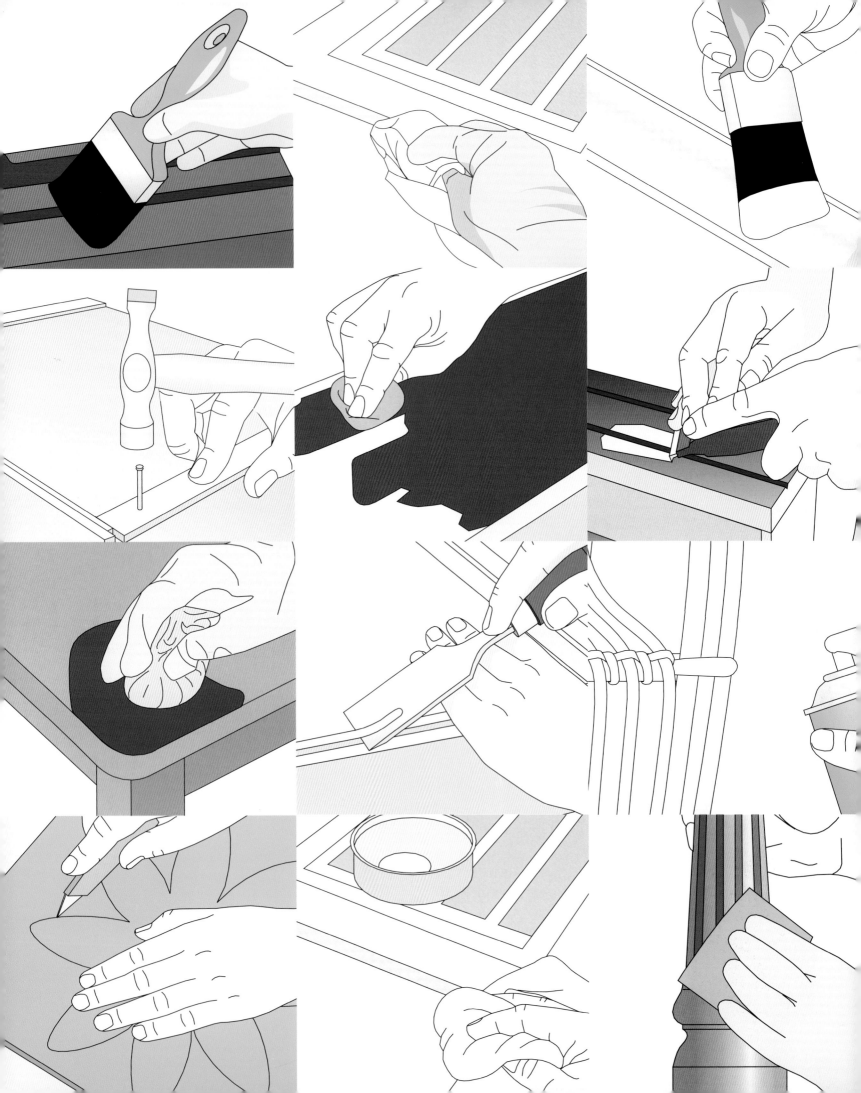

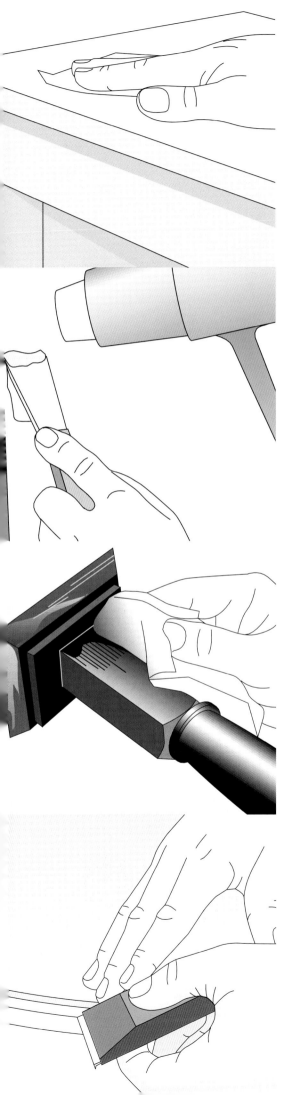

PREPARING A PIECE OF JUNK FOR TRANSFORMATION TAKES TIME AND PATIENCE. IT ALSO REQUIRES SOME BASIC SKILLS AND KNOWLEDGE OF DIY TECHNIQUES. THIS CHAPTER PROVIDES A SIMPLE GUIDE TO THE TOOLS AND EQUIPMENT YOU WILL NEED, TOGETHER WITH DETAILED ADVICE FOR CREATING THE PERFECT SURFACE FOR DECORATIVE WORK.

Basic Techniques & Equipment

Preparing the Surface

ALL DECORATIVE FINISHES, no matter how simple or complicated they are, require a well-prepared surface. Although sometimes boring and labour-intensive, ensuring the piece of junk is thoroughly prepared will help to avoid unwanted peeling and cracking, and prevent careful, dedicated work from going to waste. The next few pages provide a basic list of equipment that might be needed when preparing your piece of junk, together with some guidance on how to perform these simple tasks to best effect. Many are ordinary household items although others, such as masks and goggles, are vital investments for achieving the right finish – both successfully and safely. Remember that the value of good preparation can never be over-estimated.

CLEANING

JUNK, BY ITS VERY NATURE, is often dirty and sometimes greasy. Before anything else can be done, this dirt needs to be completely removed and a full assessment made of any repairs that might be needed. The chart on page 29 explains how to clean different surfaces but everybody should have a few basic pieces of equipment to hand.

WASHING EQUIPMENT

Many items of junk need a good wash before any assessment of the condition can be made. If possible, perform this task outside where making a mess won't be so much of a problem. Always have plenty of rinsing water to hand and protect clothes with a waterproof apron. Use a spare bowl, household sponge and/or scourer, together with a detergent or sugar soap solution for greasy surfaces. Some items will need more time and perseverance than others, but revealing the true surface beneath all the dirt can be rewarding.

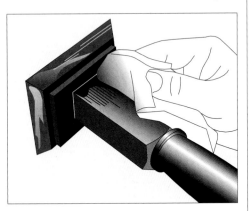
▲ Wipe all surfaces, edges and corners

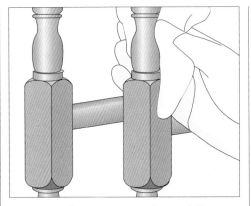
▲ Use a tack rag to remove dust and dirt

CLOTHS

Always keep old cotton shirts and sheets aside for use as spare lint-free rags. It's amazing how quickly rags and cloths need replacing so before embarking on a cleaning project, make sure that there are plenty to hand. It is also sometimes worthwhile investing in a few specialist rags, particularly those that can be used while performing decorative skills and techniques.

• MUTTON CLOTH OR STOCKINET: These are available from DIY shops and are used for polishing or general mopping up. This type of cloth can also be handy for decorative techniques, creating stipple-like textures on painted surfaces or helping to eliminate brush marks.

• TACK RAGS: Small, versatile and long-lasting, these oily cloths are ideal for cleaning wood, metal, plaster or any other surface (except glass). They will pick up and hold dust and dirt, leaving a completely clean surface to work on. Tack rags are used in most projects.

DETERGENTS & SUGAR SOLUTIONS

A range of commercially available detergents and similar products are good for cutting through dirt and grease deposits, when applied with wire wool or cloths. Check with the chart (p29) what kind of product is effective and always wear protective rubber gloves to prevent sores or chaffing. Methylated and white spirits can also be used to remove grease and grime, but always follow the manufacturer's guidelines on storage and use.

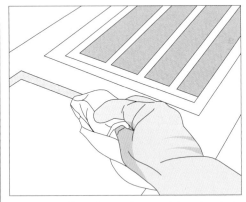
▲ Wear rubber gloves when applying chemicals

SAFETY ADVICE: Equipment

Always wear goggles and a mask whenever you are rubbing down surfaces. Gloves and protective clothes are especially important when using chemical products such as paint strippers or methylated spirit. Ear plugs are also a good idea for work with electrical equipment such as sanders. Protect all nearby surfaces with suitable covering and always provide plenty of ventilation for dust and fumes.

RUBBING DOWN

WHILE SOME PIECES OF JUNK need a simple rubbing down to get rid of loose flakes of paint, others might have several layers of varnish or paint that need removing, in order to get back to the original surface. Metal, in particular, needs a thorough rubbing down because any rust left on the item of junk will invariably recur, spoiling the finished effect. The size of the piece, the type of surface, and the desired finish will help to determine what equipment should be used, although try to have a variety of tools to hand.

ABRASIVE PAPERS

Available in most DIY stores, abrasive papers can be used to sand down a surface, distress paint, and smooth paint and varnish finishes. Most are graded either coarse, medium or fine, depending on the amount and spacing of the grit used – the higher the number, the finer and more compact the grit. Some can be fitted to electric drills or sanding machines, while others are designed to be hand held. Many people wrap the paper around a block of cork or wood for easy handling.

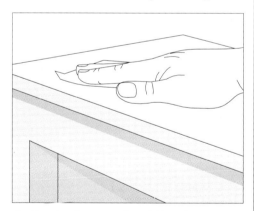

▲ Use abrasive paper for rubbing down

Also, bear in mind that some surfaces suit different types of paper more than others. For example, softwoods may need more abrasion than hardwoods.

Sanding down a surface takes patience and will often require two or more different types of paper. Use a coarse or medium coarse (depending on the roughness of the surface) grade paper to remove most of the jaggedness before finishing off the surface with a fine grade paper.

Remember to always wear a mask when using an abrasive paper, in order to avoid inhaling dust particles. It's also a good idea to follow the grain of the wood, to help prevent surface damage and scratches.

• GLASSPAPER: A soft abrasive paper containing small particles of glass that is suitable for the first stages of sanding.

• GARNET PAPER: Often reddish in colour, this paper is quite rough. However, it is more hardwearing than glasspaper, making it ideal for hardwood furniture.

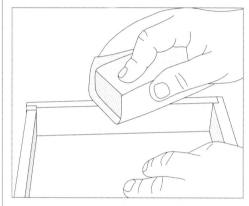

▲ Abrasive paper can be wrapped around cork

• WET-AND-DRY OR SILICON CARBIDE PAPER: As its title suggests, this paper can be used wet or dry, and is good for fine-smoothing painted surfaces. It is also particularly good for distressing stencils or hand-painted designs, although in these cases the grade should be very fine. For best results, keep the paper dry which will prevent black smudges on the decorative finish.

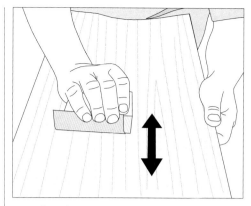

▲ Follow the direction of the grain

WIRE BRUSHES & WIRE WOOL

Relatively inexpensive and available from most DIY stores, wire brushes are particularly good for large pieces of metal with flaking paint or rust. (They can also be used instead of abrasive papers for opening up the grain on wood before liming.) Although intricate areas are best treated with handheld brushes, it is possible to get electric drills with wire brush fittings for large surfaces.

Wire wool comes in various grades of coarseness and can be used for rubbing down wood, metal and glass, as well as applying wax and distressing painted surfaces (see p71). It can also be used to apply paint and varnish removers, or be soaked in white spirit for cleaning wooden furniture. If it is used gently, fine wire wool does not scratch or mark surfaces and helps to create a very clean, smooth finish. However, the wool is made of fine steel filaments, which become loose and can be inhaled, so always wear a mask.

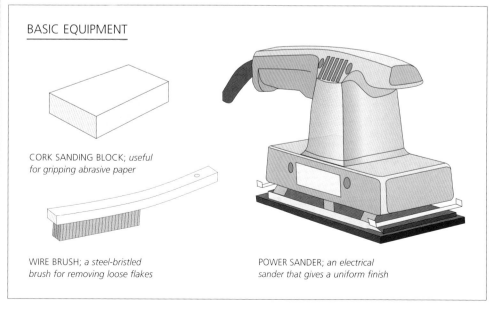

BASIC EQUIPMENT

CORK SANDING BLOCK; *useful for gripping abrasive paper*

WIRE BRUSH; *a steel-bristled brush for removing loose flakes*

POWER SANDER; *an electrical sander that gives a uniform finish*

SCRAPERS

There is a variety of scrapers available that can be used to remove surface coatings, either alone or in conjunction with a paint stripper or hot air gun. The main types are:

• BROAD SCRAPER: Wooden handled with a wide metal blade, this is designed to glide between the surface and coating.

• SHAVEHOOK: This is either completely triangular or has a combination of curved and straight blades, designed to scrape in awkward surfaces such as curves and grooves.

• SKARSTEN SCRAPER: A scraper with disposable, hooked blades that clip into a wooden handle. This can be used on flat surfaces and also on curves and in difficult grooves (see below).

USING A SKARSTEN SCRAPER

1 Starting with the flat areas, hold the scraper firmly and pull it towards you, following as closely to the grain of the wood as possible. If the surface becomes a little bumpy, turn the scraper 45 degrees and continue scraping in the direction of the grain.

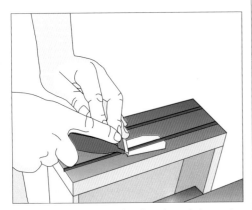

▲ Pull the scraper in the direction of the grain

2 Only push the scraper away from you in exceptional cases, such as when cleaning out grooves, as this can gouge the wood. In these instances, hold the skarsten scraper firmly and close to the blade, so that you can control the pressure.

3 Fit a serrated blade into the scraper for particularly stubborn surfaces. However, this will scratch flat surfaces so be sure to remove it after use.

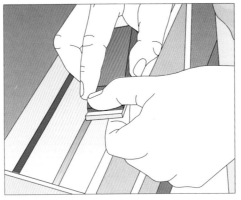

▲ Apply pressure close to the blade for grooves

HOT AIR GUNS

Paint can be softened for scraping by using a hot air gun. Much safer than a conventional blow torch with its naked flame, the air gun produces blasts of warm air, similar to that of a hairdryer. This causes the paint to soften and bubble, making it easy to insert a scraper underneath and gently lift it off. Hot air guns can also be fitted with attachments which either disperse or concentrate the heat emitted.

1 Hold the nozzle about 5–10cm (2–4in) away from the surface so that the paint bubbles and blisters, without burning.

2 As the paint layer begins to raise, lift it away with a paint scraper until most has been removed.

3 Sand down the surface with medium, then fine grade, abrasive papers and wipe over with a tack rag to remove any paint or dust residue.

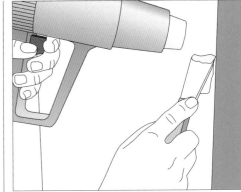

▲ Scrape away the paint as it peels under heat

SAFETY ADVICE: Lead paint

• Many old pieces of furniture will have been painted with primers, undercoats or top coats containing lead. Stripping these layers causes exposure to the lead, which is particularly harmful to pregnant women, children and pets. If you are concerned that the piece you want to strip is coated in a lead paint, invest in a special testing kit, available from most major DIY outlets.

• Blasting, burning, scraping or sanding paint that contains lead should be avoided. The best technique for removing leaded paint is to use a chemical stripper, scraping the removed paint straight into a container for disposal. If the paint is very thick, use a hot air gun to soften the coating but do not allow it to burn as this will cause harmful fumes. After removing the paint, rinse the surface well to remove any residual dust.

• Always wear protective clothing, including a face mask, when removing paint that may contain lead. Ensure that children, pregnant women and pets keep away from the area and avoid working on windy days when loose particles are likely to be blown about.

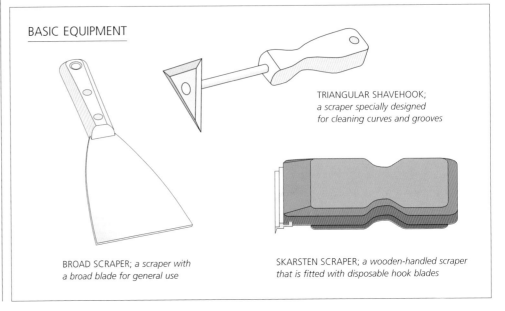

BASIC EQUIPMENT

TRIANGULAR SHAVEHOOK; *a scraper specially designed for cleaning curves and grooves*

BROAD SCRAPER; *a scraper with a broad blade for general use*

SKARSTEN SCRAPER; *a wooden-handled scraper that is fitted with disposable hook blades*

PAINT STRIPPERS

There are numerous paint strippers readily available for removing both paint and varnish. However, chemical strippers can burn if they touch the skin so always wear protective clothes and gloves. Also, ensure there is plenty of ventilation for unpleasant fumes.

STRIPPING PAINT

1 Remove any handles or hinges on the object. Then scrape off loose paint and wipe down the surface.

2 Using an old paintbrush, apply paint stripper to the piece, a section at a time. Wear waterproof gloves and work with the window open.

▲ Apply stripper with an old paintbrush

3 Scrape off all the loose and soft paint with a scraper. Use a skarsten scraper for grooves and tight areas. Remove excess stripper with white spirit, as instructed. (Avoid using water on timber as this may cause damage.)

4 When the bare surface is dry, use medium and then fine grade abrasive papers to sand it down. Finally, wipe the surface with a tack rag to remove any residue.

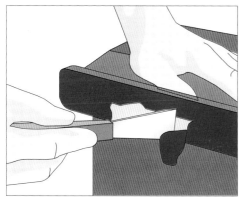
▲ Lift the softened paint with the scraper

STRIPPING SHELLAC FINISHES

1 To remove shellac finishes, including french polish, apply methylated spirit to a small section of the surface with steel wool or a nylon scourer. (Strong liquid ammonia can also be used but the fumes from these are extremely unpleasant.) Wearing rubber gloves and a face mask, rub the scourer backwards and forwards, following the grain as closely as possible.

2 As you finish scrubbing the small area, use a rag soaked with methylated spirit to rub off all excess shellac. Then move on to another area, making sure that you work on small sections at a time.

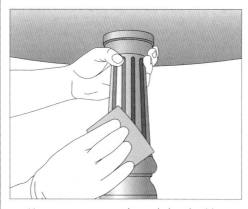
▲ Use a scourer to apply methylated spirit

3 Clean tight areas, such as grooves and curves, with a skarsten scraper. Then sand the entire surface with medium and fine grade abrasive papers.

4 If you will be using a solvent-based finish, leave the object aside for a while so that the moisture in the air can raise the grain. If you are using a water-based finish, the same effect can be achieved by wiping the surface with a dampened cloth.

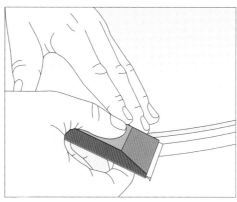
▲ Clean tight grooves with a skarsten scraper

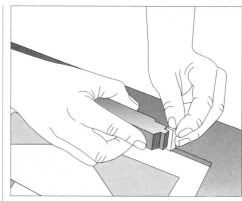
▲ Be sure to scrape out tight corners and edges

STRIPPING VARNISH

1 Sand the surface roughly with a medium grade abrasive paper. This will help the paint stripper to penetrate the waterproof coating. Then liberally apply paint (or varnish) stripper with an old brush.

2 Leave the surface until the varnish begins to bubble and lift – a process that can take 1–4 hours. Scrape off the softened varnish with a paint scraper and use a triangular shavehook for corners and grooves. Any areas where the varnish doesn't scrape off will need a second application of stripper.

3 Sand down the surface with medium and fine grade abrasive papers. Then wipe down with a tack rag to remove any residue.

HINTS & TIPS: Stripping

• If you have a large piece of furniture, it may be worth using a commercial stripping company. Some businesses use non-caustic methods which, although invariably more expensive than caustic techniques, are safer for delicate objects. Chunky pine items or pieces which aren't that valuable, can be treated with caustic chemicals. However, when the object is returned, wash it down thoroughly with vinegar to neutralize any remaining caustic soda solution. Allow the piece to dry thoroughly and sand it smooth before applying the new finish.

• If you are unsure if the surface you wish to strip is coated in shellac or varnish, try rubbing a small corner with some fine wire wool soaked in methylated spirit. If the wool becomes clogged with a brown, sticky 'gravy', the surface is coated in shellac and can be stripped by continuing the procedure. However, if the surface has been varnished, only surface dirt will cling to the wool and so paint stripper will be required.

FILLING

GAPS, HOLES AND DENTS are some of the most common defects in old pieces of junk. By filling these pits, it is possible to create a beautifully smooth finish, ready for decoration. There is a range of different fillers available.

• CELLULOSE FILLER: Popularly used for most small dents and holes around the home, this filler can be used on wood as well as plaster. Although it is not ideal for large cracks, the filler helps provide a smooth surface for rough-grained pieces of wood, and for the rough ends of manufactured 'wood' surfaces such as chipboard.

• WOOD FILLER: There are many types of specialist wood fillers available. Water-based, ready-mixed varieties are the easiest to use and are suitable for filling small holes and cracks, and sealing around bad joins in wood. They come in a variety of wood colours, as well as plain, and sand down well to a very fine, hard finish. Alternatively, some fillers are bought in powder form, which is then mixed with water to form a smooth paste.

• CHINA FILLER: A special china filler can be bought at craft suppliers and sometimes at antique centres. Use it to build up small missing areas on china edges, and to fill any cracks and chips. It takes on the appearance of china and gives a fine finish when smoothed off and hardened.

• PUTTY/FILLER KNIFE: A broad blade for forcing different fillers into difficult cavities. Although these knives are very similar to paint scrapers, their blades tend to be more flexible, helping to make the action of pushing filler into cracks, and levelling off flat against the surface, much easier.

HINTS & TIPS: Wood Filler

If you plan to leave the wood partly showing for any reason, such as liming or even colourwashing, it may be a good idea to use a tinted wood filler for filling holes and cracks.

FILLING GAPS AND HOLES

1 Sand around the outside of the hole and remove any dust. Apply some filler with a filler/putty knife. Spread the blade over the hole, pressing the paste deeply into the recess. Scrape away any excess paste and allow to dry. If the filler shrinks slightly as it dries, apply another layer as before. Then sand with a fine grade abrasive paper.

2 If areas of the wooden surface have been compressed, rather than actually gauged or pitted, try removing the dent by putting a thick, damp cloth over the area and then placing a hot domestic iron over it. The steam should help to raise the compacted wood, without needing to use filler.

HINTS & TIPS: Filling

Surfaces that are to be given a clear coating (such as shellac) can be filled with powdered pumice. Moisten a clean cotton pad with methylated spirit and dip it into sifted pumice. Coat the entire surface of the object using a circular motion, applying a gentle, even pressure. When the grain is completely covered, wipe away the excess with a clean rag.

PRIMING & SEALING

PREPARATION OF THE SURFACE includes ensuring that any decorative technique finish will be applied to a receptive base. Many surfaces, particularly wood, are porous and need sealing before final coats of paint or varnish can be applied. Even when a decorative technique has been used, it may be necessary to use a further sealant to protect the surface and prevent damage or ageing. A range of preparatory primers and sealers is available, as well as finishing sealants.

• ACRYLIC PRIMER: This quick-drying primer is generally used for sealing wood, although some brands are also suitable for metal, masonry and other materials. It is usually white in colour and very quick drying. However, if it is applied to bare wood, a further coat (or alternatively a layer of undercoat) may be required.

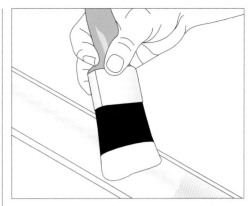

▲ Apply primer to bare wood before painting

• OIL-BASED PRIMER: A slow-drying, durable primer which is useful for surfaces that do not easily accept or grip acrylic primers, such as some metal and plastic surfaces. Oil-based primers are rarely needed for wooden furniture. The fumes emitted by oil paints are particularly strong so ensure that there is plenty of ventilation.

• RABBIT SKIN GLUE: This can be used as a preparation for gesso or as a base for gilding (see p60). The sealer can also be applied to paper to prevent the penetration of varnish or water.

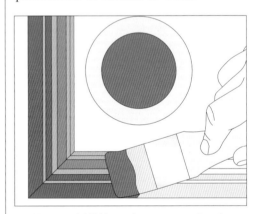

▲ Use rust-inhibiting primer on metalwork

• RUST-INHIBITING PRIMER: Sometimes known as red oxide paint, apply rust-inhibiting primer to any metalwork that you have rubbed down. This should kill any remaining rust and prevent further development. Although the primer shouldn't be needed for new galvanised metal or tin, do apply the coating to any surfaces that are likely to rust or that are to be decorated using water-based paints. It's also a good idea to use it as a base for objects that are to be gilded. Normal primer can be used on items that will definitely not have contact with water.

• SANDING SEALER: This spirit-based sealer is ideal for applying to new, stripped, dark or heavily knotted wood. (Knotting fluid, an oil-based solvent, can be used on individual knots, although it should not be used for surfaces that are to be coated in water-based paints.) Sanding sealer is also an excellent sealant for wood on which you want to apply decoupage, and provides an excellent base for waxing.

▲ Use sanding sealer on wood for varnishing

FINISHING SEALANTS

MOST FINISHING SEALANTS comprise of either varnish or wax. They work by sealing the painted, stained or natural surface so that the decorative finish is not damaged from general wear and tear, or chemicals that may come into contact with it.

VARNISHES

Unlike transparent stains that are simply absorbed into a wooden surface and require further sealing, varnishes form a clear, protective layer. Most conventional varnishes are made with polyurethane resins which provide a heat-resistant, scratchproof and waterproof finish. They can be used on painted surfaces, or on wood that has been carefully rubbed down and wiped clean with a tack rag.

The range of varnishes is enormous. They can be water- or oil-based and come in a range of finishes including matt, gloss and satin. Some tinted or stained varnishes are also available but these do not sink into the wood like ordinary stains. This means that additional coats of clear, protective varnish should be used as a sealant.

• OIL-BASED VARNISH: There are numerous types of oil-based varnish, all of which are generally slow-drying. Polyurethane types are the easiest to use and are available in matt (almost no shine), satin (semi-gloss), and gloss (high sheen) finishes. To obtain the protection of a gloss finish without the increasing shine, try applying coats of matt or satin varnish over one coat of gloss.

Sometimes available in spray cans to avoid brush marks, oil-based varnishes are usually re-coatable between 8–24 hours. These varnishes are generally more durable and heat-resistant than water-based varnishes (see below) but they can yellow with time, possibly spoiling the decorative effect. Oil-based varnishes are ideal for sealing water-soluble crackle varnish (see p72).

• WATER-BASED VARNISH: Increasingly popular, water-based acrylic varnishes are widely available in gloss, satin or matt finishes. A dead flat varnish is also available, which provides even less sheen than a matt coating. Acrylic varnishes are milky in appearance but dry to a clear finish and are non-yellowing. However, the matt and dead flat versions contain chalk which gives them a cloudy appearance when a number of coats are applied. This makes them unsuitable as a sealant for techniques that require many layers, such as decoupage. These finishes are also softer and less durable than satin or gloss varnish.

Some brands of acrylic varnish contain polyurethane for extra toughness, but most offer an average level of resistance which should be suitable for most home furniture. (Items that receive a lot of wear, such as children's toys or furniture may need stronger types.) Water-based varnish is usually dry to the touch in about 20 minutes and re-coatable after 2 hours.

HINTS & TIPS: Oil-based varnish

Several thin layers of varnish always provide more protection than a couple of thick coats. Whenever you apply a second coat of varnish, rub down the surface lightly with a very fine abrasive paper and dust off – this will ensure that the next coat adheres well.

• SHELLAC: Shellac is the naturally occurring resin of the lac beetle and is mixed with methylated spirit to form a quick-drying varnish. This traditional product is widely used for furniture restoration and french polishing, and is used as a stainer and sealant for some of the projects in this book. It should be applied to small areas of the surface by brush and then rubbed in using a round ball of lint-free cloth.

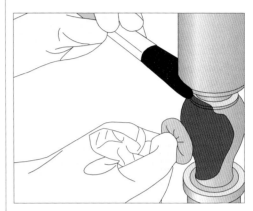

▲ Wear rubber gloves when applying shellac

Shellac comes in a variety of grades and colours and is sold under many different names. Use clear shellac sanding sealer, white french polish and white button polish for sealing wood, paper and paint. Use brown french polish or garnet polish for staining and ageing, in addition to sealing. French enamel varnish is transparent shellac with added dye and can also be used.

▲ Apply shellac to large surfaces by cloth

HINTS & TIPS: Shellac

Although it is possible to apply varnish with any soft household paintbrush, specialist varnish brushes hold more liquid and so are better for covering large surfaces. Flat hog's-hair brushes are the best, usually available from specialist craft and decorating shops.

❖ VARNISHES & WAXES ❖

TYPE	SOLVENT	SHEEN	TIP
ACRYLIC VARNISH (BRUSH)			
• FLAT	water	low	non-yellowing and quite durable
• MATT	water	none	non-yellowing and quite durable
• SATIN	water	medium	non-yellowing and quite durable
ACRYLIC VARNISH (SPRAY)	water	medium	non-yellowing and very durable
ACRYLIC VARNISHING WAX	water	medium	non-yellowing and very durable
BEESWAX POLISH	white spirit	medium	can yellow with age, quite durable
FURNITURE WAX	white spirit	medium	non-yellowing and quite durable
LACQUER VARNISH (SPRAY)	white spirit	high	non-yellowing and very durable
SHELLAC	methylated spirit	high	non-yellowing and very durable

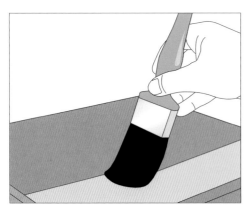

▲ Apply varnish with gentle brush strokes

• CELLULOSE LACQUER: Usually available in a spray can, cellulose lacquer gives a high sheen protective finish for water-based decorated surfaces. However, it should not be used with oil-based mediums because the cellulose thinners, which are used to dilute the lacquer, act like a paint stripper on the oil. Cellulose lacquers are quick-drying and are less likely to yellow with age.

APPLYING VARNISH

1 Prepare the surface of the object by sanding with medium, then fine grade abrasive papers. Wipe thoroughly with a tack rag, ensuring that there is no dust remaining on the surface, including any grooves.

2 Dip a thoroughly clean brush in the varnish and, without removing the excess, work the brush over a sheet of brown paper. This will expel the air from the bristles and encourage loose hairs out, preventing them from sticking to your intended surface.

3 Apply the varnish with gentle strokes, taking the brush right around the lip of drawers or doors. Try to avoid overloading the surface with varnish as this will cause runs or sags.

4 Leave the varnish to dry completely hard (possibly taking 1–3 days) before lightly sanding, dusting and applying further coats.

HINTS & TIPS: Applying varnish

Wet varnish is vulnerable to all kinds of damage. Avoid wearing woolly or fluffy clothes when you varnish and tie any long hair back to avoid unwanted deposits in the coating. Keep the room reasonably warm but do not overheat – any sudden temperature changes can cause a powdery finish.

·············· WAXES ··············

Wax finishes are usually applied over a varnish coating, helping to provide a soft sheen. The greater the number of coats, the better the sheen produced.

• BLACK BISON WAX: A blend of several waxes, black bison wax has a good resistance to water and fingermarks. It can be applied to painted furniture and creates a seal for crackled, aged and peeled-paint techniques. The wax is available in different colours although beware that some will cause yellowing.

• CLEAR WAX: Clear furniture wax is also an effective resist and can be used for creating an aged appearance on furniture. Use it over paint or wood where you don't want a colour to adhere, such as areas of wear. Clear liquid wax is particularly good for this but coloured versions are also available.

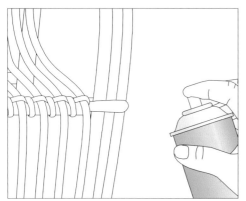

▲ Spray cellulose lacquer in a light, even coat

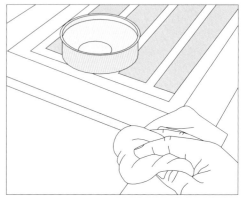

▲ Apply several coats of wax for a good sheen

APPLYING A WAX FINISH

1 To create a protective sheen on a surface, lightly sand it down with fine grade abrasive paper and then wipe off with a tack rag.

2 Apply the wax with wire wool or a nylon scourer, rubbing the length of the surface with long, straight strokes. Make sure the wax is rubbed right into the grain and try not to leave any build-up of wax on the surface.

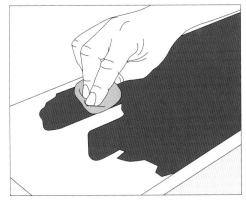

▲ Rub the wax into the grain with a scourer

3 Within a couple of minutes of application, rub the surface with a lint-free cloth to even out the coating. The surface will feel sticky but continue to rub, changing to a clean section of cloth whenever it clogs.

4 Rub the surface for as long as possible – this will help to create a polished finish. Hold the object firmly while you polish, grasping it through a clean cloth so as to prevent grease from your hand transferring to the timber.

5 Repeat the process at least once more. The greater the number of coats, the more enhanced and refined the final finish will be.

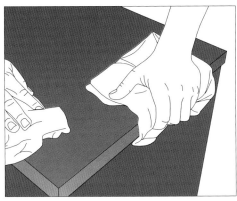

▲ Hold the item with a cloth while polishing

JOINING

EFFECTIVE STICKING TECHNIQUES may be needed for both basic repairs and decorative finishes. The type of adhesive required will depend on the job in hand, although many projects may require two or more different types of fixative.

GLUES

The strength of glue required will obviously depend upon the materials you need to stick. The main categories of glue are:

• EPOXY RESINS: These two-part adhesives set to a strong, water-resistant finish and can be used on wood, glass, ceramics and metal. Most types of epoxy resin take about 2 hours to set although weaker brands that dry in around 5 minutes are also available. Apply the glue to both surfaces and clamp (see right) until set. Avoid getting epoxy resin on the skin – it can cause dermatitis – and provide good ventilation because its fumes are toxic.

• CONTACT GLUES: These are rubber-based and lack the strength of epoxy resins, although they can be used on materials such as leather and textiles. The glue is spread on both surfaces and left to dry before the two pieces are joined. The surfaces will stick on contact so positioning must be accurate.

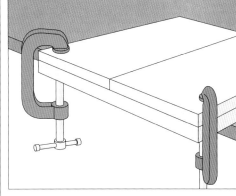

▲ Use clamps for holding glued wood together

• PVA (POLYVINYL ACETATE) ADHESIVES: Multipurpose and of medium strength, PVA adhesives are cheap and useful for sticking wood, polyvinyls, some textiles and paper. Although they are simple to apply and dry quite quickly, these glues will not work where there is damp or moisture present.

• PASTE ADHESIVES: These are weak glues that are suitable for light materials, including paper and card. Techniques such as decoupage usually require PVA or paste glues and there are numerous commercial brands available.

HINTS & TIPS: Glueing with clamps

Use G-clamps to hold surfaces together while long-drying glues (such as epoxy resin) set. Remember to place spare blocks of wood between the clamp's prongs and the object, to prevent undesired marks or damage to the surface.

BASIC EQUIPMENT

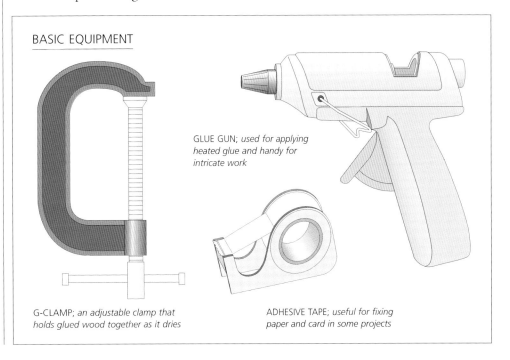

GLUE GUN; *used for applying heated glue and handy for intricate work*

G-CLAMP; *an adjustable clamp that holds glued wood together as it dries*

ADHESIVE TAPE; *useful for fixing paper and card in some projects*

GLUE GUNS

A glue gun is used in conjunction with a stick of solid glue. The small, candle-like adhesive is inserted into the gun and melted by a heating element inside the tool. It is then fed through the nozzle, in liquid form. Glue guns are particularly useful for intricate work, or for applying small dabs of adhesive. However, follow the manufacturer's safety advice and store the tool safely.

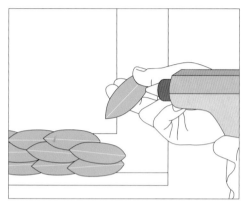

▲ Glue guns are ideal for intricate work

TEMPORARY ADHESIVES

A number of projects in this book involve using temporary adhesives. For example, tape or adhesive sprays are needed to hold stencils in position while paint is applied, or adhesive tack is required when experimenting with the position of decoupage cut-outs.

• ADHESIVE SPRAYS: A variety of sprays can be used for temporarily sticking soft materials such as paper. These are particularly useful for stencils or drawings that may need to be repositioned or adjusted several times. The thin layer of spray eventually wears off but a further coat can be applied without causing any further damage. These sprays should not be confused with fixing sprays, which are used to prevent charcoal, pencil and ink drawings from smudging. Low contact adhesive tapes can also be used but make sure that they do not lift the painted surface beneath.

• ADHESIVE TACKS: Commercial gum-type adhesives are popular for temporarily fixing light items in place. These tacks come in different strengths and, if a good quality, shouldn't mark the contact surfaces.

NAILS, PINS & SCREWS

For some basic repair work, it may be necessary to use nails, pins or screws for joining materials such as wood or metal.

• NAILS: There are numerous types of nail but general purpose varieties should cover the projects in this book. Hold nails at the base and gently tap with the hammer, before removing your fingers and hitting them home.

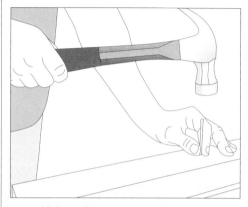

▲ Hold the nail in position and gently tap

• PANEL PINS: These light pins are used for furniture and fine joinery and should be inserted using a tack hammer. Use the cross pein (the narrow section opposite the head) for starting the insertion, which will help to prevent bashing your thumb and finger. Apply wood glue onto wooden surfaces before panel pinning.

• SCREWS: Always use screws for heavy-duty materials and functional items such as chairs or cupboard door hinges. They have a stronger clamping force than nails and can be removed or adjusted without damaging the wood. Woodscrews come in a variety of sizes and head types – ask your DIY supplier which type is most suitable for your needs.

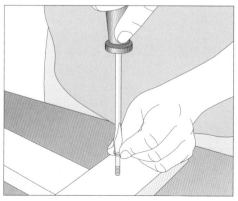

▲ Use screws for heavy-duty furniture and joins

TRACING & CUTTING

BASIC DRAWING AND CUTTING techniques are often needed for doing up old pieces of junk. Instructions for detailed work are given in the 'Decorative Techniques' section on page 30, but simple procedures to help make basic tasks easier are listed below.

PLANNING TOOLS

• RULER: Essential for both measuring and marking out designs, rulers should be sturdy and adequate in length. Centring rulers of 45cm (18in), available from graphic art suppliers, are particularly good. If you need a straight edge for cutting out, invest in a metal-edged ruler – plastic and wooden edges get sliced with the blade.

• SET SQUARE: This is useful for keeping corners accurate although a frame, book or other rectangular object can also be used for drawing edges. Transparent set squares are most useful because you can see guidelines beneath.

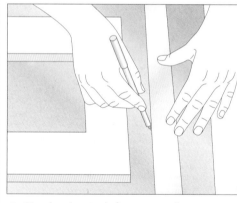

▲ Use drawing tools for accurate lines

• WATER-SOLUBLE PENCIL: This is ideal for marking wood because any unwanted lines or smudges can be wiped off later.

PLANNING A DESIGN

1 Always plan your task in advance. If you are making alterations to a piece of furniture, take measurements of all the dimensions and draw on a rough piece of paper where fixings will be required. Make sure that if the item is to be functional, any alterations you make will be of sufficient strength and adaptability. For example, if you are adding shelves to an old cupboard, think about the size of the items to be

stored and maximize the room available – although remember to allow enough space for access. Similarly, decide whether the original positions of hinges or screws really are the most useful, or whether alterations are needed.

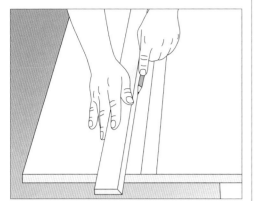

▲ Measure and mark out all dimensions

2 For large items that need matching shapes, such as two pieces of wooden scroll trim, create a template out of paper and draw around it on to your wood. This will ensure both symmetry in the shapes, and help to minimize wood wastage.

·········· TRACING ··········

Always be patient when you are tracing items and spend some time on the preparation. For example, make sure that your stencil and tracing material are securely fixed – the slightest wobble and inaccuracies begin. If the material you wish to trace on to is semi-opaque, use a light box to help you see the design more clearly. Alternatively, stick the design on a window, position your medium on top, and then trace over it.

BASIC EQUIPMENT

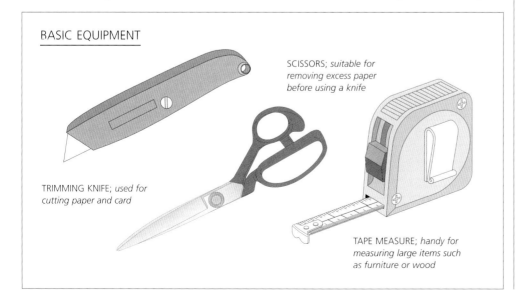

SCISSORS; *suitable for removing excess paper before using a knife*

TRIMMING KNIFE; *used for cutting paper and card*

TAPE MEASURE; *handy for measuring large items such as furniture or wood*

TRACING A DESIGN

1 Position a sheet of tracing paper securely over the design. Slowly follow the design with a pencil. For intricate patterns, rotate the design and paper, rather than your body.

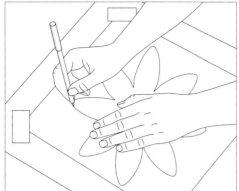

▲ Trace around the fastened design

2 Follow the outline on the reverse side of the tracing paper with a heavy (2B) pencil. Then put the tracing over your chosen surface, right side up, and follow the outline again. The heavy lead on the reverse side should transfer to the surface. Then cut out the design.

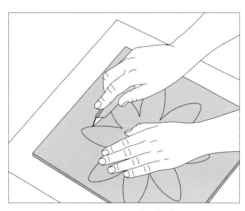

▲ Use a craft or trimming knife for cutting out

·········· CUTTING TOOLS ··········

The secret to effective cutting is sharp equipment – blunt blades cause untidy edges and slips. The projects in this book involve cutting out a variety of items including wood, paper and tin.

• SAWS: There are numerous types of saw available, both for heavy-duty work and intricate cutting. Use a fretsaw for tight curves in wood or plastic and a hacksaw or heavy-duty tin snips for cutting metal. To cut out detailed shapes, cut away most of the surrounding excess material before trying to follow the intricate outline.

• SCISSORS: Use sharp scissors and keep them aside solely for craft work, rather than odd tasks around the home that might cause them to blunt. Manicure scissors are ideal for decoupage, but ordinary scissors can be used for removing excess paper or card before using a craft or trimming knife.

• CRAFT KNIVES: Generally, craft knives and scalpels offer more flexibility and accuracy than scissors for cutting out intricate designs. Trimming knives are good for straight lines, particularly on semi-thick materials such as cardboard, but knives that can be held like a pen are better for difficult shapes. Scalpels with replaceable blades are particularly useful and, once mastered can provide crisp edges. Change the blade as soon as the cutting becomes heavy or difficult – going over a slice twice leads to rough and inaccurate edges.

• CUTTING MAT: A cutting mat is essential for protecting work surfaces. Although thick pieces of cardboard make a temporary alternative, scalpels will soon penetrate the board, blunting the blade and making a clean first cut difficult. Self-healing mats are best as they last for years and have guide lines.

HINTS & TIPS: Sawing

Mark your chosen outline in soft pencil and then position the saw on the waste side of the line. If you place the blade immediately on top of the marking, the piece will end up fractionally shorter than you intended.

Simple Repairs

ALTHOUGH SEVERELY DAMAGED furniture should be avoided, it is highly possible that your chosen piece of junk will need at least some repair work. This may involve simple tasks, such as filling holes or re-nailing some beading, or it could require more extensive work, such as repairing a drawer or replacing the panelling in a cupboard. Most tasks can be easily achieved with a little time and DIY knowledge. Using many of the basic tools already described, together with odd pieces of equipment lying around the house, you should be able to do most of the repairs yourself. This makes the final product even more rewarding, and helps to ensure that your junk item goes on to become a fully functional, as well as decorative, piece of furniture.

REMOVING OLD NAILS

OLD NAILS CAN be rusty and sharp so always take care when trying to remove them. Start by placing a piece of card or thin wood next to the nail – this will prevent the hammer or pincers from damaging the surface of the object. Then slide the claw of the hammer under the nail head and gently pull back on the hammer shaft. For

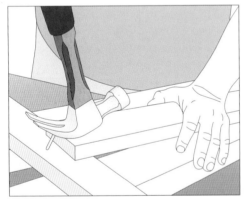

▲ Use the hammer claws to lever out the nail

maximum leverage, keep the handle almost upright. If the nail is particularly long, add more wooden blocks after each pull so that the hammer remains supported and the nail can be removed vertically. (If the nail curves, the hole will get larger.)

For nails with no head, use pincers to grip the nail close to the wood and lever it with a series of pulls. However, if the nail proves exceptionally difficult to remove, it may be worth banging it in beneath the surface and covering the mark with filler, although this will probably affect the final finish.

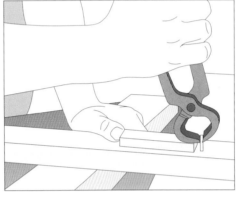

▲ Use pincers for nails with no head

WOODWORM AND DRY ROT

CHECK FURNITURE and wooden junk for woodworm by looking for holes or fresh wood dust. The parasites often attack cheaper softwood first, such as the back panelling or bottom, so even if there are no visible holes in the main sections, be sure to inspect the entire object. Any piece of furniture that shows signs of woodworm should be isolated from other furniture immediately. Squirt commercial woodworm solution into every hole and leave for 24 hours.

Dry rot tends to occur when junk is stored in warm, moist conditions. Wood that is infected will have a musty smell and may feel powdery to the touch. Untreated dry rot forms into wool-like strands that will spread across wood, masonry and metal. Any wood affected is likely to become flaky and brittle. Although affected wood must be removed, you can protect surrounding areas by using a commercial fungicide.

WOOD KNOTS

REMOVE DEAD, BLACK knots simply by carefully banging or pushing them out. 'Live' brown knots should be coated with knotting fluid to prevent them from releasing a sticky resin.

REPAIRING WARPED WOOD

ANY WARPED BOARDS of wood in a piece of furniture must be treated separately. After carefully removing the board, lay it concave-side down on a piece of wet cloth. Put the cloth (and wood) on top of a straight piece of board, covered with plastic sheeting. Clamp in place and leave overnight. The damp will help the fibres in the concave side of the wood to expand. The warp should have gone by the morning, but be sure to refit the boards as soon as possible and fix battens on the underside, to ensure a rigid finish.

TREATING BURNT WOOD

SLIGHT BURN MARKS can be treated so that some, if not all, of the dark patching disappears. Glue some garnet paper around the tip of a pencil and gently twist it over the blackened area. However, avoid sanding the nearby area as this may create more surface marks. Once the charred wood has been removed, use a cotton swab to apply a drop of bleach to the area to help lighten the exposed darker wood.

TYPES OF WOOD

ALTHOUGH BASIC REPAIRS should not involve too much carpentry, some items may need new wood fitted, such as chair struts or cupboard panels. If this is the case, it can be useful to know a little information about different types of wood and how they are commonly used. For example, antiques are likely to be made of quality hardwoods, and any repairs should involve using a wood as similar to the original as possible. The back of a fairly new, budget kitchen cupboard, however, is more likely to be made from cheap manufactured board and can be replaced with any similar alternative. Choosing the right wood will also influence the amount of money you need to spend.

SOFTWOODS

Most wood available at timber yards and DIY stores is softwood. It comes from evergreen trees, such as pines and firs, and tends to be softer than the wood produced by deciduous trees, although this is not always the case. It is used in most basic domestic furniture and can be bought with a rough edge (sawn) or refined, planed edge. Planed wood is obviously the first choice for projects in which the wood can be seen.

HARDWOODS

Much more expensive than softwoods, hardwoods come from deciduous, broad-leafed trees and tend to be only available from specialist yards. Expensive furniture, particularly that in which the grain is brought to a high polish, may be made of hardwoods, but the projects covered in this book are more likely to use softwoods. (Antiques requiring major work are best left to experts, anyway.) However, if you do use hardwoods for any repairs, make sure that all tools are sharpened to a fine cutting edge and always wear a mask. It's also worth remembering that some woods, such as teak, are naturally very oily and should be glued with a synthetic-resin adhesive. Similarly, the acid in oak can cause steel screws to stain the surrounding wood black, so use brass or plated screws for any fixings in this type of wood.

MANUFACTURED BOARDS

In addition to natural wood, there are various types of board available that are made in factories, by compressing different wood particles.

• BLOCKBOARD: In this board, several rectangular strips of wood are sandwiched alongside each other, with two double layers of pressure-bonded veneer on the top and bottom. It has good structural strength and is ideal for making additional shelving inside cupboards, or for replacing the backs and sides of drawers.

• CHIPBOARD: A cheap type of board that is sometimes used in modern cabinet making. Small softwood chips are glued together under pressure, before each side is sanded smooth. Chipboard is designed to be primed and painted, and is ideal for replacement cupboard doors which need to be both light and relatively strong and resistant.

• FIBREBOARD: Made from compressed wood fibre, this board comes in various densities. Medium density fibreboard (MDF) is the most suitable material for these projects because it is strong and has similar properties to solid wood. Fine, smooth surfaces on both sides make MDF easy to finish with paint or veneer and it is relatively cheap to buy.

• HARDBOARD: Hardboard is made from compressing softwood pulp and tends to lack some of the strength of other manufactured boards. However, it is cheap and suitable for basic tasks, such as cabinet backs or the bottoms of lightweight drawers.

• PLYWOOD: Available in sheets, plywood is made by bonding a number of thin wood veneers together under high pressure. The thickness of each veneer can vary, but an odd number is commonly used, with the grain direction alternating for additional strength. Depending on the thickness and quality, plywood can also be used for replacing cupboard doors, backs or shelves. It too can be painted or varnished to a fairly good finish.

REPAIRING A CHAIR

CHAIRS CAN OFTEN end up in a bad state of repair. Common problems, such as a wobbly leg or broken seat, often seem prohibiting and end up relegating the seat to the rubbish pile. However, a few simple repairs can give such a piece of furniture a new lease of life. Not only does this save the expense and waste of having to replace the piece of furniture – it also provides a useful base for a variety of decorative finishes.

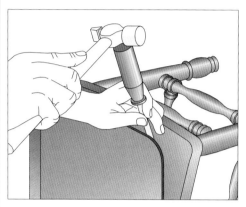

▲ Use a hammer and chisel to remove seats

1 Carefully remove chair seats by working around the main section with a hammer and chisel.

2 Pull out odd nails or screws. Any nails that are impossible to remove should be punched below the surface and the holes then filled.

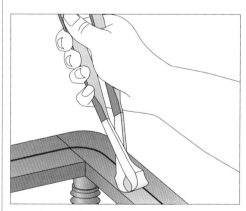

▲ Pull out old nails, screws or splinters

3 Check that all of the legs are secure. If any leg is loose, carefully detach it and, if more than one is to be removed, label it clearly so that it can be correctly repositioned. Scrape off any old adhesive and then apply fresh adhesive to the socket and end of the leg. Press the leg firmly into the socket

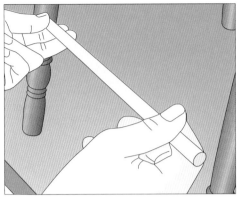

▲ Replace rails with new pieces of dowelling

and clamp the chair together until the adhesive has thoroughly dried. Repeat the process for the other legs.

4 To fit a new rail between the legs, measure the distance between the legs, plus the depth of one hole (which the rail will fit into). Cut a piece of dowelling rod to this measurement. Put a small amount of adhesive into each hole, fit one end of the rail into one hole, work the other end into the other hole, then centre the rail and allow the adhesive to dry. Sand or darken the wood to match the rest of the chair.

5 To replace the seat, make a template of the seat shape with paper and check that it fits in place. Use it to cut out the shape from plywood (about 9–12mm ($^3/8$–$^1/2$in) thick plywood is best). If desired, cut out the same shape in foam and glue it to the plywood. Cover the foam with thick calico, pulling it tight and stapling it to the bottom of the plywood.

Then cover the whole piece with a fabric of your choice, making sure that the material is pulled taut over the foam and wood. Replace the new seat into the chair frame, inserting new nails if permanent fixing is required. The chair is now ready for decoration.

HINTS & TIPS: Repairing a chair

If a chair leg wobbles, position it on a piece of flat board to determine which legs are short. Push bits of thin cardboard under the short leg until the chair is even and use the depth of this cardboard to gauge how much should be cut off of the remaining legs. However, always leave valuable antique chairs to an expert.

REPLACING HINGES

HINGES ARE ANOTHER common problem in many junk items. Rusty, distorted or half broken hinges prevent easy use of doors and can cause damage to wooden surfaces. Always remove and replace broken or damaged hinges, rather than simply trying to restore them. However, make sure that new hinges are the correct size and match.

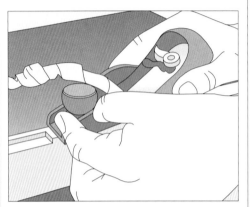

▲ Plane away excess wood around the hinge

1 Remove the old hinge and then plane away any excess housing which is not needed for the new hinge.

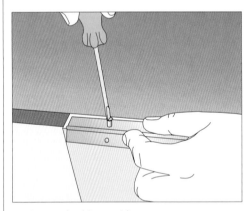

▲ Fasten the hinge with new screws

2 Screw in the replacement hinge, with new screws, into the old holes. Remember to make sure that the screw head lies flush with the hinge.

HINTS & TIPS: Hinges

Cleaned brass handles or hinges can be sealed with brass lacquer, helping to keep the shiny lustre. The lacquer is available in spray cans, but should be applied with a fine paintbrush to small surfaces such as screw heads. Hinges should also be oiled occasionally to keep the movement of the joint clean and easy.

REPAIRING DRAWER RUNNERS

DRAWER RUNNERS in old pieces of furniture are often worn away so that the drawers are difficult to pull out and push in. These are surprisingly easy to repair, and help to restore the piece of junk back to a functional piece of furniture. However, always check drawers for woodworm or dry rot (see p26) before engaging in such repairs.

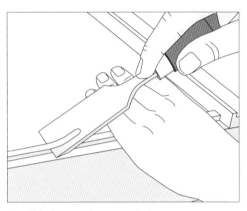

▲ Chisel away the worn timber

1 Use a chisel to pare away the worn timber of the runner until the runner is level once again.

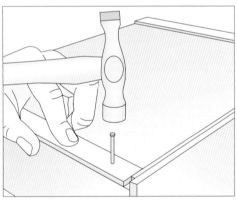

▲ Fix a strip of wood to the correct depth

2 Nail or glue a thin strip of hardwood to the runner to build it back up to the required thickness. Sand it smooth to ensure easy movement.

SAFETY ADVICE: Chisels

Chisels should not be needed for many of the projects in this book, but they can be useful for some basic repair work. Always take special care when using a chisel, making sure that the piece of wood is secured. Hold the chisel firmly and from behind – never use a steadying hand in front of the blade in case it slips.

SURFACE PREPARATION

SURFACE	CLEANING	SANDING	BASE COATS
CHIPBOARD			
• WOOD VENEERED	Wipe with damp, but not wet, lint-free rag	Fine grade abrasive paper	If necessary, apply acrylic wood primer, emulsion or oil-based undercoat
• MELAMINE-COATED	Wash with sugar soap solution, using a lint-free rag and allow to dry	Fine grade abrasive paper	As above
HARDBOARD			
• PAINTED	Wash with sugar soap solution, using a lint-free rag and allow to dry	Fine grade abrasive paper	As above
METAL			
• BARE	Brush off any rust, wipe with white spirit and wire wool	Wet-and-dry paper	Metal primer or rust-inhibiting primer, followed by acrylic primer for water-based paint
• COATED	Wash with sugar soap solution, remove any coating with an appropriate stripper	Wet-and-dry paper	As above
MDF			
• PAINTED	Wash with sugar soap solution, using a lint-free rag and allow to dry	Fine grade abrasive paper	If necessary, apply acrylic wood primer, emulsion or oil-based undercoat
• UNPAINTED	Wipe with damp, but not wet, lint-free rag	Fine grade abrasive paper	Acrylic wood primer, emulsion or oil-based undercoat
PLASTICS	Wash with sugar soap solution, or white spirit	Wet-and-dry paper	As above
PLYWOOD			
• VARNISHED	Brush well with stiff brush then Wash with sugar soap solution and a lint-free rag	Fine grade abrasive paper	Acrylic wood primer, and oil-based undercoat where necessary
• UNPAINTED	Wipe with damp, but not wet, lint-free rag	As above	Acrylic wood primer, and oil-based undercoat
WOOD			
• PAINTED	Wash with sugar soap solution, using a lint-free rag and allow to dry	Remove loose flakes with a scraper and stripper then use coarse, medium and fine grade abrasive papers	Acrylic wood primer, and oil-based undercoat where necessary
• UNPAINTED	Wipe with damp, but not wet, lint-free rag	Fine grade abrasive paper	Acrylic wood primer, and oil-based undercoat
• SEALED	Wash with sugar soap solution, using a lint-free rag and allow to dry	Remove loose flakes with a scraper and stripper then use coarse, medium and fine grade abrasive papers	Acrylic wood primer, and oil-based undercoat where necessary
• VARNISHED	Brush well with stiff brush then Wash with sugar soap solution and a lint-free rag	As above	As above
• WAXED	As above	As above	As above

Most people admire decorative techniques and yet many think they could never create a similar effect themselves. In fact, many of the most eye-catching finishes are remarkably easy to achieve, with a little patience, practice and time. This chapter provides a complete guide to the tools and techniques you will need to create a range of decorative finishes.

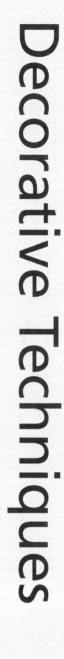

Decorative Techniques

Using Paint & Colour

Virtually every project in this book involves some painting. Whether applying a base colour for techniques such as decoupage, stippling paint through a stencil or painting a fine, decorative design by hand, the likelihood is that you will need a paintbrush at some point. The range of paints and painting materials is ever-expanding and it can be difficult to identify the most suitable products for your project. Although there is rarely a right or wrong answer, some products, methods and tools are definitely better suited to some techniques than others. Furthermore, mixing different types of paint can cause problems – for example, oil-based and water-based products should be kept apart – so plan ahead and think about the finish you want to create.

▲ Paints come in a diverse range of colours

TYPES OF PAINT

THE RANGE OF PAINTS available for achieving different decorative techniques is vast. Although some are designed to be used for specific styles of painting, most can be adapted or added to other mediums, creating an even greater array of potential results. Most people develop a favourite medium and stick to this, but it can be interesting to experiment and try all different types of paints. The following pages provide a basic guide to most types of paint, together with some advice on how they they can be used. (See the chart on page 34.)

HINTS & TIPS: Buying paint

Most specialist, decorative paints can be bought in craft shops. However, it's worth checking at a local DIY store to see if a cheap alternative can be found. These shops are increasingly stocking specialist paints – and they are often much cheaper.

EMULSION PAINT

Relatively inexpensive, emulsion paints are available in matt or satin finishes and a variety of different colours. They are most commonly used for painting walls, but can be applied to furniture pieces – 250ml (8fl oz) tester pots are ideal for small items. Emulsion paints can be thinned with water to make a wash, or tinted with acrylic paints, universal stainers or powder pigments to make a range of unique colours. They dry by evaporation of the water inside the mixture, so keep windows closed when you are applying the paint, but then open them as soon as the work is finished.

TRADITIONAL PAINTS

A recent development in the production of paints, these paints are a variation on ordinary emulsion. Natural pigments, rather than the synthetic ones used in normal paint production, are used to make the mixture. The paints also contain chalk, a traditional ingredient used in paint-making, and

▲ Traditional paints contain chalk

▲ Add pigment for bold emulsion colours

dry to a completely matt finish that appears considerably lighter than the colour in the pot.

Most of the paints include modern binders and, although they have the feel and look of those used in the past, they have the advantage of a greater degree of durability. However, they are easily marked so painted surfaces need protecting with wax or varnish. Applying varnish and waxes over traditional paints will darken them and take away their chalky appearance.

Traditional paints are a little more expensive than standard emulsion paint but they are definitely worth the investment, if you can afford them. The colours have a wonderful softness and subtlety, which makes them ideal for isolated projects such as furniture and junk. Furthermore, the paint handles very well when creating a distressed finish. These paints are very quick-drying and are usually re-coatable within about half an hour. They can be thinned with water and tinted in the same way as ordinary emulsion paint.

ARTISTS' ACRYLIC PAINT

This paint is very quick-drying and durable. Its concentrated colour makes it ideal for many types of surface decoration, including stencilling, printing and general detail painting. It can also be used to colour acrylic glaze, although the paint should be watered down a little first, to avoid making a streaky effect.

Acrylics are also ideal paint bases, and can be rubbed back to create an old, distressed look (see p71). Although they are less cost-effective for covering large surfaces, they can be used on smaller items, or watered down to make general washes. Acrylics are usually available in tubes or jars, and some specialist types, suitable for work such as fabric painting, are now available. Acrylic paint can be quite harsh on brush hairs, so make sure brushes are cleaned thoroughly after use.

ARTISTS' OIL PAINT

Conventionally used for fine art, oil colours can also be used to tint any oil-based paint or glaze. However, they are slow-drying and will slightly delay the drying time of anything with which they are mixed. Paintbrushes must be cleaned with white spirit, before ordinary water and detergent is used.

The most subtle of paints, artists' oil colours can be used for almost any decorative finish, from barge painting to stencilling, although many people prefer to use quicker drying media, such as acrylics. If you want to keep the effect simple and clean, however, there is often nothing better than simply using oils to paint some scroll work or decorative feature, on to an old varnished piece of junk.

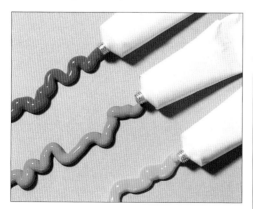
▲ Oil and acrylic paints often come in tubes

ENAMEL PAINTS

Providing a glossy finish, enamel paints are smooth and fairly quick-drying, which makes them ideal for decorative finishes such as barge painting. Although many manufacturers provide specific cellulose thinners to use as a solvent, these are often harsh on brush hairs and many people find that white spirit makes a reasonable and gentler alternative.

GLASS PAINTS

Made with resins that give brilliance and transparency, glass paints are also very durable and adhere to almost all surfaces. In addition to glass, they can be used on most plastics and acetate, although you should test a sample piece of plastic surface before beginning the final piece. Used from a spray can, glass paints create a lovely frosty effect. If they are squeezed straight from a tube, they can be used to create straight lines or edges for outlining patterns.

GOUACHE COLOURS

Although relatively expensive, these colours are extremely strong and are ideal for tinting water-based paints and glazes. They can also be used for simply painting a design on to a surface.

OIL-BASED HOUSEHOLD PAINTS

Oil-based paints come in flat, eggshell, and gloss finishes. However, gloss paint tends to create a crisp, clean effect which is not ideal for making an item look worn and old. For this reason, most people using these paints for decorative finishes tend to use flat or eggshell oil-based paints, both as base coats and to make glazes for the decorative finishes.

Oil-based paints give a much tougher finish than emulsion paints and are particularly useful in light-coloured glazes where scumble glaze (see glossary), and the addition of varnish, would be too yellowing. The only drawback to oil-based paints is that they take a long time to dry and need 24 hours between coats. To tint oil-based paints, use artists' oil paints or universal stainers, which are stronger and cheaper than artists' colours but not quite so subtle.

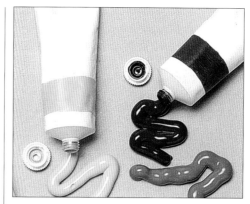
▲ Artists' paints have a greater range of colour

SPRAY PAINT

Available in easy-to-use cans, spray paint is produced in a large range of colours and finishes. Acrylic water-based spray paint, specifically intended for use in interior decoration, is ideal for almost all surfaces, including wood, metal, plaster, plastic and glass. It can be used for small projects such as stencilling, as the main colour for doors and shutters, and is especially suitable for children's trunks and toys because it is non-toxic. You can also buy spray enamels for metals and glass, pearlized finishes and polyurethane varnishes. Apply the paint in several thin coats rather than one heavy one, so as to avoid paint build-up and runs.

HINTS & TIPS: Spray paint safety

Drying paint should always have plenty of ventilation. However, when you are using spray paint, keep a window open during application and wear a protective face mask. Bear in mind that effective spray painting requires several consecutive layers, so work on a warm day during which the window can be kept open. Avoid working in strong draughts or breezes as the movement of air could affect the direction of the paint.

▲ Spray paints are ideal for stencilling

❖ TYPES OF PAINT ❖

TYPE	SOLVENT	TIPS
ARTISTS' ACRYLIC PAINT	water	Durable and quick-drying, can be used for basic painting or as a tint for glazes and water-based paints
ARTISTS' OIL PAINT	white spirit	Good quality paints most suitable for simple artistic effects. They can also be used to tint glazes
EGGSHELL	white spirit	A good, basic top coat that has less sheen than gloss but is more hard-wearing than emulsion
EMULSION	water	Available in matt or satin finishes, this paint is quick-drying and can be diluted to make washes
GLOSS	white spirit	A suitable paint for high-finish top coats, which need to be resistant to dirt and wearing
GOUACHE	water	Strong colours that can be applied as paint, but which also make ideal tints for glazes
OIL-BASED PRIMER	white spirit	Contains more oil than normal undercoats so it creates an effective sealant, although it is slow to dry
UNDERCOAT	white spirit	Provides a solid base for gloss or eggshell paints. Can be slow-drying

.... POWDERED PIGMENTS ....

Natural earth and mineral pigments come in powder form and can be mixed with other paint colours, acrylic and PVA mediums, and wax. They are available in an excellent range of colours from good art and specialist decorating shops.

Earth pigments are natural colours such as ochre, umber, red and sienna. Their usage dates back to prehistoric times when they were incorporated in many art forms, including cave and rock paintings. Mineral pigments have also been used as a method of colouring from ancient times, but their sources are now considered to be semi-precious stones, so the colours are now produced synthetically.

Experiment when adding pigment to any medium because it's easy to add too much or too little and create the wrong colour. Mix thoroughly to make sure the colour is even and there are no lumps. Make a very small mix first to avoid wasting materials and, when you are happy with the colour, then prepare a larger amount.

.... PRIMER ....

Usually oil-based, primers are applied to raw wood to help seal the surface and prepare it for additonal paint coverage. Its oil content makes primer ideal for very porous surfaces, but it can be slow-drying.

A different type of primer, rust-inhibiting primer, is used as a base paint for metallic surfaces. It should be applied as soon as any rust has been removed from the item, helping to prevent further corrosion. (See page 20 for more information.)

HINTS & TIPS: PVA & Acrylic Mediums

These water-based mediums can be used as glues or varnishes, but they can also be mixed with acrylic, gouache, universal stainers or powder pigments to make paints and washes. Artists' acrylic mediums are very useful for extending acrylic paints and for mixing with pure powder pigment to make concentrated acrylic colour. Oil-based mediums are also available but, like oil-based paints, they take a long time to dry. However, they do provide a resistant finish.

▲ Use powdered pigments for extra colour

▲ Add pigments in small quantities

PAINTING TOOLS

ANY VISIT TO A CRAFT shop or hardware store will reveal the vast array of painting tools available. Finding the right tool can be difficult and expensive – many manufacturers will lead you to believe that a different tool is required for every task. In fact, many pieces of equipment are quite adaptable. Providing they are cleaned and well-maintained, brushes should last for several years, developing a worn comfortable feel for the user – much like the junk itself!

If you are first embarking on a decorative project, assess what tools are required and make sure you are adequately equipped. However, avoid buying a brush in every size available – think about the specific effect you want to achieve and consider whether using the edge of another brush, or perhaps an old butter knife, might work. As you practise more techniques, your collection of tools should grow, but avoid investing in unnecessary equipment. Remember, the ethos behind the idea of doing up old junk is resourcefulness!

ARTISTS' BRUSHES

There is a diverse range of artists' brushes available. Even standard brushes, which are suitable for basic paint application, vary quite considerably in size and quality. It is well worth remembering that while cheap brushes seem more appealing to the purse, they are more likely to lose hairs frequently and possibly ruin the painted effect.

Although good quality brushes require more expense and maintenance care, it is often a false economy to invest in the cheapest brushes available. However, this does not mean that the best brush is always the most expensive. If possible, go for a brush that is 'middle–of–the–range', or ask shop staff for practical advice.

• BASIC ARTISTS' BRUSHES: These come in a variety of shapes. 'Flats' have a square end, helping to produce thin imprints, whereas 'filberts', which are also flat, gently taper into a conical shape. Round, finely pointed brushes are ideal for painting intricate designs, although these must be stored carefully as they are prone to easy damage.

• HOG-FITCHES: Good, all-purpose brushes, hog-fitches are generally used for oil painting and can be round, flat, or dome-shaped. Extremely versatile, they may be used for painting narrow bands of colour, applying glue, waxes and gilt creams, touching up paint and tamping down metal leaf.

HINTS & TIPS: Brushes

Brush hairs can be synthetic or made from animal hair. Synthetic brushes are ideal for acrylic painting, although they must be thoroughly cleaned after use – acrylic paint that has been left to dry can not be removed. For watercolours and soft techniques, quality animal hair brushes are best. Expensive types include sable or badger, but cheaper hog or squirrel hair is available.

Fine artists' brushes   *Sword liners*   *Hog-fitch brush*   *Soft-haired mop*   *Artists' brushes*   *Hog's hair varnishing brushes*   *Artists' brushes*   *Stippling brushes*

▲ Use large stippling brushes on main surfaces

• STIPPLING BRUSHES: Stippling is the term used for finely lifting on or off very fine speckles of paint. Stippling brushes have stiff, dense bristles in a squared-off shape, and come in a variety of sizes. They are useful for many paint techniques, and are particularly good for merging paints and removing hard lines and edges. A good quality decorating brush or a round continental brush can be used as a cheaper alternative.

• SWORD LINERS: These long-haired, soft brushes are tapered and angled, enabling them to produce many widths of line simply by varying the pressure applied to the brushstroke.

• SEA SPONGES: For sponging effects, natural sponges are the most popular tool. This is because their absorbency and irregular natural structure create attractive patterns. Always clean out natural sponges thoroughly after use – they are relatively expensive and should ideally be re-used several times.

• FLAT-HAIRED SYNTHETIC BRUSHES: Useful for applying two-part crackle varnish and acrylic goldsize, flat-haired synthetic brushes are very soft and leave no brush marks on the surface. Once used for varnish or goldsize work, they should be cleaned and kept aside purely for those tasks.

• SOFT-HAIRED MOP: Usually made from squirrel or camel hair, mop brushes are round and are primarily used to apply metallic powder to gold size during gilding. Thay can also be used to remove surplus gold or metal leaf, as described on page 62.

• DRAGGING BRUSHES: Sometimes known as floggers, dragging brushes are used for graining. They have long hard bristles that are dragged through wet glaze, creating the effect of long, straight, prominent lines.

• BRUSH CLEANERS AND RESTORERS: There are many kinds of brush cleaner available from hardware and paint stores that quickly remove oil-based paints and varnishes. Use a restorer following the cleaning to soften the bristles and give your brushes a longer life. If you have invested in expensive paintbrushes, it's worthwhile cleaning and restoring them.

• KITCHEN PAPER: This is invaluable for applying shellacs and polishes, for rubbing in and wiping off paint, mopping up spills and buffing waxes.

• PALETTE KNIFE: Flexible-ended palette knives can be used for both applying wood filler (see p20) and mixing oil colours on a palette. Finely shaped varieties can also be used for applying paint, producing an interesting texture and style.

• PAINT KETTLE: Although it is possible to paint out of a tin, using a paint kettle or paint tray allows you to use small amounts of paint at a time. This helps to keep the remaining paint in the tin clean and free from air. (Exposure to air will cause a skin to form on the surface of the paint inside the container.)

Use smooth pieces of dowelling or old wooden spoons for stirring paint and make sure that kettles (or paint trays) are cleaned thoroughly after use.

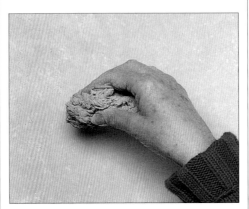

▲ A sea sponge makes an interesting texture

▲ Pull dragging brushes through wet glaze

• RADIATOR ROLLER: Suitable for large furniture surfaces, as well as walls and doors, radiator rollers are ideal for quick, simple coats of paint. Most can be fitted with a variety of replaceable roller sleeves.

HINTS & TIPS: Paint brush budgeting

Basic surface painting, such as emulsion, traditional paints and primers, can be performed using relatively cheap household paintbrushes. Have two or three brushes of different sizes – 2.5cm (1in), 4cm (1½in) and 5cm (2in) are good – to make flat, edged and rimmed surfaces easier to cover.

HINTS & TIPS: Applying paint

• Every paint comes with a specific set of instructions. Always read the label thoroughly and observe recommended drying times – even if a paint feels 'touch-dry', it is unlikely to be ready for re-coating until the manufacturer's time recommendation has passed.

• Always work in a well-ventilated area. The air should be a comfortable temperature; too hot or cold and the paint is likely to dry unevenly and cause problems of cracking or peeling later.

• Ensure the surrounding area is adequately protected, with plenty of spare cloths and cleaning materials to hand. Even decorative painting, using a small pot of paint, can be vulnerable to accidents and spillages.

• Most paints need to be stirred thoroughly. If this is the case, use a completely clean, dust-free stick, such as a piece of wooden dowelling or an old wooden spoon. Re-stir the mixture for every subsequent application.

• Prepare the surface thoroughly between coats. Glossy surfaces will need to be lightly sanded and cleaned, to ensure that the next coat adheres properly.

❖ PREPARATION FOR PAINTING ❖

TYPE	PREPARATION
METAL	Apply an appropriate metal primer, then the base colour
PLASTER, MASONRY AND CEMENT	Apply two coats of the base colour
PLASTICS AND CERAMICS	Sand the surface or apply a bonding medium (eg PVA), then two coats of base colour
WOODWORK	Fill, seal, sand and apply two coats of base colour

▲ Mask off areas with paper and/or tape

APPLYING PAINT

MOST PEOPLE WILL automatically paint in even, straight lines. It's a good idea, however, to brush with, rather than across, the grain on wood and it's not necessary to attempt uniformly even strokes. In fact, you can quite happily paint in a relaxed, more random way and this will give more texture and character to the surface of the piece.

Furniture that does not have a grain, such as whiteboard, can still be given a wood-like appearance by brushing in the direction that a grain would most likely follow. When painting metal and smaller decorative items, try painting in a completely random way, cross-hatching brush strokes. This leaves brush marks going in all directions and creates a lovely texture that looks good when used with antiquing glazes. Put a generous amount of paint on the brush and spread it evenly with long, simple strokes. Work in sections (unless instructed otherwise) and lay off excess paint with firm, even strokes.

▲ Paint in the direction of the grain

MASKING

Masking tape comes in a variety of thicknesses and is ideal for masking off areas that are to be coated with spray paint, or for securing stencils. However, it can sometimes be too sticky, taking off a layer of surface paint as it is removed. To avoid this, try de-tacking the tape by pressing it against a cotton cloth, before applying it to the surface.

Remember that masking tape should not be used for producing clean, straight lines because paint often bleeds underneath it, ruining the finish. If the surface is smooth, such as glass, clear adhesive tape can be used.

▲ Rub down wooden surfaces before painting

▲ Make sure that metallic surfaces are primed

CHOOSING COLOURS

THE VARIETY OF COLOURS now available in different paints and mediums can make choosing a final shade difficult. Many people tend to play safe and choose neutral colours which, while unadventurous, do increase the likelihood of creating an effect that will look good in any room. However, although it is important to make sure that the final piece fits in with its intended environment, it can be fun to experiment with a range of different colour possibilities.

In order to mix colours effectively, it's useful to understand how they interact.

PRIMARY COLOURS

The three primary colours, blue, red and yellow are the source of all other hues. By mixing one primary colour with another, ie blue with yellow, you create what is known as a secondary colour (in this case, green). The range of subtle shades of green that can be mixed is vast. If blue is mixed with yellow in a ratio of 2:1 (or vice versa), you create an intermediate colour. (The same applies to the other primary colours.) Finally, a tertiary colour is created by mixing the three primary colours together in different percentages. As an exercise in trying to find the right colour combinations, it can be useful to examine a colour wheel. This shows the primary, secondary and intermediate colours positioned in equal segments.

COMPLEMENTARY COLOURS

These are colours that appear opposite each other in the colour wheel; very simply, red is opposite to green, yellow to purple, and blue to orange. These colours react strongly with each other, often becoming more vibrant if they are set side-by-side.

If complementary colours are mixed in equal quantities they become dark grey and muddy, but a touch of one to the other will darken and tone it down without making the colour look dead.

▶ On the right is a suggested selection of useful acrylic pigments you can buy for making your own colours

Yellow ochre

Ultramarine blue

Raw sienna

Prussian blue

Burnt sienna

Cerulean blue

Red ochre

Veridian blue

Venetian red

Oxide of chromium

Cadmium red

Raw umber

Alizarin crimson

Burnt umber

COLOUR MIXING

THERE ARE NO RULES about which colours should or should not be mixed together. Many unlikely combinations can produce very interesting shades – it is simply a question of experimenting and developing an eye for colour. With practice, you may find that you come

to 'know' immediately how a certain colour will be affected by adding another pigment to it.

Remember when mixing paints that the texture and viscosity need to be as similar as possible. For example, artists' colours should be thinned down before being added to a glaze – if they are added straight from the tube, the paint will be too thick and the colour will not mix consistently. If you are planning on creating subtle variations of a hue, add tiny amounts of the darkener/lightener at a time. Although

it is possible to keep adding more tint or shade, it is impossible to remove any excess, once it has been added.

HINTS & TIPS: Shading & tinting colour

A 'shade' is made by adding black to a colour, helping to darken it and reduce its vividness. A 'tint' is created by adding white to a colour. This reduces the strength of the original hue and tends to make the colour more opaque. However, for a bit of variety, try adding raw umber to a colour. This will tone down any pigment, even white, immediately giving an aged appearance.

▼ The first three rows show colours mixed with their complementary colour, raw umber, black, and then white. The last two rows show different combinations of blues, yellows, and reds

NATURAL PIGMENTS

NATURAL EARTH PIGMENTS, which are warm and soft, tend to be quite easy to live with and are extremely adaptable. These colours have been used in paint-making for centuries; they are literally made of finely ground earth and are very inexpensive. With the addition of white they make very pretty pastel shades. Cooler shades of green and blue can also be chosen, from beautiful mineral colours.

MIXING PIGMENT WITH PAINT & PAINT MEDIUM

ONE ECONOMICAL WAY of creating a vast range of hues is to add powdered pigment to a paint medium. It can be added to emulsion or traditional paint, although do this gradually with thorough mixing, to avoid thickening the paint too much. (Remember that even if the paint looks adequately mixed in the pot, it may look less so when painted on to a surface. However, this unevenness of colour adds to the object's charm and gives a more authentic appearance of ageing.)

▲ Mix coloured pigment with medium gradually

Artists' acrylic colours and universal stainers can be used in place of powered pigment. Most types of pigment and medium are compatible with each other, so enjoy experimenting with different variations. Do, however, make sure that you are using all water-based (or oil-based) products. Also, when you are mixing pigment with paint, work in a room that is well-ventilated and take care not to inhale the pigment powder, as it can be toxic.

▲ Artists' colours can be used in medium

For darker or more intense shades, pigment can be mixed with PVA medium or glue and water, or with artists' acrylic medium. This will create a rather plastic paint without texture, but it is good for painting detailed designs. When diluted, it is also ideal for colourwashing and glazing. If you are using acrylic scumble glaze for a textured effect, you will only need to add a small amount of pigment and it is not necessary to add water.

PAINT FINISHES

PRACTISE A NEW PAINT technique on a painted piece of hardboard or medium density fibreboard (MDF), until you are happy with the result and feel proficient enough to use it on your own piece. These boards can be re-used; simply wipe off the oil or acrylic glaze with a damp cloth and white spirit.

When it comes to the final surface, be confident and enjoy experimenting. Most mistakes can be easily rectified – but many of the techniques described are unlikely to reveal faults. If you are doing glaze work, avoid patching up areas until the whole surface is dry.

▲ Verdigris makes an attractive finish

BAGGING

BAGGING

A simple way to create a marble or stone finish, bagging involves pouncing a plastic bag over a recently glazed surface. The bag gently lifts and redistributes the glaze creating a soft, luxurious texture.

COLOURWASHING

Fast and simple, colourwashing involves lightly covering the surface with a glaze using rough, varied brush strokes. Once dry, the criss-cross marks of the brush should be visible. Then apply another coat of glaze, crossing the earlier brush marks. The final effect should be soft, yet quite lively. For a more vivid surface, try using contrasting glazes.

CRACKLING

Crackling is one of the easiest paint effects to master, providing painted surfaces such as furniture, picture frames or small shelves with an interesting surface texture. A crackle finish is achieved by applying a layer of crackle medium sandwiched between two coats of colour. As the top coat of paint dries, small cracks appear, exposing areas of the base colour. See the section on crackle glaze on page 72.

VERDIGRIS

Verdigris is a popular paint finish that simulates the natural weathering that occurs on copper, bronze and brass. While a true verdigris finish develops after years of exposure to the elements, decorators can re-create the effect by a clever use of acrylic paints. Green emulsion glaze is applied to a bronze base, and then light blue and green emulsions are roughly painted on top. Whiting can then be applied.

HINTS & TIPS: Choosing colours

As the glaze for colourwashing is very transparent, choose a lighter or darker version of the base for a subtle effect, or a strong contrast for a lively effect. Remember that the base colour will be visible in some areas, so a blue wash over a red or pink base will appear violet in some parts and blue in others. Always experiment on a sample board first to see what effect you can expect when the job is finished.

DRAGGING

Dragging produces a soft, subtle finish to many different surfaces. A stiff-bristled brush is dragged through wet glaze, creating a soft, grained texture with fine lines.

LIMING

Liming is a traditional technique, best suited to open-grained timbers such as oak, maple, pitch pine, elm and ash. Apply liming paste to the wood and then seal with sand sealer. Rub down the surface with fine grade abrasive paper and then varnish, creating a soft, whitened effect. (See the 'Carved Linen Chest' project on page 168.)

MARBLING

Although there are a number of different marbling effects, most can be achieved by simply applying 2–3 soft glazes in uneven patches onto a wet base. Softly merge them with a clean rag and then with a soft-hair brush. To create a veined effect, use a sword liner brush to quickly draw some veins along the surface and then soften with a sea sponge. With practice, and an emphasis on random application, the marbled effect should gradually come together.

RAGGING-ON & OFF

Another simple technique, ragging-on involves gradually applying glaze with a piece of scrunched-up fabric to the coated base. To create a varied pattern, undo and re-scrunch the rag every time you need more glaze.

Apply the glaze to the base-coated surface and, while the glaze is still wet, scrunch a piece of material into a ball and dab it over the surface to remove areas of the wet glaze. Turn the pad constantly to avoid a mechanical, repetitive look. Use different materials to achieve variations in texture.

SPONGING-ON & OFF

Sponging-on produces a crisp, mottled texture. Glaze is applied using a sponge and two or three different glazes.

Sponging-off involves dabbing a surface, coated in wet glaze, with a damp sea sponge. As the glaze lifts, the base coat beneath should be visible through the soft texture.

▲ Paint can be applied following the grain (left), or cross-hatched for texture (right)

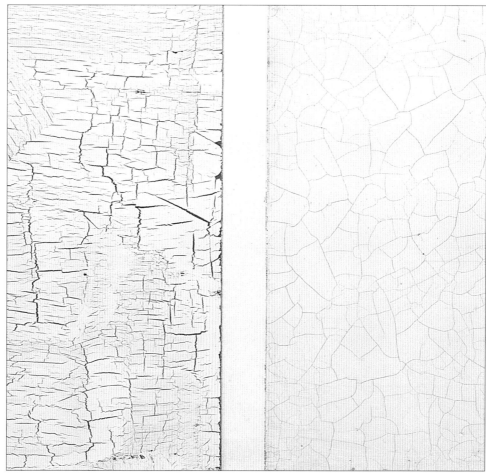

▲ Crackled finishes can be created with two-part crackle varnish (left), or crackle glaze (right)

Decoupage

A FRENCH WORD MEANING 'to cut out', decoupage is the art of cutting paper images, glueing them to a surface and giving them several coats of varnish until the design looks handpainted. Decoupage was particularly popular in the 17th and 18th centuries as a pastime for ladies of the French and Italian courts. It was still popular in Victorian times, which saw the advent of colour printing and dye-cut scraps. Decoupage is currently enjoying a huge revival, partly helped by the increasing availability of exciting gift wraps and printed images. It's an easy technique to achieve but it is time consuming – a typical project needs about fourteen different treatments. However, spending time on the project will ensure a professional finish.

MATERIALS & EQUIPMENT

THE MOST OBVIOUS starting point is finding the piece you wish to decorate. Almost anything can be decoupaged, no matter what its age or material, but have a think about what kind of object might be useful, or what would look good in your home. Remember, also, that the shape and size of the object may further influence the pattern and design you wish to create.

Old items can be found in junk shops and at antique markets, but craft stalls are also an excellent source of suitable wooden and cardboard objects. By using fabric instead of paper, decoupage can even be extended to decorating old wicker furniture and baskets.

Once you have decided what to decoupage, you will then need to consider more specific equipment, as described below. For equipment and materials used in stripping and preparing items, prior to priming, see page 16.

▲ Books often contain ideas and designs

SOURCES OF CUT-OUTS

The range of different wrapping and gift papers is now so vast that it's highly possible you'll find a good design simply by walking into a local card shop. However, there are many other useful sources of attractive designs. Calendars, children's books, posters, gardening manuals and magazines are all useful sources, as well as specially published decoupage books, which provide a selection of prints that can be cut out, photocopied, enlarged or reduced according to your needs.

Decorative maps, calligraphy, hieroglyphics or border patterns can also be used for the technique, as can paper scraps – which was one of the popular options of Victorian times.

HINTS & TIPS: Picture cut-outs

Avoid using cut-outs which have heavy print on the reverse side. Although sealants do help prevent print showing through, heavy ink can still be visible through thin paper and will ruin the design.

▲ Rolls of gift wrap make ideal cut-out sources

BRUSHES

It is useful to have a range of different brushes for the decoupage process. Try to ensure that they are of the best quality possible – poorer quality brushes tend to shed hairs which can spoil the varnished surface.

• ACRYLIC PAINTBRUSH: Although any artists' brush can be used for painting, decoupage tends to be applied to acrylic-painted surfaces. Acrylic paints can be very harsh on fine brushes such as sable so, if you plan to do a lot of decoupage work, it may be worth investing in paintbrushes that are kept aside purely for this technique.

• SQUIRREL MOP BRUSH: This is ideal for coating large surfaces with emulsion paint because the soft hairs help to ensure a really smooth finish. Again, although the brush is not vital for decoupage work, it will help to ensure a really fine surface for cut-outs and varnishing.

• GLUE BRUSH: Always have a separate brush for applying glue. Although a cheap one will suffice, make sure that the bristles are a suitable size. (Delicate cut-outs will tear if large brushes are used on them.)

• VARNISHING BRUSH: A good quality, silky paintbrush is adequate for applying varnish and saves the expense of buying specialist equipment. However, make sure the brush is always cleaned thoroughly to prevent stiffening.

ADHESIVES

Decoupage cut-outs require two types of adhesive – temporary tack for the initial arranging and paste or spray glue for final sticking.

• ADHESIVE TACK: This is ideal for sticking cut-outs into temporary positions as you arrange the design. Avoid cheap brands as they are likely to be very greasy, and could mark the paper cut-outs.

• PVA GLUE: Flexible and reasonably fast-drying, this glue dries to a clear finish and should work for most decoupage processes. Sprays can also be used, although they are less versatile for reglueing edges and borders.

ABRASIVES

Different grades of abrasive paper or wire wool are needed at all stages of decoupage, from smoothing the initial surface to rubbing down the final layer of varnish. Wet-and-dry abrasive papers can be used for rubbing down wood, metal or oil-based paint surfaces. However, avoid using them on emulsion paint surfaces, or on varnish that is covering prints, as it is difficult to see the depth of abrasion through the wet 'slurry' that occurs.

PAINTS

The type of paint you use for the base can vary although always check that your washes, sealants and decorative paints are all compatible. Remember to prime new or stripped wood (see p20) so that the grain is adequately sealed, and give new, stripped or unpainted metal a coat of rust-inhibiting primer.

• EMULSION PAINTS: Thinned down and built up in layers, emulsion paints make a marvellous base for decoupage. They are porous, however, and need sealing with an acrylic sealant before decoration is applied.

• OIL-BASED HOUSE PAINTS: Use flat or, eggshell finishes for items that need to be hardwearing. However avoid using gloss oil-based paint as the high sheen makes the surface too slippery and glue-resistant for decoupage.

▲ A range of tools is required for a professional decoupage finish

▲ Spend time cutting out intricate shapes and patterns

43

• ARTISTS' OIL COLOURS: These are useful for mixing with oil-based paints to provide more colour variation. However, they are slow-drying and will slightly delay the drying time of the original paint. If they are used on their own to colour cracks or make antiquing fluid, these paints will need at least a couple of days to dry thoroughly.

• ARTISTS' ACRYLIC PAINTS: In terms of decoupage, these paints are most useful for adding finishing touches. They can be used to highlight cut-outs or applied over emulsion or oil-based paints for extra detail.

• OIL-BASED AND WATERCOLOUR PENCILS: These are ideal for colouring prints and cut-outs. However, take care when using watercolour pencils not to get the paper too wet – otherwise the cut-out may wrinkle. Pencils are also useful for repairing any accidental damage to prints which might occur during the rubbing-down process.

CUTTING & ROLLING EQUIPMENT

Complex decoupage designs are worth spending some time over. Always keep cutting instruments sharp as this will both improve the quality of the shape and help to minimize the likelihood of accidents (blunt instruments tend to slip more easily).

• KNIVES: Most craft knives are not sharp or flexible enough for decoupage projects. However, slim metal scalpels that take renewable blades are ideal – although the technique does require practice. Remember to use a good cutting mat to protect the work surface.

• SCISSORS: Most household scissors are too large and cumbersome for intricate shapes, although they can be used for cutting pieces into more manageable sizes. Use a sharp pair of curved, cuticle scissors for cutting elaborate patterns.

• ROLLERS: Use a small rubber roller for going over cut-outs that are stuck in place. This is particularly important for large pieces because excess glue or air can get trapped beneath the paper.

▲ Cut-outs can be sealed before varnishing

SEALANTS

Available in spray or tin form, sealants have many uses. They can be used to seal porous surfaces, such as emulsion-painted wood, to prevent subsequent layers of glue or varnish sinking in, and also to fix and seal hand-coloured prints so that the colour does not bleed when glue or varnish is applied. Although they are not vital in decoupage, it is worth taking the time to seal cut-outs before applying varnish. This is because the sealant makes paper less absorbent, thus helping to strengthen delicate designs.

VARNISHES

Varnishing is the defining stage of the decoupage process. If it is carried out with patience, varnishing creates a wonderful, luminous hand-painted quality. Remember that for a professional finish, a minimum of five separate coats will be required. Each layer will obviously need sufficient drying time, and, after the third application, the surface should be lightly rubbed down between coats. Some varnishes have a yellowing effect on the underlying surface so be sure to choose your varnish type carefully.

▲ Protect cracked finishes with varnish

• ACRYLIC VARNISH: This varnish is the best product for retaining original, underlying colours. However, it is not very hard-wearing or resistant so apply at least one coat of yacht or polyurethane varnish to the top layer of acrylic varnish. This will provide a tough finish, suitable for hardworking surfaces such as tables and trays.

• POLYURETHANE AND YACHT VARNISHES: These varnishes have a mellowing effect and, if that is the desired finish, can be further enhanced by using an antiquing technique (see p37). Polyurethane varnish is available in matt, satin or gloss finishes and is sufficiently tough for most household uses. However, yacht varnish, which is only available in gloss, is even more resistant but will, subsequently, create an even stronger yellowing effect to the decoration beneath.

• CRACKLE VARNISH: This varnish is ideal for pieces that are to have a cracked and ancient appearance, particularly those with classical designs. (The 'Floral Place Mats' on page 140 use this technique.) Remember, however, that the cracked finish will still need a couple of coats of protective of varnish. (Crackle varnish is distinct from crackle glaze – the medium applied between coats of paint for a crackled effect.)

HINTS & TIPS: Using varnished glass

One useful way of identifying how final colours on a decoupage project will look is to view them through a varnish glass.

1 Simply take a piece of picture glass 15 x 10cm (6 x 4in) and apply a coat of polyurethane varnish, using strokes in one direction. (Be sure to leave one end of the strip clear so that you can grip the glass.)

2 Once dry, apply a second coat of varnish in the opposite direction. Continue until you have built up at least six coats of varnish.

3 To use the tool, simply hold it over any base coats or cut-outs that are being considered for a specific project. Looking through the varnished glass, you should get an instant idea of how the colours will look when the project is eventually finished and varnished. (This can be invaluable for working out a colour scheme and for mixing different hues.)

WAX

If you have the time, applying one or two coats of wax to the final piece will help to ensure a really deep sheen. Wax is particularly effective on surfaces that have been sealed with either matt or satin varnishes and provides an easy to clean finish. However, the item will need to be rubbed down with fine grade abrasive paper or wire wool, before the wax is applied. Use tinted wax (see p73) for an antiqued finish.

PREPARATION

As WITH ANY DECORATIVE technique, solid preparation of the surface will greatly influence the success of the final finish. Basic tasks such as stripping, rubbing down and filling (see p17) all need to be tackled before the more creative process can begin. Remember that many decoupage finishes benefit from their extremely smooth appearance, so be prepared to rub and sand down the wood or metal base adequately. Treat any rust spots or woodworm with an appropriate treatment and fill holes with filler before sanding. If the object is metal, apply rust-inhibiting primer to ensure that rust won't become a problem in future years. Once all of these procedures have been completed, be sure to clean away all dust and debris.

APPLYING THE BASE COAT

Once any necessary primers and undercoats have been applied, the object will be ready to receive its base coat. Use oil-based paints such as flat or eggshell finish for items that are likely to receive a lot of wear or be chipped

▲ Rub down the surface following the grain

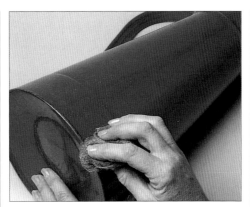

▲ Use wire wool to remove rust

easily. Remember that these take time to dry, however, and each coat must be gently rubbed down with fine grade abrasive paper and then tacked off.

For a more traditional technique, use water-based paints which have been diluted with a little water (about a tablespoon of water to half an average-sized jar). Once the paint has been adequately mixed, apply it evenly, in the direction of the grain. Check for drips

▲ Apply rust-inhibiting primer to metal surfaces

and allow to dry. Once two or three coats have been applied, rub down with fine grade abrasive paper and wipe with a tack rag. Then repeat the entire process, rubbing down and tacking between coats, until you have built up a perfectly smooth, even surface. Depending on the make of paint, between six and ten applications will be needed.

HINTS & TIPS: Using an undercoat

Apply undercoat to a primed wooden surface for extra sealing. Although it is not always necessary to use undercoat paint on a sound painted or varnished surface, it does make a useful 'masking' coat if the existing colour is particularly intrusive.

COLOURING A PRINT

Although there is a vast array of wrapping paper that can be used for decoupage, a more traditional method involves colouring and applying prints. Make sure that any print you wish to use is of no particular value and ensure that your design will fit and work on the chosen object. Then, before cutting it out, apply colour to any dull or black and white areas. You can use ordinary pencils for this, but for a more traditional effect, use oil-based or water-based pencils.

If you are using oil-based pencils, aim for plenty of variety in tone and leave small amounts of white uncovered to keep the picture vibrant. Avoid being too subtle with your colouring technique – very delicate colours tend to disappear or lose their hue under several coats of varnish.

Use short strokes packed close together, ensuring coverage and control. If you are grading a colour from light to dark, let longer and shorter strokes gently dovetail into one another where the light starts to merge into the dark. For a more uniform effect, keep the strokes going in the same direction, like the original shading strokes on the print. Once complete, spray sealant (sparingly) over the print. Leave the print to dry before cutting it out.

Use water-colour pencils in the same way, although avoid filling in large areas. Instead, use a fine artists' brush to gently apply water to the colour, spreading it across the design in long, soft movements. The tone can be varied by altering the amount and depth of colour that is spread across the pattern. However, do be careful not to get the paper too wet as it is liable to crinkle.

▲ Colour in cut-outs for extra decoration

CUTTING & ARRANGING THE DESIGN

PERHAPS THE MOST FUN STAGE of the process, cutting and arranging the design is where creativity and inspiration come to the fore. Remember to cut large pieces into more manageable sizes, before beginning the intricate work of cutting out a design.

When using a scalpel, work on a cutting board and, wherever possible, move the paper rather than the knife, which should be cutting towards you. Similarly, if you are using a pair of scissors, gently move the paper into position as you cut, rather than attempting to steer the scissors.

▲ Carefully cut out the decoupage shapes

Always cut the smaller 'inner' pieces of background away first and leave the outside contours until the end. Similarly, leave any flimsy, delicate pieces well supported by adjacent background until the last minute. Once cut out, store each piece carefully where it cannot get lost or creased. Flat, plastic display pages are useful storage places as they are waterproof and can be checked for contents without causing damage.

▲ Arrange the design with adhesive tack

▲ Glue the cut-outs into position

Take time to arrange the design, perhaps experimenting with different positions by using adhesive tack on the back of each piece. Try to give a focal point to the design, rather than scattering the cut-outs at random, and think about how different shapes and colours interact with each other. If it helps, add finishing touches, such as colour, to the cut-outs at this stage.

GLUEING THE DESIGN

There are two different methods for applying glue in decoupage. One involves spreading small amounts of glue on to the object before laying each piece into place, and the other is simply to apply glue to the back of the cut-out, before positioning it. Both techniques have different advantages and disadvantages, but applying glue to the cut-out is likely to minimize the presence of unwanted adhesive.

Before glueing on to an emulsioned surface, lightly spray the surface with sealant. This will make the paint less porous and provide more time for arranging the design. Then glue each piece on to the object, making sure that the cut-outs are absolutely smooth and that all the edges are stuck down.

Go over larger cut-outs with a rubber roller to squeeze out any air bubbles or deposits of excess glue. Press down on the edges of each cut-out with a fingertip, checking vulnerable sections such as thin strips or spiky protrusions. If you find a loose edge, take a small amount of glue on the end of a cocktail stick/toothpick and slide it under the paper, holding it down for a second or two with your fingertip. Wipe off any excess glue with a soft cloth wrung out in warm water.

▲ Wipe away excess glue

HINTS & TIPS: Applying glue

Use aluminium kitchen foil as a base for cut-outs when applying glue. This will both help to protect the work surface and make lifting the coated paper easier – the shape will not stick to the metallic surface. When the foil becomes sticky, simply throw it away and use another piece.

VARNISHING

THE AIM OF VARNISHING in decoupage is to submerge the design completely. The finish should be totally smooth so that the edges of the paper cut-outs can not be felt. This takes numerous layers of varnish which will, of course, require adequate drying time.

Apply the varnish with generous strokes, catching any drips or runs. If you are using polyurethane varnish, apply two coats before gently rubbing down and wiping with a tack rag. For water-based varnishes, apply three or four coats before rubbing and wiping down. After this, whatever the type of varnish, always gently sand down and wipe off between further coats. About six to ten coats will be needed.

▲ Apply varnish to the whole surface

FINISHING

ONCE THE VARNISHING is complete, lightly rub down the surface once more and wipe off with the tack rag. It is then a good idea to apply a protective coat of wax, helping to ensure the durability of the decoupage finish. A number of antiquing techniques can then be used.

CREATING A PLAIN ANTIQUED FINISH

A basic antiqued effect can be achieved simply by coating a darkish glaze over the object. The mixture is left to stain the surface, before being gently rubbed away to reveal a darkened hue beneath. The secret is to highlight corners and edges – places where time would have caused a build-up of dirt, or where areas would have gradually become worn. However, keep the effect subtle and avoid over-using the stain.

MIXING THE PAINT

Squeeze into the bottom of a jam jar about 2.5cm (1in) of raw umber oil paint and about 6mm (¼in) of black. Add a little white spirit and mix into a smooth creamy paste with an artists' paintbrush. Gradually add a little more white spirit until your mixture is slightly thinner than single cream.

APPLYING THE ANTIQUING

Using a normal household paintbrush, paint the mixture over the entire piece, poking it well into any nooks and crannies and especially around locks or handles. With a dry, clean brush, work over the surface, redistributing the antiquing mixture and wiping off any excess with the brush.

DISTRESSING THE FINISH

Cut some nylon tights or stockings into medium-sized pieces and form them into wads. Take one of the wads and begin rubbing the surface in a circular motion. Rub off more of the antiquing mixture in places where the item might have become worn, and leave traces of fluid in areas where dirt is likely to have collected. Change the nylon wads as they get saturated in mixture. When you are satisfied with the effect, leave to dry and then apply a coat of varnish.

CREATING A 'CRACKLE' VARNISH FINISH

Crackled effects (such as the one used for the 'Floral Place Mats' on page 140) are popular for finishing many decoupage projects. Sometimes known as 'craquelure' the easiest method is to use a ready-made kit which is available in most craft shops.

APPLYING THE COATS

Apply the oil-based varnish to the surface and allow to dry to the point of tackiness. Then paint on the second varnish, which is water-based and fast-drying. The cracks appear on the surface after the second coat has dried because the oil-based coat beneath is still drying and 'on the move'.

For large cracks, the oil-based coat should be very tacky when the water-based coat is applied. However, for smaller cracks, leave the second coat until the oil-based varnish is almost dry. (Test the varnish in an unobtrusive spot until you are sure that the base coat has dried appropriately.) Reluctant cracks can be encouraged by using a hair-dryer, but avoid creating a heat that is too intense as this may ruin the surface. (See the 'Ageing Techniques' section on page 71 for further advice.)

FINISHING

Once dry, the cracks will need emphasizing to ensure that they are visible. To achieve this, cover the item with antiquing mixture (or gold), leave for a couple of minutes, and then wipe off with a soft cloth. Allow the surface to dry and then varnish.

HINTS & TIPS: Finishing

Always rub down the varnish layers very gently – the paper cut-outs are close to the surface and may get caught with the abrasive paper. If this happens, the resulting white marks can usually be disguised by smudging on some oil-based or watercolour pencils. Remember to seal the repair with a spray of acrylic sealant, before continuing.

▲ Gold can be used for highlighting cracks

▲ Apply antiquing fluid before wiping it away with a brush or cloth

Stencilling

HIGHLY VERSATILE AND USEFUL for repeating images, stencilling is a simple technique that can create some quite stunning results. The practice actually dates back to ancient times – the Egyptians of 2000 years ago used geometric stencils to create magnificent borders in their tombs and palaces. Most modern stencilled designs are characterized by their sectioned appearance. Colours are applied in layers and clear divisions are made between different segments. Look at the stencilled pattern of a flower, for example, and you will note that each petal is cut as an individual part of the design, and that the flower head, stem and leaves are all quite separate. The simple, but stunning effect of stencilling can be achieved quite easily to decorate various surfaces.

EQUIPMENT & MATERIALS

COMMERCIALLY PRODUCED, pre-cut stencils and stencilling kits are available in most craft stores. However, it can be more original – and interesting – to make your own, personal stencils, using a range of basic materials.

STENCIL CARDS

Stencilled, painted shapes are created by cutting out the desired pattern on a stencil card. In other words, wherever there is a hole in the card, paint will appear. The type of card (or transparent sheet) that is used, however, will influence how quick and easy the pattern is to create.

• OILED MANILA CARD: The traditional choice for stencilling, oiled manila card is tough, durable and surprisingly easy to cut. However, it tends only to be available in A2 and A3 sheets, which can be restrictive if you wish to make large repeats. Symmetrical patterns also require careful tracing (see p24) on to the card, using a reverse tracing technique. This is because the card is opaque and can not be laid over the design on a light box, as other transparent materials can.

• ACETATE SHEETS: One of the most durable of stencilling materials, acetate is often used for commercial stencilling projects. Its transparency enables you to see exactly what you are doing, and assists with positioning on the object. However, acetate is extremely smooth, and so it can be common for blades to slip on the surface. Always take care when cutting out a pattern and apply even pressure to the knife at all times.

• PLAN TRACE: A tracing paper that combines the best properties of both acetate and manila card, plan trace can be easily cut, is translucent and extremely tough. It may also be used in photocopiers, making copying, enlarging or reducing of designs much simpler, and its fine density ensures that cut outlines are neat, clean and crisp.

▲ Plan trace is both durable and easy to cut

CUTTING TOOLS

Accurate cutting is vital when making a good stencil so spend plenty of time on creating the right shape. Always use sharp blades in a scalpel and ensure that they fit the handle properly. Use a proper cutting mat, which will protect the surface and minimize blunting of the blade. Scissors can be useful for large, flowing designs but, with practice, scalpels produce a much cleaner cut.

HINTS & TIPS: Stencilling

• Stencilling should involve a light, soft blending of colours to give highlighted and shaded areas. Oil-based media are good for creating this effect because they blend well and can cover large areas.

• Position overlay stencils carefully to avoid smudging the pattern underneath and don't overload the brush – paint is easy to apply but sometimes difficult to remove. If you require a second colour without gaps or bridges, make two separate stencils. The first stencil will be used for the background colour, and the second design positioned over this to add the other colours.

▲ Oiled manila card is opaque but easy to cut

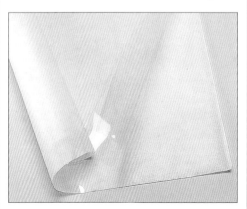

▲ Acetate sheets are tough and durable

PAINTS

Specialist stencilling paints are available but it can be cheaper and more creative to experiment with other types. Almost any paint can be used, although some have more advantages than others.

• EMULSION PAINTS: Available in a variety of colours and handy, tester-size tins, emulsion paint is water-based and easy to use. It comes in two different finishes, matt and vinyl silk, which can create their own interesting effects when used in conjunction with each other. For example, stencilling a design in a slightly darker shade of vinyl silk, on to a matt base of the same colour, can simulate rich damasks or brocades. Alternatively, by isolating and stencilling one element in vinyl silk, you can lend a feeling of movement to the overall design, as the light is reflected by the paint's slight sheen.

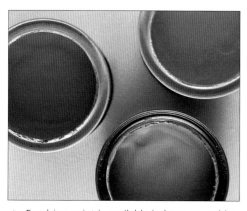
▲ Emulsion paint is available in large quantities

• ARTISTS' ACRYLIC PAINTS: Perhaps the most flexible and manageable of paints for stencilling, these paints are suitably hardwearing yet water-based. They can be used neat or diluted, although very diluted mixtures are more likely to run under the stencil card.

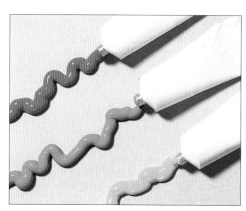
▲ Acrylic paints come in a range of colours

▲ Mix spray paints with successive coats

• SPRAY PAINTS: Ideal for people who find hand-applied methods difficult to master, spray paints are available from art, craft and model shops in an increasing colour range. Although they are appropriate for most porous surfaces, however, car sprays should be used for stencilling on surfaces such as glass, ceramics or metals.
  Always apply spray paints in thin, even layers – almost a dusting – so as to avoid runs and dribbles. To achieve this, hold the can as far from the stencil as possible, using additional paper masking around the main stencil card.
  Spray colours can be mixed by using successive, very lightly sprayed coats because the paint hits the surface in tiny pin-prick spots, which are easily offset by using different hues. Only ever use spray paints in well-ventilated conditions and always wear a mask.

• ALKYD PAINTS: These provide many of the qualities of oil paints with as fast a drying time as acrylic. The texture is buttery, so they do need to be thinned with white spirit or turpentine substitute for stencilling.

• OIL PAINTS: The choice of purists, oil paints are the trickiest type of paint to use for stencilling and they dry extremely slowly. However, for people who are practised in oil paint application and mixing, these paints can create beautiful transparent effects when mixed with a little varnish or oil painting medium. Extreme care must be taken in removing the stencil after applying paint. Oil pigments remain unstable for at least four hours, which means that accidental smudging, by lifting the card too soon, is a hazard.

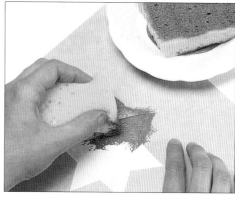
▲ Sponges make ideal paint applicators

PAINT APPLICATORS

Paint can be applied through a stencil in a variety of ways. Using a sponge is quick, cheap and easy, but brushes also provide a variety of different effects. Although a proper stencil brush is ideal, an ordinary brush can be adapted by binding the bristles (see below) or cutting them down. Alternatively, a rag dipped in drying paint will give a direct imprint. This can be used to create an interesting random effect, especially over a base, opaque colour, to create a decorative, finishing touch.

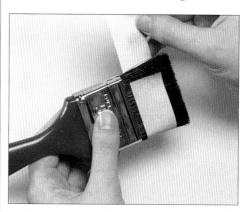
▲ Bind tape around bristles to make them stiff

❖ MAKING YOUR OWN ❖
Stencil & Paint Applicator

Before embarking on a large stencilling project, it's useful to try out the technique with a few simple tools. Try making your own stencil by cutting out a simple design on an empty cereal packet. Although the waxed side is ideal for stencilling, the porous side will need to be varnished to help make it waterproof. For the paint applicator, cut off about a third of a kitchen sponge. (Avoid sponges with large holes as these will cause a build-up of paint.) Use the rest of the sponge as a paint reservoir (see p54), which will help to ensure a regular flow of paint.

DESIGNING A STENCIL

INSPIRATION FOR A stencil design can come from virtually anywhere. For many people, ideas for repeating patterns spring from existing home decoration, such as wallpaper or upholstery, or from various soft furnishings around the home. If this is the case, the simplest technique may be to trace the pattern direct.

Try focusing on the more dominant elements in the room and remove them from surrounding shapes to see how they work alone. Remember, also, that single motifs are likely to need less reworking than a stencil that is to continuously repeat. For border patterns, use leaves or scrolls as connecting links.

▲ Carefully trace over the design

Flatten out the design, then carefully trace it accurately line for line (see p24), using a soft fibre-tip pen or soft pencil. Take out any small or complicated shapes that might prove impossible to reproduce – the idea is to create a design that is derived, rather than directly copied, from the existing decor. If necessary, take another sheet of tracing paper and make a new tracing, which uses the main design elements.

▲ Simplify the traced design

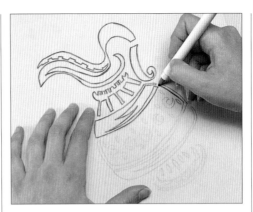

▲ Draw around the areas to be cut

Remember that stencils use 'negative space' – that is to say, it's the area you cut out that creates the pattern. So negative space should always be completely surrounded by positive space (the uncut remainder of the stencil). There should be a constant border that is not cut or broken by the intrusion of another shape.

In some cases, it will be necessary to create your own borders or 'filaments'. For example, a bunch of grapes gains its original form through shape and colour. To convey the shape of grapes, it will be necessary to create filaments that define the outline of the bunch and, within that, a few odd grapes. (See the 'Vine Leaf Table' project on p114.)

The same principle applies to more complicated flower or leaf shapes. For your stencil to work properly, you will need a space of around 5mm (^{1}/10in) between each cut. Smaller filaments are liable to break and may allow paint to seep behind the stencil, causing the picture to 'bleed'. For this reason, try not to leave too many 'floating' or unsupported filaments. Bridges that are in isolation tend to make weak joins, which will move or break as paint is applied through the stencil.

HINTS & TIPS: Drawing filaments

Make sure that each negative space is constantly bordered by positive space. Then map out where you want your filaments to go. To make the process easier, follow the design line for line with an extremely thick marker pen. (A wide nib will give you the thickness of each filament in one line, without having to draw intricate shapes.) However, do make a mental note to take care when cutting; you must cut either side of the line rather than down the middle.

SCALING UP AND DOWN

Some designs need to be enlarged or downsized from their original trace.

• PHOTOCOPYING: After measuring the desired size, photocopy the design to the nearest possible setting, keeping any intermediate-sized copies as they may prove useful later. It's also a good idea to take a few copies at the correct size, ensuring that there will be sufficient versions to adapt for the final stencil.

• GRIDS: These can also be used for scaling designs. If the original design is 20cm (8in) high and the required size is 40cm (16in), draw a grid over the pattern using squares measuring 1 x 1cm (^{1}/2 x ^{1}/2in approx). On a separate sheet of paper draw another grid, each of whose squares is exactly double, that is 2 x 2cm (1 x 1in approx). (Draw the grid in ink so that as the design is transferred in pencil by freehand, mistakes can be erased without affecting the grid markings.) Then, either by eye or using a ruler, assess the position of each line within the squares on the smaller grid. Sketch the overall shape onto the larger grid, enlarging the lines to the correct size.

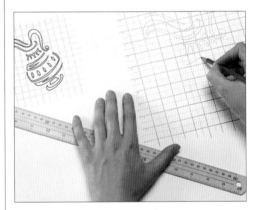

▲ Use a grid for enlarging designs

HINTS & TIPS: Reversing the design

If you come across a design element that is perfect in size and shape for the stencil but is pointing in the wrong direction, trace it and reverse the paper, creating an exact mirror image. Remember that although stencil cards can be reversed, the first side will be coated in paint and may ruin the surface. It is therefore adviseable to cut out two stencil cards, marking one as the correct position, the other reverse, and then use each accordingly.

▲ Pantographs can be used for enlargements

▲ Make a final trace of the refined design

• **CREATING A GRID:** The least reliable and accurate of methods, the design can be transferred to card simply by drawing a grid on the card and copying the pattern. (Using the same technique as that described for scaling up and down.) However, this technique does require freehand skills and leads to fuzzy lines which can be a hindrance for accurate cutting. Going over the 'proper' pencil lines with a heavy felt tip pen may help.

• **PANTOGRAPHS:** These can also be used for enlarging images. Although using one of these gadgets effectively takes practice, the result can be a very accurate, refined enlargement (or downsizing) of the original design. As you follow the outline of the smaller image, a pencil, rested in the pivoted levers draws the same outline but to a specified scale. Once mastered, the device can be used for basic outline positioning, before the remaining image is drawn freehand. Interestingly, many people find that using a pantograph has actually helped them to improve their hand and eye co-ordination.

dipped in ink — remember that making a trace will not damage the original underneath so be as relaxed and loose as possible. The original, disjointed pencil marks should be replaced with elegant lines, as you become increasingly familiar with both the tracing technique, and the design itself. With confidence, your lines will become more constant and the design should start to flow a little more freely. This final version was known in the Italian Renaissance as a 'cartoon'.

To check the symmetry of the design, and to identify any mistakes, unwanted marks or poor proportions, try turning the picture over and viewing it from the back.

TIGHTENING THE DESIGN

Once traced, it's a good idea to assess the stencil design in its intended position. The early stages of simplification can make the design seem a little sparse but, if it is to form a repeating pattern, hold two or three copies close together in order to see how the overall shape will appear. If large blank spaces are likely to occur, return to any under- or over-sized copies and see if the design can be elaborated with additional flourishes. In particular, think about the elements bordering the design in the original pattern. If necessary, trace additional sections and create further stencils but remember that much of the attractiveness of stencilled patterns come from their relative simplicity.

• **MAPPING PIN:** Although it's quite labour-intensive, this method can be fun and was favoured by stencillers in the Renaissance. Position the design on top of the card and push through the lines with a series of pin-pricks. Judge the distance between the holes carefully — too far apart and they will leave only the barest of impressions; too close and the card could end up becoming excessively perforated.

Ordinary needles and pins tend to produce holes that are too fine for this exercise. However, mapping pins, with their stout heads and long sharp points, generally make neatly rounded holes and are ideal for transferring designs through to the stencil card beneath. Ensure that the design and card are adequately anchored together, so that the original picture does not slip and alter the accuracy of the pin-pricks.

▲ Put the design together to check for gaps

TRANSFERRING THE DESIGN

If possible, photocopy the final design on to a sheet of plan trace. This will ensure that there is a back-up copy of the design, just in case anything should go wrong during the cutting stage. For transparent stencil cards, such as plan trace or acetate, the design can be immediately cut out (see p52) but for manila stencil cards, there are four different methods for transferring the design, each described here.

MAKING THE FINAL COPY

Once the design is at the correct size, make a fresh trace so that the lines are totally clean and refined. Use fluid motions on the tracing paper with a soft pencil or small watercolour brush

HINTS & TIPS: Transferring the design

With any transfer method, ensure that neither the design, trace or card can slip, causing a distortion of the image. Use a temporary adhesive to keep items in place but ensure the tack is easy to remove.

▲ Follow the outline with a series of pin-pricks

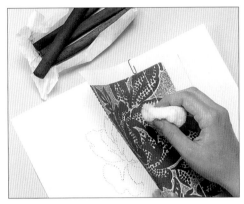

▲ Rub charcoal through the pin-pricks

• CHARCOAL: A more faithful transfer can be achieved by rubbing charcoal through the pin-pricks on to the card beneath. (Use a piece of cotton wool to gently force the powdery charcoal through.) This method is ideal for repeating designs because the pin pricks need to be made only once – any number of transfers can be made simply by reapplying the charcoal.

• PENCIL OR CARBON PAPER: One of the simplest techniques involves liberally shading the back of the pattern with a very soft pencil. Then the design is positioned, right-side-up on the card, and the lines are retraced using a harder pencil or ball-point pen. The pressure of this nib should transfer the graphite from the other side. However, the transfer may be difficult to see on particularly dark manila cards. In these cases, position carbon paper between the design and the card, and trace around the lines. The carbon will be transferred from its backing, onto the card surface. Remember that typewriter carbon paper, as opposed to plain carbon paper, is actually more sensitive and therefore most suitable for this kind of work.

▲ Carbon paper can be used for transferring

CUTTING THE STENCIL

Always use adequately sharp tools for cutting out stencils and have a cutting mat underneath any knives. Start with the more intricate shapes as these tend to pull at the card. (Avoid beginning with long or flat areas as these may distort or even tear as smaller, adjacent sections are cut.)

It is generally a lot easier to cut towards the body but keep the knife as close to an upright position as possible, in order to reduce the likelihood of slipping and causing injury. Steady the stencil by keeping your free hand behind the cutting blade. Some longer lines are best cut by keeping the knife in a constant position and moving the stencil card. This tends to be less tiring and increases the flow of curved lines. Remember that shapes do not need to be cut exactly as they are drawn – it may help to make a series of short cuts, rather than one or two long ones.

▲ Cover uncomfortable handles with tape

• SCALPELS: These knives should require the minimum of pressure. If you find yourself having to apply force, the blade is probably becoming blunt and should be changed. If the handle feels awkward, increase its size by applying a liberal wrapping of adhesive tape, helping to make the slim stem easier to hold.

HINTS & TIPS: Cutting mats

Cheaper alternatives to self-healing cutting mats include unwanted vinyl floor tiles, the underside of rubber-backed carpet tiles, several sheets of heavyweight card or the covers of unwanted hard-backed books. However, these may cause the blade to blunt and inhibit free movement of the knife.

▲ Keep the blade movement steady

CUTTING THE STENCIL TO SIZE

Having cut the design into the stencil, cut the stencil itself down to a more usable size. If the design is to fit a specific area, it's a good idea to cut the stencil to fit exactly. For a repeating border around a room, the top edge of the stencil must be exactly square, in order to stop the design wobbling or running out as you follow the bottom edge of the moulding. Marking the middle line of the stencil will make it easier to position. To do this, draw a square around the motif. By joining each corner diagonally, you will find the exact centre of the design. Using a set square, you can then mark off the vertical and horizontal mid-lines.

If the design is for a repeating border, trace one half of each of the neighbouring motifs either side of the stencil. This will help with lining up the stencil for paint application.

HINTS & TIPS: Accidental cuts

Broken or accidentally cut filaments can be mended using masking tape. Make a rough or oversized splint with the tape and then cut the masking tape down to fit, ensuring that you don't break the outlines.

▲ Mend broken filaments with masking tape

PREPARING THE SURFACE

IT'S IMPORTANT TO ASSESS the suitability of the surface to be stencilled. Water-based paints never adhere properly to an oil-based surface and tend to wear very easily so are best avoided. However, oil-based paint does adhere to surfaces coated with water-soluble emulsion paint. Remember that finishing off a stencil technique with a couple of coats of varnish will help to provide a tough protective shell.

Before stencilling, make sure that the surface is clean and totally free of dust. Any project will profit from a little time spent on preparation (see page 16) and some thought over the base coat. For example, a stencilled design can be beautifully offset by using a slightly clouded paint effect for the base surface. Simply thin down the paint with water or white spirit (depending on its base) and apply it unevenly with

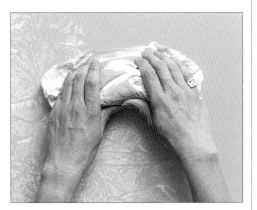

▲ Agitate the surface with a dry cloth

broad strokes from a large paint brush. Then rub or agitate the painted surface with a dry cloth.

Alternatively, for oil-based surfaces, mix some oil pigment or paint in varnish. This will provide even more time and flexibility, allowing the paint to be moved around to create a range of different finishes. For example, rags or natural sponges leave exact imprints, allowing the base colour to come through. A vigorous dabbing with a dry stiff brush held at right-angles to the surface will create an all-over stippled finish that's ideal for small objects, such as mirror frames or door panels. If the varnish is difficult to handle on larger areas, add a little refined linseed oil which will slow down the drying time

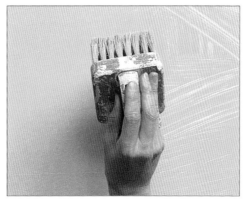

▲ Surfaces can be stippled with a brush

even further and keep the mixture workable. The same principles can be used after stencilling to create a softer or antiqued effect.

Frottage can also be effective. This involves applying the surface with wet glaze, before immediately pressing a sheet of brown paper down onto it. Then lift the paper, to reveal a random, mottled effect. Alternatively, try a basic colourwash by simply applying the

▲ Frottage produces a random effect

glaze with a rag. The more you rub the paint into the surface, the more delicate the finish will be.

Although a plain base can be used, these painted effects provide an unusual, decorative base for stencilling projects.

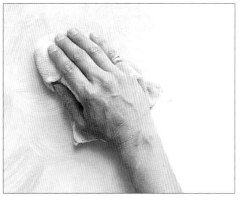

▲ Colourwashing makes an effective stencil base

POSITIONING THE STENCIL

THERE'S NOTHING WORSE than a stencil that is obviously supposed to be right in the middle of a surface and is quite obviously not. Similarly disconcerting is a crooked motif or border that starts dropping halfway across a surface. To avoid this, identify the middle of the design and gently mark a straight rule, mid-line. Then marry up the middle of the stencil with the surface marking. For smaller flat surfaces, a set square can be used to ensure the centre line is a true right angle.

One of the cardinal rules of stencilling is always to start in the middle and work outwards. This ensures that the design is correctly balanced within the perimeters of the surface – even if the repeating stencil has been designed to fit exactly from corner to corner. By starting from the middle of the surface, any small fractions or gaps are kept to the less visible perimeters.

FIXING THE STENCIL IN PLACE

SMALL SQUARES OF MASKING tape can be used at each corner of the stencil to hold it in place but do check that the tape will not mark or remove any of the existing surface paint. Avoid drawing pins which leave permanent holes, and adhesive tack that tends to raise the stencil away from the surface, allowing paint to seep or dribble.

However, the best type of adhesive is non-permanent adhesive spray, such as that used for mounting photographs. Avoid overspraying as an excessive layer can work as a paint remover, lifting the

▲ Use marker lines to position the stencil

▲ Tape the stencil into position

paint surface below. If the stencil needs to be reapplied several times, wipe off the adhesive and apply a new coat – avoid adding continuous layers. Also, take care when removing the stencil as delicate filaments may tend to stick to the surface and tear on lifting.

▲ Use adhesive spray for several applications

HINTS & TIPS: Stencilling around corners

• Stencilling borders around corners is particularly difficult, especially when it comes to matching up the design. To avoid mistakes, try the following method: Having calculated where the stencil is to go and how many times it is to repeat, make a mental note of any halves or fractions of the design that will be needed to fit into corners. Ensure that every section of an area that takes a full repeat has been tackled, before attempting to bend the stencil for fitting into corners. This is because bending stencils reduces their strength and lifespan, and can distort the design.

• Bending the design around a corner is best done in two stages, with time allowed for the first half to dry before applying the stencil to the adjacent surface. You will be surprised how much a corner will disguise inconsistencies, providing the top and bottom correspond with the stencil levels on the neighbouring surface.

APPLYING THE PAINT

PAINT CAN BE APPLIED in a variety of manners for stencilling. For sponging, it is a good idea to use a 'reservoir' – a spare piece of sponge that acts like an ink pad, helping to prevent irregular ink flow. Simply place the reservoir sponge in the bowl of paint and squeeze it firmly until it has taken up most of the mixture.

Then gently dab the reservoir sponge with the applicator sponge, until this too has taken up the paint. Dab the applicator sponge on a clean sheet of newspaper or an uncut part of the stencil, to check that the paint isn't oozing or dribbling. A clean crisp imprint means the sponge is ready for use. Then, starting in the middle of the largest cut, apply the paint with the sponge, working back so that, by the time the sponge reaches the edges, a minimum of paint is being applied. The paint can be built up in layers, but this simple technique is ideal for a first practice run. It not only helps to provide a sense of what a sponged finish will look like – it also reveals the final shape and image of the cut-out stencilled design.

▲ Use the reservoir for collecting paint

Smudgy edges are caused by a build-up of paint. Avoid this by starting in the middle of the design and gradually working outwards, gently pushing the paint towards the outside edges. If the design begins to look a little insipid around the sides, try applying further, light layers. Always allow each layer to dry, however, and aim for numerous light coverings, rather than one thick coat, which is likely to cause a build-up of paint and smudging.

Before deciding on a final method of paint application, it's a good idea to experiment with different techniques. Each method creates a slightly different effect, and it can be useful to try out the whole range of techniques before deciding on the final finish you want to create. Remember that all stencilling methods produce a slight clouding, but this is characteristic of a carefully worked piece and contributes to the three-dimensional charm of the decorating technique.

▲ Stipple the paint through the stencil

USING A BRUSH

If you are applying paint by brush, remove excess paint from the bristles on newspaper before working through the stencil. Keep the brush at right angles to the surface, otherwise stray hairs may sneak behind the stencil and mark the surface. Gently stipple the paint through the stencil, working from the centre outwards to help avoid paint build-up and smudges. Keep a small dish or saucer of water and lots of washing up liquid to hand. If small smudges or dribbles occur, a timely wipe with a cotton bud should remove any problems or stray marks. However, most mistakes can be rectified with a fine artists' brush once the paint is dry.

Other variations of brush application include feint oil painting and shadow stencilling. Feint oil application involves using artists' oil bars, rather than conventional paint. The oil bar is rubbed onto a pallette and then a stiff brush is swirled into the colour. Use this brush to lightly press the colour through the cut-out stencil in short, circular motions. The final effect should be a feint finish, softer than usual paint, together with gentle brush marks.

▲ Feint stencilling

Shadowed stencilling involves applying paint or artists' oil bar colours in the same way. However, after the first application, the stencil is removed and repositioned about 2mm (¹/₁₆in) over the right- or left-hand edge. A lighter shade of the same colour, or perhaps a subtle shade of grey, is then applied between the edge of the first coat and the border of the stencil. This creates a three-dimensional effect, providing the original stencil shape with a soft, decorative shadow.

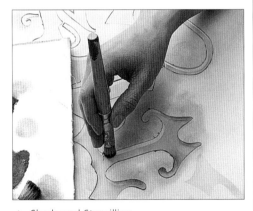

▲ Shadowed Stencilling

USING SPRAY PAINT

Spray paint tends to be very fine and can travel into the smallest of areas. For this reason, always provide plenty of masking around the outside of the stencil, to protect the surrounding areas. This can make using registration or centre marks difficult so avoid using sprays for tight, repeating patterns. As with brushed or sponged stencils, any build-up of paint near the edge can lead to drips or dribbles, so keep the spray as fine as possible. Hold the cannister at a sufficient distance from the surface and apply several even coats, rather than one thick layer. See page 49 for more information.

HIDDEN STENCILLING

The most subtle of stencilling techniques, this method is ideal for very soft finishes and projects that are designed to blend into a room, rather than stand out. It is achieved by coating the base surface in a very lightly coloured glaze. Once this glaze has dried, the stencil is positioned over the surface and the same glaze is applied through the cut-out, using a stippling motion. The stencilled effect is created by the double layer of glaze.

▲ Hidden Stencilling

REVERSE STENCILLING

A very simple version of stencilling, this technique does not require as much planning as other techniques and it is far less time-consuming. This is because the design does not need any filaments – the images are, effectively, cut out silhouettes.

Reverse stencilling is ideal for small projects in which the cut-out will only be used once. Although the stencil can be removed and reused, it must be totally cleaned between applications. This means that acetate or plan trace, rather than oiled manila card, are most suitable.

The idea is to cut out the stencil shape as a block – what is known as negative space in other stencilling methods actually becomes positive space. The chosen colour of the stencilled design should then be applied to the object's surface. It is not necessary to coat the whole item, only the areas in which the stencil is to appear.

Once the base paint has dried, position the stencil over the top and stick it temporarily into place. Then use a brush to gently apply the top coat

▲ Stick the cut-out in position

around the cut-out, taking care not to lift the egdes. Once these areas have been carefully covered, you can coat the rest of the surface more liberally. If it helps, go over the stencil itself, but make sure that the brush or roller action does not lift or move the cut-out stencil beneath.

While the paint is still wet, carefully remove each cut-out. (It may help to locate and lift the corner with the tip of a scalpel.) Take care not to smudge the wet surface paint, or damage the

▲ Stipple around the edges of the cut-out

cut-outs. Then leave the surface to dry. Remember to wash the stencils thoroughly, if you plan to re-use them for later projects.

▲ Carefully lift the cut-out with a knife

VARNISHING

ANY STENCILLING PROJECT that might receive heavy wear should be varnished for protection. High gloss finishes should generally be avoided in favour of satin or matt varnishes, which are available in polyurethane (white spirit soluble) or acrylic (water soluble). Polyurethane or acrylic are both equally good, although polyurethane is not entirely clear and will yellow the stencil slightly. This can often be a bonus in that it will remove the 'edge' on over-bright colours and slightly age the finish. Enhance this by adding a little oil paint (any of the umbers or siennas are particularly good), diluted well with turpentine substitute.

▲ Varnish over stencilled designs

Always stir varnish thoroughly before use because the formulation can settle, especially if it has been left too long on the shelf. Short strokes with a brush held at right angles will provide a more consistent finish. Aim for a series of thin coats rather than a thick, syrupy layer which may eventually crack or cause discolouration.

Alternatively, use liming wax to protect the surface, such as the 'Bedside Chest' project on page 175. The wax should be applied to the whole of the surface with a cloth or some kitchen paper and left to dry for about half an hour, before being polished off with a soft, clean cloth. Liming wax tends to subdue the colour of the paint – both the base paint and the stencilled decoration – but this can be ideal for items that are intended to look slightly aged or worn. (See also the section on 'Distressing and Sanding' for other similar effects.)

▲ Use liming wax for a subdued effect

Shellac or lacquer can also be used for protecting very vulnerable or intricate stencilled patterns. The gold leaf and gilding used for the 'Lacquered Butler's Tray' (p129), for example, are coated with protective lacquer before normal coats of varnish are applied.

Conversely, the stencilled patterns on the 'Glass Cupboard' (p195) are left untouched. This is because the designs were spray painted (and should therefore be quite resilient), and because the surface is vertical and is unlikely to be touched or damaged with constant use. Furthermore, if your stencil is made of acetate and carefully cleaned, it can be retained and used for 'touching up' areas that begin to show wear, at a later date.

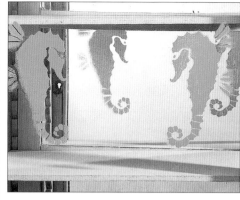

▲ Vertical stencils may not need protection

DISTRESSING & SANDING

FOR A LIVED-IN FINISH, distress the glaze or varnish coating with a stiff dry brush before it dries completely. To eliminate any dust particles that have lodged in the wet varnish, gently sand each coat with a fine grade abrasive paper and build up a series of coats.

HINTS & TIPS: Storing stencils

If a stencil is to be re-used, make sure that it is stored flat. Fix soggy stencils to a glass or ceramic surface with temporary adhesive spray, as this will hold them flat while they dry. Excess paint should be carefully wiped off before storage; a light dusting of talcum powder will absorb any retained moisture.

▲ Ornate designs, such as this cherub on page 182, can be stencilled

Mosaic

MOSAIC IS A DECORATIVE art form with a history dating back many thousands of years. Small individual pieces of glass, marble or broken china are joined together to form a single image, pattern or variety of designs. Mosaics can be either simple or complex, and they can be used to decorate virtually anything, from floors to tables, vases to picture frames. They are especially good for enlivening flat surfaces, particularly because the most effective mosaics tend to use a variety of colours. The ragged, natural look of mosaic also means that anyone, no matter how skilled in artistic effects, can produce surprisingly attractive results. By experimenting with different designs, mosaic work offers the chance to create totally random patterns.

EQUIPMENT

THE MAIN PIECE of equipment, the mosaic pieces, can be sourced from a variety of places. Tesserae (small squares or cubes of glass or marble) are usually sold in sheets but it is also possible to buy mosaic tiles in bags of assorted colours. It's worth remembering that vitreous glass and china have a lustre which is long-lasting so, providing the grouting is treated properly, these finishes should be resistant to both heat and water. Alternatively, broken china or coloured wall tiles can be used although beware of splinters and serrated edges.

It is even possible to use a mixture of tesserae and broken ceramics. However, mixing media of different finishes is likely to create an uneven surface – which could be a problem for objects such as table tops. Nevertheless, flower pots, picture frames and various other items can be cheaply and easily enhanced with a variety of tiles, ceramics or tesserae.

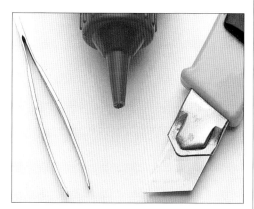
▲ Various tools for mosaic work

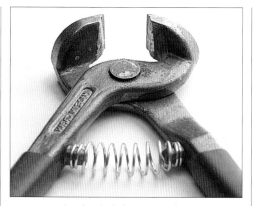
▲ Use spring-loaded tile nippers for shaping

TILE NIPPERS

A good pair of tile nippers is vital for creating mosaics. Available from most DIY stores, these tools fracture, rather than cut, tiles. Tile nippers are spring-loaded so that as they are gripped closed, the jaws do not quite meet as normal pliers; instead there is a gap of about 2mm ($^1/_{16}$in). This means that the jaws fracture, rather than cut through, the actual tile, allowing you to gradually nibble around and create shapes. Remember that mosaic materials contain glass or china powder and so small clouds of dust will occur as a tile is cut. Hold the piece at waist level to avoid inhaling the powder and, if possible, wear a protective mask.

PROTECTIVE EYE WEAR

It can be common for tiny shards of glass or china to fly into the air when you are working with mosaics. Always wear protective eye wear when you are nipping or cutting tiles, and warn other people who are likely to enter the workroom.

ADHESIVES & GROUTING

Use high-bonding PVA glue or ceramic tile adhesive for fixing tiles and sealing exposed tile edges. (It may help to hold and transfer glued pieces with tweezers.) For grouting, the ready-made, indoor grouting available in most DIY shops is ideal, although concrete will provide a stronger finish for any projects that are likely to be left outdoors. Both mediums can be coloured with dyes or paints, (special powder dyes for concrete are available), so the choice of finish is almost infinite.

> ❖ MAKING YOUR OWN ❖
> *Concrete Grouting*
>
> To make your own concrete grout, make a 50:50 mix of sieved sharp sand and cement powder. Gradually add water but keep the mixture relatively dry – it should be crumbly to the touch, rather like breadcrumbs, and definitely not as moist as pastry. An optional dash of washing-up liquid will make the mixture more elastic. Always wear gloves to avoid irritation from the materials.

▲ Protective glasses are vital for mosaic work

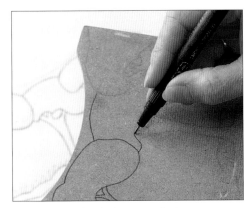

▲ Draw out the design onto the base

PLANNING THE DESIGN

As WITH ANY DECORATIVE project, always plan out a mosaic design and think about the total desired effect. Keep the design relatively simple – much of the effect from mosaics derives from the interaction of colour and simple shapes. Remember also, that perfect, rounded shapes are quite difficult to achieve when cutting brittle objects. In fact, most rounded finishes in mosaic patterns are achieved by creating long shapes. Numerous pieces of tesserae are positioned side by side at gentle angles, helping to create long, flowing curves, rather than small, compact ones.

Draw out the design on the surface base so that there will be adequate guidelines for the final pattern and make some rough calculations about the number of tesserae, in different colours, that will be required. Then score the surface of the object with a craft knife, keeping the scored lines quite close together. These will provide channels in which the glue can set, helping to increase the strength of the bond between the tiles and surface.

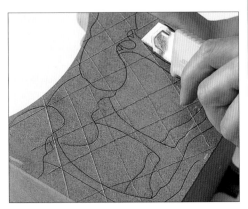

▲ Score the surface for better adhesion

CUTTING THE TILES

IT'S A GOOD IDEA to practise cutting tesserae with a few spare tiles, so that you begin to recognize the way pieces fracture and break. Hold the nippers just on the edge of the piece and gently squeeze them together. At the same time, squeeze the tesserae in your free hand, trying to apply the same level of pressure as that which you are applying to the nippers. This should help the tesserae to break cleanly in straight, simple cuts. Intricate shapes are achieved by several small nips, rather than one large one.

▲ Use the nippers to nibble at the tesserae

Some types of tesserae are more difficult to work with than others. For example, broken china is particularly easy to nip, while very glossy pieces, such as vitreous glass, can be very difficult. Some objects can be made more manageable by breaking them with a hammer, before beginning with the nippers. Glass pieces with a slightly granular finish, tend to be much easier than smooth finishes. It can also help to freeze glass tesserae for a while – the pieces are much easier to break when they are cold.

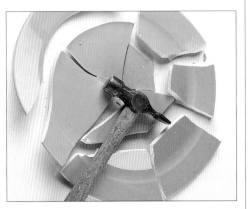

▲ Use a hammer to reduce large pieces

▲ China breaks into random pieces

GLUEING THE TILES

ONCE THE CUTTING technique has been mastered, begin to cut out the pieces for the final design. It may be easier to cut several pieces, glue those into position, and then cut some more, in order to rest your hands from the tile nippers. Simply

▲ Position a few pieces of tile at a time

apply some glue to the back of each piece and position it on the surface, gently pushing down to ensure that the glue seeps into the scored surface. Do not worry about uneven gaps between pieces – these will be filled with grouting to create the slightly ragged effect that makes mosaics so endearing.

▲ Do not worry about gaps between pieces

GROUTING THE MOSAIC

MIX THE CONCRETE by slowly adding water to a bowl of ready-mix powder, or to a 50:50 mix of sieved concrete and sharp sand. If you want to colour the grouting, add the dye at this point and stir thoroughly. Then rub the concrete mixture firmly into the gaps between the tesserae, making sure that it goes right down between each piece. The grouting helps to hold all the pieces in place, as well as to decorate the mosaic. Before the grouting dries, wipe the object with a damp – not wet – cloth until it is as clean as possible.

▲ Mix the grouting

If ready-mixed grout has been used, leave the object to dry for about 8 hours (or whatever the manufacturer's instructions state). However, if concrete has been used, the mixture will need to 'cure'. Curing is a chemical reaction between the concrete mix and the water, and it must occur before the concrete has been allowed to dry fully. For this reason, keep the object damp for about two days. Wrap it in damp (not wet) cloths and then tie a plastic bag securely around the outside. The plastic will help to retain moisture.

▲ Apply the grouting between the tesserae

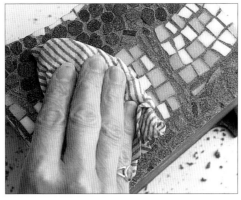

▲ Wipe the surface before the grouting dries

After two days, uncover the item and leave it to dry naturally. If the mosaic requires further cleaning, apply water and then add a little patio cleaner, which contains hydrochloric acid, on to the surface. As soon as the mixture stops fizzing, scrub away any marks with a stiff brush. Rinse the piece well and leave it to dry.

▲ Wrap the item in a damp cloth while curing

HINTS & TIPS: Broken china mosaics

It can often be easier to use concrete for sticking broken pieces of china, particularly for large mosaics. Simply cover the whole item with concrete, press the china pieces into the mixture and leave to cure and dry in the usual way.

MOSAIC PROJECTS

THE RANGE OF ITEMS that can be decorated with a mosaic finish is vast, but picture frames and flower pots (as shown in the projects in this book) are two particularly popular types of junk. However, always try to keep a flat finish on objects that are to be handled frequently. Also, bear in mind that items that are to be stood outside should be sealed to make them waterproof.

▲ Picture frames make ideal mosaic bases

▲ Mosaic pieces can be complemented with further decoration

Gilding

OPULAR THROUGHOUT the world for thousands of years, gilding was even used to decorate the jewellery of the Incas and the ornaments of ancient Egyptians. Although the term is commonly associated with the application of gold, gilding can involve all kinds of metal leaves and powders, including silver, bronze, aluminium and platinum. Gilding often provides the perfect final touch to a room, whether it is used on a picture frame, vase or storage box. Creating the impression of an object made of solid, precious metal, the technique involves applying a very thin layer of gold to any base – even something as flimsy as papier-mâché. There are a variety of different methods for creating this effect, including gold leaf, gilding cream and metallic powders.

MATERIALS & EQUIPMENT

THE EQUIPMENT AND TOOLS you need to create a gold effect will depend on the type of gilding you choose to use. Even so, you should not need to invest too much money in order to produce a stylish, extravagant effect. Many of the basic pieces of equipment include abrasive papers, soft cloths and good quality paintbrushes.

However, while some techniques, such as gilding powder, can be used with ordinary household varnish, other methods such as gold leaf application tend to require specialist glue. Before deciding on which technique to use, it may be a good idea to think about how much equipment you want to invest in, how much time you wish to spend on the project, and how intricate you want the final effect to be.

ABRASIVE PAPERS

The variety of abrasive papers needed will depend upon the surface of the piece of junk that is to be gilded.

▲ Always sand surfaces before gilding

▲ Use sharp, clean cutting equipment

However, it is useful to have a range of coarse, medium and fine grade abrasive papers to hand, and to work through the appropriate different levels, always finishing with a fine grade paper.

Wet-and-dry paper is also useful, particularly very fine grades such as 1200 or 1500. Used like ordinary abrasive paper, wet-and-dry should be rubbed over a slightly wetted surface to create a really smooth finish.

CUTTING MATERIALS

Only relevant for gold leaf applications, cutting materials can include scissors or a sharp craft knife. For the best results, however, it is worth investing in a gilder's knife, a long metal bar with a sharp edge. This knife can be used both to lift sheets of gold leaf, and to cut the medium in one sharp pull, rather than in a sawing action which would cause the leaf to tear and damage. Always allow for a reasonable overlap when cutting gold leaf. Any excess can be removed as the material is gently pressed into position.

▲ Abrasive papers and bole for preparation

PAINT

Depending on your piece of junk and the desired finish, you may find it useful to apply a coat of bole to the surface prior to gilding. Bole is a special type of background paint that works both as a filler for slightly rough surfaces and as a paint base. It comes ready-mixed and, once applied, is ideal for sanding down to a very smooth finish. Alternatively, a satin-finish paint, not matt or gloss finish, can be used as a base coat. However, make sure that the paint has the same base (either oil or water) as the gilders' size (see below).

ADHESIVES

Ordinary, household varnish can be used to make gilding powder adhere to a surface. However, gold leaf requires a special type of adhesive known as gilders' size. The medium is used both to stick gold leaf into place, and to seal gilded and normal surfaces. It is available as a water- or oil-based product and, depending on the brand, can require drying times ranging from

▲ Gilder's size for gold leaf application

20 minutes to 24 hours. Larger items, such as ornate cornices, will require a size with a longer drying time (see box). Gold leaf must be applied before the size is fully dry, but when it is still tacky (much like gold powder to a varnished surface). Too early and the leaf will be marked by the wet size underneath, causing the gold to appear lifeless and dull. If it is applied too late, the leaf may not adhere to the surface properly, causing a poor and untidy finish.

BRUSHES & APPLICATORS

Brushes are needed for both tidying gold leaf, and for applying gold powder. They should be as soft as possible – pony-hair or squirrel brushes are ideal. If possible, keep gilding brushes aside purely for that job. Any residues of paint will cause the brushes to stiffen and damage subsequent gold leaf or powder work. Wash gilding brushes only rarely; it is far better to

---

HINTS & TIPS: Gilders' size

• The faster the gilders' size dries, the smaller the risk of dust settling in the surface. However, quick-drying size is more fragile and prone to cracking. It is therefore important to try and find a happy balance, perhaps opting for a medium-length drying size but ensuring that the surrounding area is totally free of dust or other pollutants. For example, keep draughts to a minimum and avoid wearing loose or woollen clothing.

• To see whether the size is ready to receive the gold leaf, create a spare trial patch, preferably on a similar surface, and attempt to apply gold leaf at timed intervals. When it adheres comfortably to the patch, the real object will also be ready to receive the gold leaf.

---

tap them clean and gently shake out any metallic dust. If possible, invest in the best quality brush you can afford.

Use cotton buds for gently pressing gold leaf into position, particularly in difficult or intricate areas. Velvet can also be used for pressing gold leaf over large surfaces, and for polishing gilded surfaces to a shiny finish.

THE GOLD EFFECT

Gold leaf, gilding cream and gilding powder all have their different advantages. For example, while leaf is more time consuming and complex to apply, it provides a long-term finish which is less likely to lose its lustre than other forms. Gilding cream is a popular choice for small projects or highlights – it is conventionally used for patching up gold work – whereas gilding powder is considerably more messy than the other methods, but it can be carried out with basic metallic powders and household varnish.

• GOLD TRANSFER LEAF: This is available from specialist paint suppliers or gilding shops. Transfer leaf is a very thin layer of gold or brass, supplied in small squares and lightly attached to tissue backing with a layer of wax film. Professional gilders use specially designed cushions for applying leaf transfers, but it is possible to create a good finish simply with a soft brush.

Try not to touch the metallic surface until it is in place on the object, as it will stick to your fingers. Many people find the easiest way to lift the sheets is to use the bristles of a soft brush that has been swept across their cheeks. The light coating of grease should provide just enough adhesive.

▲ Gold leaf transfers

▲ Metallic effects can also be made using cream

• GILDING CREAM: Commonly used by gilders for repair work, gilding cream is particularly handy for patching areas where the size dries and cracks. The cream can also be used for small highlighting work, such as the 'Folding Filigree Screen' project on page 90.

• GOLD POWDER: This can be used as a quick alternative to leaf transfers, although it tends to be more messy and will definitely require a protective varnish cover. The powder is applied to a surface that has been coated with varnish – the varnish should be allowed to semi-dry so that it feels tacky.

Gold powder can also be used to patch up cracks in gold leaf gilding. However, it's important to ensure that the powder is an exact match of the shade of the gold leaf.

VARNISH

In addition to working as an adhesive for gold powders, varnish should be applied over a gilded surface in order to avoid tarnishing and damage. For an aged finish, use clear spray varnish or clear gloss wood varnish (oil-based), mixed with burnt sienna or raw umber artists' oil paint (see p63).

▲ Protect gilded surfaces with a coat of varnish

APPLYING GOLD LEAF

IT'S ALWAYS WORTH looking at the finish on gilded articles in stores and antique shops to see how slight imperfections are a common feature. Although the aim is to create as refined a finish as possible, using sheets of leaf will inevitably create some joins and overlaps. Notice, however, that these are barely visible when the piece is looked at in its entirety.

Always ensure that the work environment is as dust-free as possible. Remember that wet size will be vulnerable to dust and particles for up to several hours so, if you are worried about dust rising and then settling on the piece, try damping the floors with a water spray, or putting down wet towels. Also, make sure that your tools are totally clean and ready to hand, to avoid disruption later.

▲ Gently rub down the surface

Take some time to sand down the item to a really smooth finish. Leaf transfer is so thin that any rough patches will show through and mark the gilded surface. Once sanded, remove any dust residue with a tack rag. Wipe ridges and crevices clean with a cotton bud.

If the item is large, or is to be totally covered in gold leaf, it may be worth applying one or two coats of bole, or a paint in the colour of your choice. If the size for the leaf transfer is oil-based, make sure that the paint you use is also oil-based. Once dry, sand the surface with fine grade abrasive paper and fine wet-and-dry paper.

Then use a soft brush to apply a thin layer of gilding size to the surface. Try to avoid leaving brush marks in the coat. Although the size will be milky on inital application, it should dry to a clear, slightly petrol-like colour.

Very carefully cut a single sheet of gold transfer leaf to the required size. Remember to leave some excess on each edge, so that each piece overlaps on the surface and can be trimmed later. However, bear in mind that transfer leaf will adhere to gilding size on contact, so avoid leaving so much excess that unwanted pieces stick to the surrounding wet size.

Press the leaf face down on to the tacky size, keeping the backing paper in place, and rub it with a cotton wool ball, soft brush, or piece of cloth to ensure that it is firmly in position. Then gently peel away the backing paper, taking care not to lift the leaf from the object's surface. Repeat this process until the whole item is covered with gold leaf transfer.

Gently press the leaf flat with a soft brush. Although wrinkles may appear, these should disappear as the surface is brushed clean. Then, gradually brush away any overlaps and excess pieces of gold. Any large pieces, known as skewings, can be kept for patching up corners and crevices. Continue working around the surface, gradually

▲ Brush away excess pieces of gold leaf

brushing away wrinkles, loose flakes and lumps. As you work around the object, small faults, such as cracks or gaps may become apparent. These can be repaired, using the same technique described above, with the skewings. Alternatively, while the size is still tacky, touch up any cracks or gaps by gently brushing gold powder over the top of them.

▲ Touch up areas with gold powder

Leave the item to dry fully – you will need to follow the guidelines on the size tin – and then polish it very gently with a piece of velvet or cotton wool. However, the gold surface will still be vulnerable to breaks or tears so avoid using rough movements.

▲ Apply a coat of bole as a base

▲ Press the leaf onto the surface

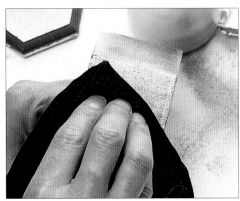

▲ Gently polish the gold surface

Although the object is now gilded, it will not be able to withstand scratching or heavy handling. The surface is also liable to tarnish with time. It is therefore important to protect the surface with a few coats of varnish. Either spray the surface with lacquer or varnish, building up several thin coats, or try using the ageing technique which is explained below.

AGEING THE PIECE

TO GIVE THE GILDED finish an appropriately old and time-worn appearance, try adding some stain to the protective varnish. This can be applied all over the item, or simply to areas that would age and wear naturally, such as exposed corners.

First, apply one coat of clear, oil-based varnish to the surface and leave

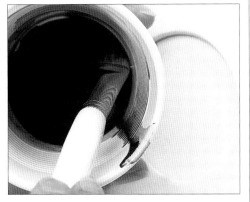

▲ Mix a small amount of colour to the varnish

to dry completely. Then mix a small amount of artists' oil colour – either burnt sienna or raw umber – into a small pot of varnish. Apply two coats of this mixture to the item, allowing each application to dry thoroughly. Then add a little more artists' colour to

▲ Apply two coats of the stained varnish

▲ Wipe off excess varnish with a cloth

the mixture to darken it even further. Apply this to creases or moulded areas of the surface, and to any areas where dirt is likely to have settled over time, such as edges, grooves or handles. Finally, wipe away some of the varnish with a soft cloth. The idea is to leave darkened varnish only where age may have led to tarnishing or grime.

QUICK GILDING WITH CREAM

FOR A FASTER gilded effect, or for items that can not be sanded, such as papier-mâché, gilding cream can be used. (The cream is also ideal for creating gold highlights on painted surfaces.) Cheap and easy to obtain, the finish will not polish to as high a sheen as leaf transfer, but it still creates an effective, metallic surface.

The item can be varnished with spray varnish or aged with a stain/varnish mixture as before. In the case of this star (see p65), the darkened varnish sits comfortably in various crevices creating natural low-lights and shaded areas.

Begin by painting any raw surface with bole, or the chosen paint colour of your choice. Once this has dried, use

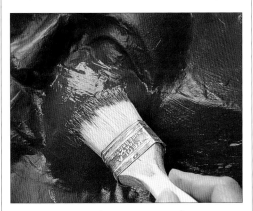

▲ Apply a coat of bole to raw surfaces

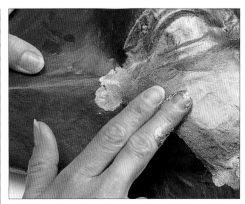

▲ Rub gilding cream over the shape

your fingers to gently rub gilding cream all over the surface. Be sure to cover all crevices and intricate areas – if necessary, use a cotton bud to insert cream into difficult gaps.

Allow the cream to dry for the recommended time (usually about 2 hours) and then buff the surface gently with a soft cloth. This will help to give it a slight shine and lustre.

▲ Polish the surface with a soft cloth

QUICK GILDING WITH POWDER

ANOTHER VERY QUICK and satisfying way of applying a gold finish, gilding powder is slightly less messy than gilding cream. It is also suitable for items that will have to stand up to quite a lot of wear and tear, such as lamps, handles and doorknobs. However, the actual powdering does create quite a bit of dust so it may be wise to do any projects involving gilding powder outside. As with other gilding methods, apply a base coat of colour, or a couple of coats of bole to seal the surface. When the paint is dry, apply a thin layer of gilders' size and leave to dry until it is just tacky.

▲ Apply size to the painted surface

Dip a clean, dry brush into the gold powder and gently brush it on to the tacky size. Apply the gold powder fairly thickly as it will soak into the size. Brush away the excess until you can handle the item without too much powder coming off.

If you prefer, use different coloured metallic powders for a varied effect. To do this, simply apply different colours directly to the surface and mix them together as they stick to the size.

▲ Apply the gilding powder with a brush

Once dry, apply a coat of clear protective varnish to the object. If the item is to receive a lot of handling, use several coats, allowing sufficent drying time between each application.

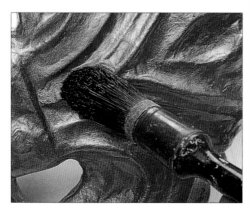

▲ Apply a coat of protective varnish

▲ Powder, leaf and cream may be used together

MAKING METALLIC PAINT

POWDERS CAN ALSO be used to make metallic paint for touching up cracks and patches on leaf transfers. Alternatively, it can be used as paint for gold edging and for adding small decorative details or motifs to a painted piece of furniture.

To do this, put about a tablespoon of metallic powder into a dish and slowly add a little linseed oil, mixing well until the mixture is smooth and similar to the consistency of double cream. Then add about four drops of paint driers to the mixture – otherwise the linseed oil will not dry. Make sure that the mixture is strong, as well as smooth and free flowing. If it is too weak, the gilding will appear rather weak, lacking vibrancy or definition.

Once prepared, the paint can be applied with a very fine artists' brush to cracks and gaps in gilded surfaces, or as decoration to painted objects. Bear in mind, however, that any mixture comprising of solid, metallic particles will dry to a slightly distressed finish, and will not create the unmottled sheen achieveable with leaf transfer.

▲ Mix metallic powder with linseed oil

▲ Add paint driers to the paint mixture

OBJECTS FOR GILDING

GILDING CAN BE applied to almost any surface, providing the base has been adequately prepared (see p16). It tends to be most effective when it is used in small areas, such as for highlighting trims or borders, or on small room accessories such as lamps or frames. Gilding techniques can even be used on natural items such as shells or stones.

▲ Apply gilding to small items for greater impact

Whenever you use gilding as a decorative effect, try to resist the inclination to over-use the colour. Gold, together with silver, bronze and other metallic colours, tends to look its best when it is used sparingly. Use the metallic colours for highlighting and allow surrounding colours to bring out the lustre of the gilding.

HINTS & TIPS: Colour variations

Gilding does not have to be gold. Leaf, powders and creams are also available in silver, aluminium and copper, while creams come in a myriad of shades, including pewter, which is particularly effective for door handles.

▲ Transform old trays with gilding

TRAYS

One item that many people don't think of highlighting with gold or metallic colours, is a household tray. Although it is true that gilding will be vulnerable to constant use, an occasional tray can be transformed with gold highlighting and a protective coating of varnish or lacquer. See the 'Lacquered Butler Tray' on page 129, or the 'Gold Leaf Tray' project on page 138, for ideas on how to gild such items.

LAMP BASES & VASES

Always popular in metallic colours, vases make ideal bases for gilding techniques. Lamp bases are also perfect for the effect because they tend to reflect warm, glowing shades when the bulb is switched on. Gilding the inside of the lampshade will further enhance this glow. Similarly, candlesticks can be easily transformed with the use of silver or gold leaf, as well as gilding cream or powder.

BOXES & TRINKETS

Suitable bases for first projects, wooden or papier-mâché boxes can be enhanced with gold leaf transfer. These make ideal gifts or general containers for jewellery and trinkets.

PICTURE & MIRROR FRAMES

Plain or ornate, frames are among the most popular objects for gilding. Intricate areas can be patched up with gilding cream or powder, although leaving some cracks in the gold leaf will help to create the appearance of ageing. Even a decorative gold border, such as the one stamped on to the mirror on page 110, helps to add a subtle finishing touch to the surface.

▲ Use gold to highlight room accessories

▲ Transform old containers with gilding

Stamping

PRINTING DESIGNS on to items of furniture or walls is not a new idea, but it has enjoyed a revival in recent years. It is an excellent technique for creating repeating patterns on flat, painted surfaces, and tends to be less intricate than some other decorative methods such as stencilling. Stamping designs can be simple or complex, and much of their effect comes from a fairly relaxed, random application. This means that you rarely have to worry about achieving symmetrical effects, or measuring accurate spacing for each stamp motif. Although rubber or wood are conventionally used for stamping techniques, it can be interesting to experiment with other mediums such as metal, sponge or even halved vegetables (see below).

STAMPING MATERIALS

A RANGE OF DIFFERENT materials can be used to make printing stamps. The type of material you choose will influence the texture and definition of the print, as well as the durability of the stamp itself. For example, stamps that are to be used consistently should be hardwearing and easy to clean and maintain. Small, one-off projects, however, could be decorated using quick homemade stamps that will be disposed of after use.

• RUBBER STAMPS: The most common type of stamp, rubber print blocks are able to withstand constant use over a length of time. Although ready-made, rubber stamps can be very sophisticated, large objects may need more than one design and this can prove to be quite costly. It is therefore often more economical, (and creative!), to make your own rubber stamp which can be adapted to your personal needs and decorative taste (see right).

▲ Professional rubber stamps can be reused

▲ Use sponge for a textured finish

• FIRM SPONGE, CORK AND LEATHER: These are less durable than professional rubber stamps but, cleaned properly, they should last for a sufficient length of time. Material such as these also tend to create a textured finish, creating a far more craft-like appearance to the chosen surface.

• POTATOES: Many firm vegetables, such as potatoes or carrots, can be used for cheap, basic stamps. However, they only work for one-off projects, creating a semi-textured finish.

• STAMP PADS: Ink stamp pads are available from most craft or stationery stores and are ideal for quick, simple stamping. Originally designed for fabric decoration, they are quick-drying and leave a good hardwearing finish on wooden surfaces.

• PAINT: Virtually any kind of paint can be used for stamping, although the type of surface on which the stamp is to be applied, will influence the choice.

MAKING A RUBBER STAMP

TO MAKE YOUR OWN rubber stamp, work out a rough design on paper. Then transfer or copy the design on to a piece of rubber, on the side which will form the top of the stamp.

Make sure that the design is simple and clean. The decorative effect should come from repeating motifs, rather than from complex shapes.

············ CUTTING THE STAMP ············

Use some PVA adhesive to apply a piece of foam to a wooden block. Do not worry about keeping the foam neat – it can even be in several pieces – because it will be positioned behind the actual stamping surface.

Then carefully cut out the rubber design using sharp scissors or a craft knife and cutting mat. Use the same adhesive as before, stick the cut-out pieces of the rubber on to the foam. Press firmly and add extra glue to any areas or edges where the rubber does not adhere properly.

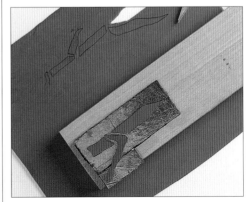
▲ Position the rubber cut-outs on the foam

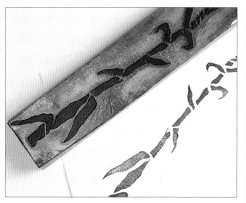

▲ Try out the stamp on rough paper

TESTING·THE STAMP

Apply an even coat of artists' acrylic paint to the rubber stamp with a chunk of smooth sponge. Then turn the stamp over and press firmly onto a spare piece of paper. This image is how the final pattern will appear, so make any changes to the shape at this stage.

Once satisfied with the rubber design, cut away the excess backing foam with a craft knife. This will help the stamp to stand proud of the block and prevent paint straying as the stamp is applied and gently rocked on the final surface.

HINTS & TIPS: Planning ahead

Before ordering supplies, decide on the finished size of the design. Order extra rubber, in case of mistakes, and one wooden block for each stamp. These blocks can be re-used, even if the particular stamp design is no longer needed.

HINTS & TIPS: Making a mirror image

For a mirror image of the design, make another stamp by simply printing the first one directly on to another piece of rubber. Cut around this image and stick down.

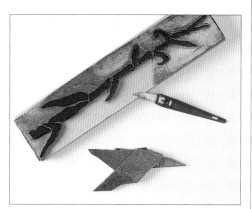

▲ Cut away the excess foam

APPLYING THE STAMP

Dab artists' acrylic colours with either a sponge or brush onto the stamp. (Other paints can be used but they should be both opaque and thick – about the consistency of double cream.) Test the stamp on some spare paper to remove any excess paint, before pushing the design down onto the surface of the object.

Gently rock the stamp to ensure even pressure (it may help to practise this technique on spare paper first). Then, holding the surface steady with your spare hand, carefully lift the stamp in one swift, single movement.

▲ Push down on the stamp with even pressure

Depending on the type of stamp material, it may be possible to reapply the stamp a few times before more paint is needed. Sponges, for example, absorb considerable amounts of paint and will not need new paint after every application. If this is the case, remember to press lightly for the first print and then gradually apply harder pressure for the next few applications, in order to try and keep the depth of colour even.

MAKING A POTATO STAMP

CUT THE POTATO in half and wipe off the moisture. Cut around the template (such as the ivy leaf shown below) with a craft knife on to half a potato. Then cut away the background so that the design to be printed stands proud. (See page 110 for more information.)

HINTS & TIPS: Potato stamps

Vegetables give off a fair amount of water, so you will need to blot the potato with tissue occasionally to prevent the paint from diluting or smudging.

▲ Cut around the template on to the potato

Barge Painting

ARGE PAINTING DECORATION is the term used to describe the decorative finish traditionally associated with narrow boats. Like any folk art, however, the decorative effect can be achieved on a range of furniture or junk items. Traditionally, the themes for canal boat decorations are limited to scenes with castles and groups of roses and daisies. Yet there's plenty of scope for variation, both in terms of the designs and the actual methods of painting. Although the roses demonstrated here might not suit the item you wish to decorate, the actual method of painting can be used to create other designs or variations. Remember that traditional background colours for barge painting are dark, providing a suitable base for bold, striking colours.

TYPES OF PAINT STROKES (see opposite)

ROSE PETAL STROKES

1 Paint the rose petals in this order: first the two central petals then, working from left to right, the three large outer petals, followed by the three smaller ones. Apply the stamens last of all, when the roses are completely dry.

Hold the brush upright and press it down so that half of it is flat against the surface. Then pull the brush towards you, lifting and curving it so that you finish the stroke with only the point touching.

USEFUL DECORATIVE STROKES

2 Hold your brush upright so that just the tip touches the surface. Then, moving from left to right and curving the line, dip the brush down and back up to finish on the tip again.

DAISY & BORDER STROKES

3 Press the first quarter of the brush on to the surface and move the brush back lifting it at the same time. As you gently pull the stroke across, you should finish on the tip.

THIN STROKES FOR STAMENS

4 Press the first quarter of the brush on to the surface and move the brush back lifting it at the same time, so that you finish on the tip.

SMALL ROSE PETAL STROKES

5 These are made using the same technique as described in step 1, but by using less brush and curving upwards.

LEAVES

6 Starting and finishing on the point of the brush, pull the brush towards you, flattening it while curving it out and in. Start at the same point and make the second stroke in the same way, but this time curve out in the opposite direction. Then fill the centre.

LONG & CURVED STROKES

7 These are made in the same way as step 2, only your brush must be well charged with paint and you should lift the brush gradually as you move towards the point.

HINTS & TIPS: Painting techniques

There is no need to be mathematically exact when painting in this style. Any discrepancies will actually help to replicate the naivity of true barge painting. However, do make sure that the base circles for roses are sufficiently distanced to allow room for the petals, but not so far apart that they look isolated. The same goes for the leaves and the daisies.

▲ Bargeware painting is ideal for decorating kitchen containers

1

2

3

4

5

6

7

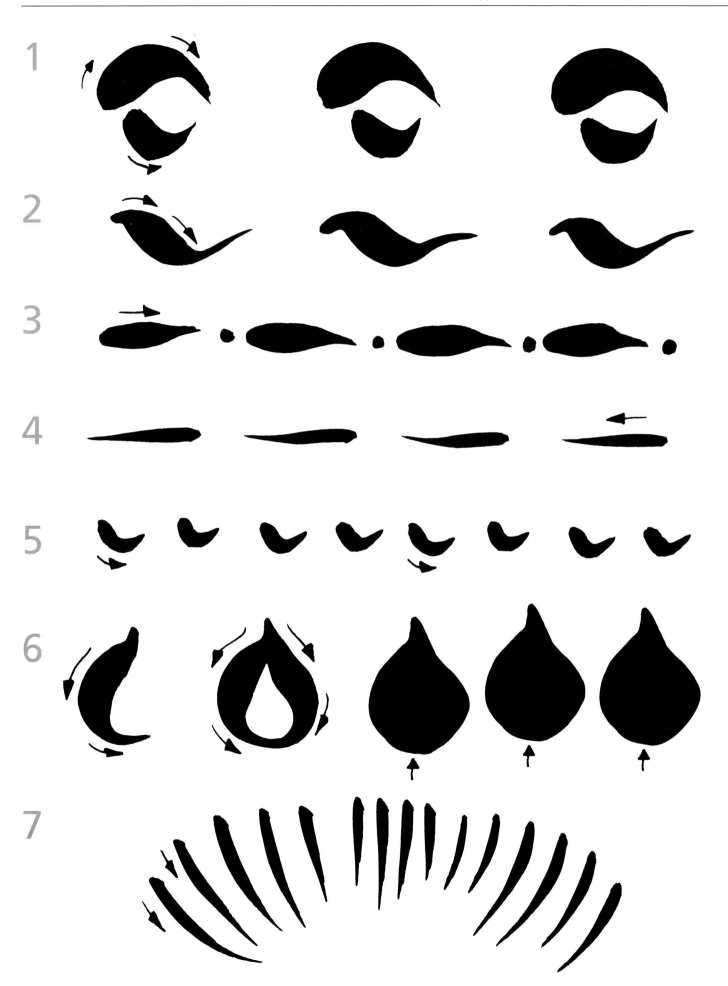

• WHITE ROSE: Start the rose with a pink circle, made by mixing bright red and white together. Make the shadows with bright red and the top petals with white. The stamens are painted yellow.

• RED ROSE: Start the rose with a crimson circle and add a little black to this to make the colour for the shadows. Paint the top petals with bright red and the stamens in yellow.

• YELLOW ROSE: Start the rose with an orange circle and paint the shadows with crimson paint. Using a clean brush, paint the top petals and the stamens in yellow.

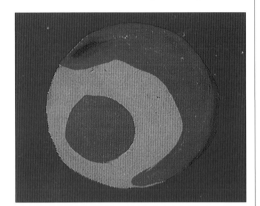

▲ Start with a red and pink centre

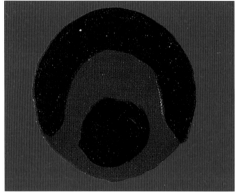

▲ Create a crimson and black centre

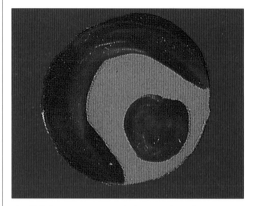

▲ Paint an orange and deep red centre

▲ Add white top petals and yellow stamen

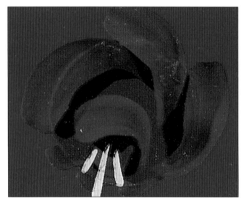

▲ Paint on bright red petals and yellow stamen

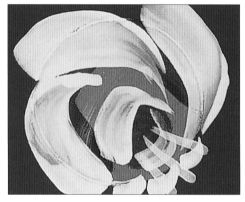

▲ Add yellow top petals

Daisies are begun by painting a circle of white petals. These can then be highlighted with an optional pale blue. The yellow centre has a small bright red brush stroke flicked around one side. These simple flowers are ideal.

motifs for separating or connecting other decorative features, and work well alongside other flowers such as roses. You may find it easier to practise these designs, before moving on to more intricate flowers and patterns.

The leaves are painted in lime green with a small smudge of tan paint at the base. The veins are painted in yellow. All the filling lines and trimmings are usually painted in yellow, but you can intersperse another colour around them.

▲ Paint out the white petals

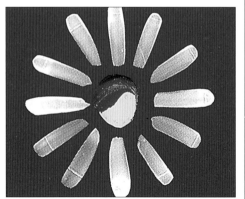

▲ Add a yellow and red centre

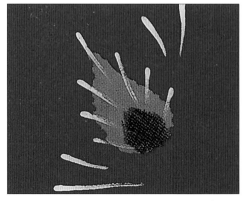

▲ Add yellow veins to the lime green leaf

Ageing Techniques

MANY PEOPLE LIKE to complete a decorative project with an aged finish. Creating an antiqued effect helps to conceal damage or wear that can not be repaired, as well as ensuring that the furniture retains a sense of history and charm. (Afterall, the piece wasn't always considered to be junk!) There are numerous methods for giving an aged appearance to a piece of furniture. These can be carried out at different stages of the decoration process, and some are more complex than others. In addition to the techniques described here, try general highlighting with paint.

BEFORE PAINTING

A PIECE OF NEW or raw wood can be made to look older by darkening it with brown shellac solution or by staining it with a water-based wood dye, such as walnut brown. The wood will need to be porous and, if it is untreated, first cleaned with a mild detergent solution to remove any grease or dirt. It is also possible to use oil-based dyes although these will obviously require more careful preparation. For further ageing, throw a bunch of keys at the surface, or manually create rough, damaged edges – the reverse techniques of usual surface preparation!

AFTER PAINTING

SURFACES THAT ARE coated in paint can be made to look older by gently distressing the paint. Use abrasive paper, silicon carbide finishing paper, or wire wool dipped in either methylated spirit (for emulsion paint) or water (for traditional paints), to create a distressed finish. These all have a slightly different effect on the paintwork and can be used in combination to achieve the desired result.

It can also be useful to apply a wax resist to areas where you plan to rub back, before the paint is applied. This will help to make the rubbing-back process a little easier.

▲ Use methylated spirit on emulsioned surfaces

ANTIQUING GLAZE

APPLIED EITHER DIRECTLY on to paint or over varnish, antiquing glaze offers an old, aged with dirt, effect for most types of surfaces. The antiquing glaze is made by mixing colours such as raw umber pigment or rottenstone, (sometimes to a glaze medium such as the one used in the 'Seashore Cabinet' project on page 192).

Apply the mixture with either a cloth or brush and then, almost immediately, wipe the excess away with a clean rag or piece of nylon. However, leave the glaze in darker, recessed areas.

The transition between soft and dark areas can be harmonized by blending the glaze with a soft mop brush, or by adding a second, almost transparent glaze to the dry antique glaze surface.

▲ Rub down edges with wire wool

▲ Apply antiquing glaze for a subtle browning effect

The fly spots visible in old furniture can also be imitated by spattering some thinned-down paint over the wet glaze. This is achieved by loading the tips of a brush, such as a fitch brush, with thinned paint and softly rolling your finger over the tip, so that the paint spatters over the glaze. A concentrated mix of raw umber, or raw umber mixed with black, is particularly suitable. Alternatively, spattering a little methylated spirits over an oil-based glaze will create an effect similar to that of antique stipple (see below).

However, before any antiquing glaze is applied to a decoupage project, make sure that the surface has been given two or three protective coats of varnish. Otherwise, the glaze will penetrate the paper cut-outs and cause discolouration.

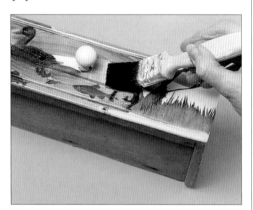

▲ Stain decoupage projects after varnishing

ANTIQUE STIPPLING

THIS EFFECT IS ASSOCIATED with the gradation of colour from dark to light. Any object that has been used over time will show more wear in some areas than others – piano keys, for example, or door handles. This subtle effect can be imitated by stippling colour into a wet glaze, creating both dark and light surface patches.

After coating the surface with an untinted oil glaze, apply a pale glaze in the areas where the surface should be lighter. Then apply a darker glaze with the same brush, into the remaining areas. Stipple the darker glaze into the light glaze, remembering to clean the brush before returning to the dark patch. The effect should be very delicate and can be enhanced by spattering thinned paint over the top.

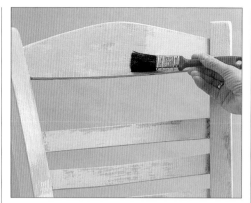

▲ Brush crackle glaze over the rough paint

CRACKLE GLAZE

THIS MEDIUM IS APPLIED to painted furniture to create the impression of old, cracking paint. It is simple and easy to apply, and can be used with most types of paint, although the amount of cracking between different brands of paint varies.

First, coat the object with one rough layer of paint. Keep the paint patchy so that both bare wood, and the paint beneath, will be visible through the cracks. Then apply a thick layer of crackle glaze with an ordinary household paintbrush and leave to dry.

Then apply a second coat of paint over the surface. This application can

▲ Apply a second coat of paint over the glaze

again be random, but try to cover most of the first colour. Once this coat has dried, use a medium grade abrasive paper, wrapped around a sanding block, to distress the finish. Patches of bare wood and the original layer of paint should become visible.

HINTS & TIPS: Using crackle glaze

When painting or varnishing over a crackle glazed surface, work quickly and try to avoid going over areas more than once. This is because chemicals in the paint or varnish, together with the movement of the brush, could actually reactivate the glaze, causing the paint to slip. Similarly make sure the final surface is coated with a water-based varnish, otherwise the paint may activate the glaze.

▲ Distress the surface with abrasive paper

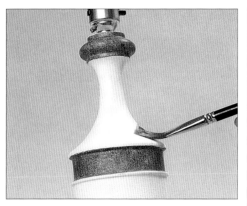

▲ Apply two-part cracke glaze with a brush

TWO-PART CRACKLE VARNISH

CRAQUELURE DESCRIBES the fine cracks that cover the surface of old oil paintings. The cracks are formed by the gradual and unequal shrinkage of layers of paint under the varnish. This effect can be imitated by using two coats of varnish – one quick-drying and one slow-drying.

First, apply a slow-drying oil-based varnish to the object's surface. Allow the coat to dry to the point of tackiness before applying a water-based varnish over the top. The two coats will dry at different rates, causing a cracking effect.

The size of the cracks depends upon the thickness of the layers of varnish –

▲ Highlight cracks with antiquing glaze

thin layers produce small cracks, thick layers tend to produce wider lines. The length of time allowed between coats also influences the effect. The greater the length of time between the first and second varnishes, the finer the cracks that are produced. It is therefore adviseable to practise the technique before using it on the final object.

Although a hairdryer can be used to speed up some of the drying, too fierce

▲ Different tinted waxes can produce a variety of finishes

a heat will create an unnatural effect and spoil the final finish. Once dry, coat the item in a coloured glaze, such as diluted raw umber artists' oil. Use a clean rag to wipe off the excess glaze, so that the stain remains only in the cracks. For a finishing touch, add a little more white spirit to the glaze, dip a stencilling brush (or any brush with stiff bristles) into the mixture and run your finger through the hairs, causing the paint to spatter onto the surface. Once dry, apply a coat of protective, oil-based varnish to seal the surface.

Craquelure can be used on porcelain or wood, and it is particularly effective on decoupaged pieces, because it helps to age the surface and unite the different shapes.

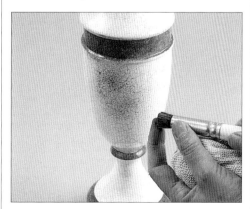

▲ Spatter antiquing glaze for a mottled effect

HINTS & TIPS: Highlighting craquelure

Craquelure surfaces do not have to be highlighted with conventional shades such as raw umber (for ageing) or gold. In fact, bright colours such as vermilion can be just as effective, helping to create a striking, lacquer-style finish.

TINTED WAXES

A LARGE VARIETY of brown or antiquing furniture waxes are available which can be used on their own, or in combination with the varnishes and glazes already described. Walnut shades are particularly good for ageing paint surfaces, both because of their antique colour, and by the feel and subtle sheen they impart. Bear in mind that antiquing waxes may have a yellowing effect on the painted surface beneath.

If the wax is to be applied to a varnish finish, make sure the base is a matt varnish, so that the wax can adhere properly. Alternatively, rub a satin finished surface with fine wire wool to help remove the shine, before applying the wax. Apply the wax evenly with a rag or kitchen paper and leave it for about half an hour before buffing to a good sheen.

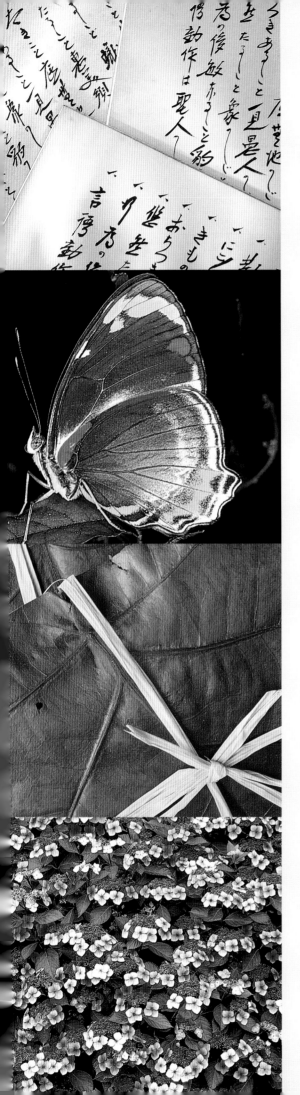

FINDING INSPIRATION FOR A
PROJECT SHOULD ALWAYS BE
A SPONTANEOUS EVENT. IDEAS
TEND TO SPRING FROM THE MOST
UNEXPECTED OF PLACES, AND
THE MORE UNUSUAL THEY ARE, THE
MORE INDIVIDUAL THE PROJECT IS
LIKELY TO BE. ALWAYS BE ON THE
LOOK OUT FOR INSPIRATION, AND
FOLLOW YOUR INSTINCTS. THE NEXT
FEW PAGES PROVIDE A FEW BASIC
IDEAS WHICH SHOULD PROPEL YOU
ON TO BIGGER AND BETTER THINGS!

Sourcing Inspiration

Shapes & Patterns

INSPIRATION CAN OFTEN come from seeing patterns, shapes and colours working together in combination. Look at different fabrics and ceramics, photographs and pieces of equipment, and think about how individual lines and marks work in conjunction with each other. Simple shapes and random patterns are often excellent sources of creative ideas. Try imagining how they would work in a fragmented mosaic or perhaps as a repeating stencil. Even simply playing with the pattern in paint can be enlightening.

Shapes and patterns can be naturally occurring, such as the amazing marks on a butterfly's wings, or manufactured, such as the intricate mechanism of a clock. They can derive from positioning similar or different objects together, or possibly even from

looking at one item from a certain angle or in a particular light. Everything, from the floor to the sky, a brick wall to a tree, produces an infinite variety of intricate patterns. Always be on the look out for different ideas and be open to adapting different shapes. The tiniest flower bud or a large cloud in the sky, the panelling of a fence or the ripples of a river, can all present a range of unusual patterns. Examine how even angular lines can suggest soft shapes, how simple spirals can draw in your line of vision, and how random marks work together when studied from a sufficient distance. For practical purposes, decide what type of effect you wish to achieve and see if there is a specific type of shape or pattern that is associated with this feel. For example, regimental stripes tend to be clean and official while swirls are more casual and relaxed. Patterns that are

rigid can be difficult to achieve on uneven surfaces, so think about the item of junk you wish to decorate and use this as part of the inspiration for adapting a pattern or design. Remember that there are no rules when it comes to creating ideas.

Simply take the time to look around, see what suits the object, think about what you like and what has the potential to be adapted, and experiment with shapes and patterns until you find the right inspiration for creating your own perfect design.

Texture

EVERYTHING WE TOUCH, from the paper in this book to the bark of a tree, has a unique texture. Many decorative techniques are created by playing with texture. Whether creating designs with thick, oily paint, waxing a fine, ultra-smooth finish or ageing a piece of wood by making it look rough and battered, texture is often the main motivation behind a final finish. From a mottled vegetable skin to a piece of Chinese silk, some natural, weather-beaten wood to a rusty old chain, different textures provide a range of colours and sensations.

Texture is not only something to be felt. Different textured surfaces will reflect different amounts of light, or create a three-dimensional sense to an otherwise flat area. This means that texture can also influence colour, causing one basic hue to take

on a range of subtle variations as the shape and feel of the surface alters and contours. Texture can be totally smooth, such as the soft, luxuriant feel of a piece of silk, or very tactile, like the flaking paint of an old wooden surface. It is present in everything, although it can be common to miss its presence by looking at the colour or shape of an object in greater detail. Bear in mind, for example, that when you look at the variations in colour and pattern of a cross-section of fruit, the surface will also feel different in certain areas. Similarly, a group of objects, arranged on top of each other in a haphazard fashion, will have a different texture to the surface of one single object held in your hand. This never-ending variety in tone and texture is an ideal starting point for thinking about the decorative finish you want to create. Do you want a smooth, glossy

finish or an aged, antique effect? Do you want to create the impression of texture with stippled paint techniques, or do you want to try and remove the suggestion of contour, by making a totally smooth, decoupage finish? If you are copying the

shape of a certain object onto the surface, would imitating the texture of the item help to convey the artistic impression? Next time you think about creating a decorative finish, examine the range of textures you can use to create it.

Nature

A CONSTANT SOURCE of inspiration, nature is diverse, readily available and ever-evolving. Plants, trees, flowers and animals all offer a range of inspiring colours, shapes and themes for different decorative designs. Furthermore, no matter where you are, nature is never far away. From rolling fields and forests, to urban parks and gardens, an ocean brimming with aquatic life, to a single tree playing host to insects, birds and moss, evidence of nature can be found everywhere. Even the fruit in a supermarket display conveys some sense of natural life and growth.

Remember that you don't need to investigate large areas to source a multitude of ideas; single objects can present numerous variations of colour and texture. A single apple, for example, adopts a variety of textures, shapes, colours and patterns,

according to whether it is whole, peeled, cut in half or sliced into segments. Even the core and pips offer further variation. Then think about the range of apples available – the different colours and sizes that can be bought, the different tastes and uses you associate with each piece of fruit. Even the way in which the apple is displayed in a shop, laying with numerous other pieces, creating a variety of contours and patterns, may present some useful ideas. Furthermore, the original source of the object could prove useful. In this case, we associate apples with trees, in particular orchards, but the amount of subsequent tangents is innumerable. Try applying this kind of lateral thinking to any aspect of nature, from fish to flowers, seeds to wild animals, oceans to deserts. Every element of nature can be seen from numerous different angles; movement, growth, colour,

texture, pattern, light — the list is endless. Add to this the human influence on nature — the ripples created by disturbing a pool of water, for example, or the way in which a plant can be encouraged to grow around man-made structures — and you

will see how nature really can ensure that you never run out of ideas. By thinking laterally, every trip to the coast, walk in the park or visit to the grocers could present a host of inspirational ideas.

Light & Colour

IKE NATURE, light and colour are everywhere. From the vibrant hue of a red rose bud, to the rainbow colours caught in a soap sud, the effects of light and colour can be found wherever you look. In fact, all colour is contained within light – it is as light bends, gets absorbed or is bounced off of a surface, that colour becomes visible. Colours can evoke memories and emotions, funny moments or favourite hobbies. Different amounts of light will also influence these associations, such as soft, warming light or bright vibrant sunshine.

Colour can be strong and bold, or soft and subtle. It is commonly associated with emotion – whole therapies based around the influence of colour now exist. Blue, for example, a favourite colour of many people, is often used for its harmonizing

qualities, while red suggests strong passion and yellow is appreciated for its sunny, vibrant feel. The chances are that the colours you use for a project will correspond with, or complement, the existing colours of the surrounding room. However, it's worth thinking about how different light affects colour and how this could influence your finish. Practical aspects, such as the way in which direct sunlight causes bleaching on most surfaces may influence how you decide to distress or antique a painted finish. The way in which light and shadows interact could provide ideas for how to colour decoupage prints, or how to paint freehand pictures in a three-dimensional way. Even the way in which light bounces off of a surface, highlighting some colours and subduing others, may provide inspiration. Furthermore, bear in mind that colours are constantly interacting with each

other, producing an infinite range of hues. A deep blue positioned next to a vivid red will look considerably different when it is placed next to a yellow, green, or even when it is left on its own. Add to this, the range of effects created by different

intensities of light shining on the blue, and you will see that colour and light are perfect themes for experimenting with design. Look around and see just how much colour and light influences your life.

Seasons

THE DIVERSITY AND CREATIVITY offered by nature extends to the change in seasons. Look out for the changes in plants and animals, the cycle of colours and textures, and the different appearances that one scene can adopt at different times of the year.

Think also about how we use seasonal associations, from the availability of different foods at certain times, to the colours and fabrics we like to wear. Changes in season present a whole host of different textures, appearances and sensations – and all can provide an ever-evolving wealth of inspiring ideas.

Although most people associate seasons with certain concepts, Christmas and Easter, for example, or particular weather, the diversity of each season is vast. Different months present the growth and arrival of different fruits, vegetables and plants, as

 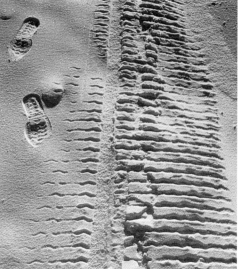 

well as a change in temperature or type of activity. For example, while summer sunshine may bring thoughts of hazy, relaxing days on the beach, winter snow could suggest crisp, morning walks or cosy retreats by the fireside. Autumnal harvesting or spring chicks, summer holidays or winter ski-ing are all common images, but the effects of different seasons is vast. Take, for example, a simple flower. In one season it will be just beginning life, appearing small and fragile as its shoot gradually reaches for more light. As the year progresses, the plant will become stronger, producing a bloom and asserting a presence in its surrounding environment. Another season on and the flower will be starting to wilt, losing its vibrant colour and gradually reducing back to a browning stem. A few more weeks and the flower may no longer be visible at all, as the

browning leaves die completely and the flower awaits the next seasonal cycle. Add to this the way in which the flower catches different lights or the way in which the head opens and reaches for the light, then gently wilts together as it dies. Even the

way in which dew gently hangs from the petals in early sunrise demonstrates how seasons bring a constant sense of change and evolution. Think about how these changes can influence your choice of colour, texture and decorative technique.

Art & History

EVERYDAY OBJECTS provide perfect, easily accessible, sources of inspiration. From a pile of stacked up books, to a favourite work of art, an old birthday card to the wallpaper on your walls, everything we use can help to influence an artistic design. In fact, studying the room and objects that will surround your piece of junk can help to suggest suitable themes. Variations on hobbies and interests, or the extension of an existing style, may all help to create a personal, highly individualized design that suits both you and your environment.

Art and history is a diverse term, encompassing a range of potential themes. For some people, it will be associated with classical concepts and ideas, such as antique furniture, Grecian mythology or Roman architecture. For others, the themes can

be much more personal, such as family photographs, aspects of cultural identity or even childhood memories. There is obviously no right or wrong way of thinking about art and history, but it can be useful to think about what the themes mean to you. Some people find inspiration in prints, antiques and architecture, others find it in their favourite pop band or fiction novel. Ideas can be visual or conceptual, audible or textural. The contours on old maps, for example, or the symmetry of an old clock face can make ideal decorative patterns for different furniture pieces. Alternatively, books may provide inspiration, either by content or by the visual pictures or calligraphy that is used. Even the plot itself may present some suitable ideas for decorating themes! Many pieces of junk are used to store old or favourite items, so see whether the function

of the furniture also presents some ideas. For example, a cabinet used to store fossils or shells could be decorated with similar motifs, or a jewellry cabinet could be given gilded highlights to match the gold inside. Remember, also, that favourite

heirlooms needn't be valuable or ornate. Objects aged by time, such as tin containers or mossy, terracotta pots, can present just as many ideas for colour, texture and themes as classical pieces of art, history and culture.

Arguably the most sociable and lively room in the house, the living room should be comfortable and stylish, reflecting your individual character. Finishing touches, whether a decorated picture frame or stylish lamp, help to personalize the room and make ideal projects for trying out a range of artistic techniques.

Living Room Projects

Folding Filigree Screen

THIS OLD SCREEN was covered in numerous layers of uneven brown paint. However, gently rubbing down the old paint revealed a stylish surface that could easily be given a new lease of life with a coat of midnight blue. The edgings and intricate areas were highlighted with gilt wax cream, which helps to accentuate the delicate cut-out patterns. A small gold star motif was then stamped around the border. This type of screen looks best against plain walls or draping fabric, or in front of a window so that the wonderful patterns are emphasized.

❖ YOU WILL NEED ❖

Medium and fine grade abrasive papers

Tack rag

Bowl of soapy water and old toothbrush

Protective sheet

Midnight blue acrylic or
water-based matt emulsion paint

Household paintbrush

Artists' brush

Ruler and chalk

Motif stamp

Stamp roller or art brush

Gold watercolour paint or craft paint

Saucer or small container

Gilding cream

Spray polyurethane varnish in satin finish

1 Rub down the screen with medium and then fine grade abrasive papers to remove all paint build-ups and flaking paint. Wipe down with a tack rag and then clean the screen with warm soapy water, using an old toothbrush to get into the corners and crevices. Allow to dry thoroughly.

2 Cover the floor with a plastic sheet or newspaper and paint the entire screen with two coats of midnight blue paint, using an artists' brush to paint into the crevices and cut-out patterns. Remember that the screen may be easier to paint if it is laid flat on the floor, or if a spray can is used – but ensure adequate ventiliation.

3 Measure the frame surrounds of one entire section and divide this equally to space out the gold star stamp pattern. (As all three panels are the same, you will only have to work this out once.) Then make light chalk marks to indicate where the stamp must be positioned.

4 Pour a small amount of gold paint into a dish. Work paint into the roller until it is fully coated and then roll this over the stamp. Press the stamp in position and remove using one swift action. Alternatively, simply dip an artists' brush into the gold paint and apply a coat of this to the stamp. For a very definite motif, re-coat the stamp with paint after each application and clean off any residue occasionally.

This old screen had very intricate detail

5 Apply a small amount of gilding cream to your thumb and forefinger and smudge it into all cut-outs and edges. Leave to dry and buff gently to a soft sheen. Then spray the screen evenly with one coat of satin varnish and allow to dry thoroughly.

HINTS & TIPS

- For a weather-worn, stamped, effect, add more gold paint to the stamp only every 2–3 applications.

- Stamps are available from most craft shops but many suppliers will make stamps according to your own design. Alternatively, make your own vegetable stamp, as explained on p110.

For further paint technique projects see:
Picture Frames pp100–105; Decorated Lloyd Loom Chair pp108–109; Stamped Mirror pp110–111; Verdigris Chandelier pp118–120; Display Decanter pp124–125; Shaker Chair pp126–128; Ironware Barge Pot pp164–165

▲ Apply the base coat of midnight blue

▲ Add gilding cream to the edges of the cut-outs

Calligraphy Lampshades

PLAIN, SIMPLE LAMPSHADES are remarkably easy to transform. These shades were found at a garage sale and were given a new lease of life with the use of a gold metallic art pen, a skein of garden raffia and a stick of sealing wax to give a finishing touch. The inspiration for this project came from the popular fabric and china designs which feature gold calligraphy in a variety of languages. There are a number of books on calligraphy and it's useful to look at old books, scrolls and wall hangings in museums to obtain different ideas. In addition to single characters and letters, it can be amusing to use well-known sayings or phrases from foreign dictionaries. Alternatively, why not use something less familiar to create a bit of intrigue?

❖ YOU WILL NEED ❖

Lampshades

A can of decorative gold spray

Protective mask

Protective sheeting

Fine-tip gold flow metallic art pen

Artists' mounting card

Ball of raffia (from garden centres)

Craft glue or glue gun

Scalpel and cutting mat

Wax sealing stick and stamp

Card

Glue

1 Spray the inside of the lampshades with the gold decorative spray, using protective sheeting around the shades and a mask to protect your lungs from the fumes. Take care not to get spray paint on the outer side of the shade. Leave to dry thoroughly.

2 After choosing the calligraphy design, practise creating the letters or figures with the gold pen on the artists' mounting card. Maintaining a consistent flow of ink through these pens does take practice, and it can be useful to plan the angles and positions of each character before beginning work on the actual shade.

3 Carefully draw the characters and marks onto the shades, holding the base firmly in your other hand. Take care that the ink does not smudge as you work around the circular shape – it's also a good idea to

Simple lampshades are easy to pick up at antique sales

start from the top of the shades and work down. For extra decorative effect, gently shake the pen so that gold ink spatters over the shades. However make sure that the surrounding area is well protected, and be prepared for uneven, random blobs as the ink flies onto the shade. Leave the lampshades aside to dry for about an hour.

▲ A range of decorative features can be used

▲ Secure one end and plait the raffia

▲ Fray off the ends of the raffia trim

4 Cut six lengths of raffia approximately twice the circumference of the bottom of the shade. Secure one set of ends and neatly plait three double strands to fit around the bottom rim, allowing some overlap (see picture on page 92). Glue the plait round the bottom of the shade, but fray off the ends. Stick down one set of ends and overlap the other, leaving about 3cm (1¼in) unplaited and frayed. Repeat the process for the top rim but exclude the overlap piece, simply cutting and sticking down the ends to make a neat join.

5 Melt the sealing wax on to the card by lighting the wick end and allowing the wax to drip. Quickly press the stamp in and out while it is hot. Once dry, cut around the card, close to the wax seal, with a scalpel blade – leaving the card attached will prevent the seal from cracking. Glue the seal into position over the join of the raffia as shown. By applying the sealing wax to the card you will also eliminate any risk of damaging the shade. This is because it often takes several practice runs with sealing wax before the desired effect is achieved.

▲ Use a scalpel to cut around the seal

▲ Position the seal over the frayed raffia

▲ Carefully stick the raffia around the trim

HINTS & TIPS

• Remember that the curved shape of the shade will be more difficult to write on than a flat surface, so try folding some card into a similar shape and practise the technique.

• Metallic pens must be shaken regularly to keep the flow of ink consistent. Remember to do this over the protected surface to avoid flying ink.

• Sealing wax can be bought from many craft and stationery shops, although kits for personalized sealing stamps with sealing wax are also available. Alternatively, temporarily fix an old foreign coin to a heavy bolthead and dip this in the hot wax.

For further accessory projects see:
Picture Frames pp100–105; Stamped Mirror pp110–111; Gold Leaf Tray pp138–139; Ironware Barge Pot pp164–165; Potichomanie Glass Jar pp188–189; Laundry Box pp200–201; Mosaic Vase pp227–229; Decorative Pots pp236–238

Round Coffee Table

THIS COFFEE TABLE was thrown out as rubbish during a house renovation. It had been partly rubbed down, and was filthy from dirt, dust and builders' use. However, the elegantly shaped legs with carved grooves and the beading around the top were still intact. It was decided that a plain finish, with contrasting coloured highlights, to emphasize the shape and patterns, would best suit the table. After giving it a thorough scrub down, a vanilla ice-cream coloured, water-based paint was used for the main colour. This is complemented with earthy coloured highlights – made by mixing terre verte powder pigment with the base paint. The amount of highlighting you choose to do can vary, but this table benefits from uncluttered simplicity.

❖ YOU WILL NEED ❖

Medium and fine grade abrasive papers

Tack rag

Sanding sealer

Household paintbrushes

Fine longhair art brush

Cream water-based paint

Terre verte pigment powder

Small container

Masking tape (optional)

Cream furniture wax and a clean lint-free cloth

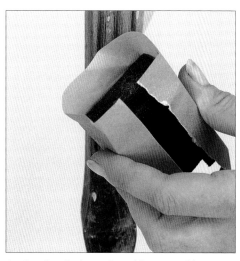

▲ Gently rub down the table top and legs

▲ Apply the cream base paint

This old table needed little more than some simple rubbing down and a new lick of paint

1 Taking care not to damage the surface, rub down the entire table with medium grade abrasive paper, ensuring that any flaking varnishes are removed and the surface is smooth. Repeat the rubbing down with fine grade abrasive paper. Wipe down with a tack rag. Apply a coat of sanding sealer over the entire surface and leave to dry.

2 Apply two coats of the cream base paint, following the recommended drying time between coats. If necessary, apply a third coat. For a very smooth finish, lightly rub down with fine grade abrasive paper and a tack rag between coats. This additional work will ensure an even surface.

3 To mix the coloured pigment, pour a small amount of cream paint into a small container and tap out a small amount of terre verte pigment powder. Mix thoroughly, adding more paint or pigment until you obtain the colour you need. The final consistency should be a little

▲ Mix the pigment with the cream paint

95

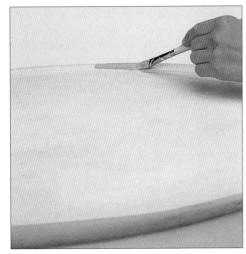

▲ Paint the top beading

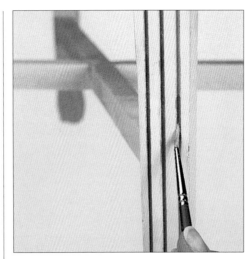

▲ Highlight the grooves in the legs

▲ Polish the table with cream wax

thicker than the original water-based paint, but keep it at a workable consistency, similar to double cream.

4 Using the art brush, apply paint carefully inside the grooves, using long continuous strokes. If the paint does not flow easily, dip the brush into water and then into the paint. If there are no grooves to guide the brush, try using masking tape to create a long, thin line which the brush can fill. Paint the top beading in a similar way. Once dry, apply a second coat of the pigment paint and leave overnight.

5 Using a soft clean cloth, apply the first coat of cream wax evenly to the entire table with a circular motion. Leave for approximately ten minutes and then gently buff with a clean cloth. This process should be repeated until you obtain a durable soft sheen finish, and will take between two and six applications. Acrylic varnishing wax offers greater durability for tables that need to be hardwearing, such as those used for children's toys or games. However, avoid using beeswax or tinted wax as these will alter the underlying base and decorative colours.

HINTS & TIPS

• When painting furniture, it's not necessary to remove all the old colour or varnish, so long as you obtain a clean, matt surface to which the new paint can adhere.

• For ideas on repeating decorative motifs, see the template section on page 242.

For further table and desk projects see:
Vine Leaf Table pp114–117; Table & Chair pp154–157; Writing Desk pp170–171; Chequered Table & Chairs pp204–206; Verdigris Table pp224–226

▲ Add small detail motifs

Needlecraft Workbox

THIS OLD WORKBOX was in remarkably good condition for its age, although it did have a split leg. Such damage can easily be fixed using the procedures described in the 'Basic techniques and equipment' section on page 14. Decoupage is an excellent form of decoration for such an object because of the numerous, interestingly shaped surfaces, all of which are framed by the main structure of the box. The soft, delicate design also complements the role of the box as useful storage for needlecraft and embroidery tools.

❖ YOU WILL NEED ❖

Fine wire wool

White spirit

Fine grade abrasive paper

Tack rag

Oil-based eggshell paint

Brushes

Acrylic paints

Sponge

Paper patterns

Scalpel, mat and scissors

Adhesive tack

PVA glue

Roller

Damp cloth

Acrylic varnish

Polyurethane clear gloss varnish

This workbox has a number of panels and different surfaces

1 Rub down the box with fine wire wool and white spirit to remove any build-up of polish and dirt, followed by fine grade abrasive paper. Use a tack rag to remove any dirt or dust residues. Then apply two coats of the chosen base paint, rubbing down and tack-ragging the surface between the first and second coats.

▲ Rub down the surface following the grain

2 To highlight the box's form, use a sponging technique around the frame and edge of the lid. Gently apply the diluted acrylic paint around the frame, twisting and turning the sponge to create a random, cloudy effect. Repeat with a second colour.

▲ Carefully cut out the decoupage shapes

3 Choose and cut out the various pieces for the decoupage design using a scalpel and cutting board, together with fine manicure scissors for intricate work. Arrange the cut-outs on the box with adhesive tack before glueing them into place. Gently squeeze out and remove any excess glue with a roller and damp cloth.

▲ Work out the design using adhesive tack

4 Once dry, give the box two or three coats of acrylic varnish. Then gently rub down the surface with fine grade abrasive paper, wipe with a tack rag and apply another coat. Continue in this way until the design is completely submerged.

HINTS & TIPS

Remember that changing the handles on items of furniture can give them a totally different look and help to create the final effect. In this case, metal handles were removed and exchanged for wooden ones, which could then be painted to become part of the overall scheme.

For further storage projects see:
Floral Cutlery Box pp134–135; Storage Trunk pp172–174; Multipurpose Chest pp212–213

Picture Frames

S IMPLE FINISHING TOUCHES to a room can make all the difference. Picture frames, for example, are remarkably easy to adapt and can be transformed using any number of different techniques. A lick of paint, a collage border of spare trinkets or a mosaic tile effect can all help to create a personalized frame that suits your chosen picture or photograph. Ideas can come from literally anywhere – spare curtain fabric, a piece of distressed furniture or even an old box of junk. Here are just a few suggestions that should provide inspiration for other, inventive projects.

Geometric Picture Frame

❖ YOU WILL NEED ❖

Frame 32 x 25cm (13 x 10in) internal,
50 x 43cm (20 x 17in) external

Blue acrylic paint

2.5cm (1in) brush

$^{1}/_{2}$ cup of scumble glaze

2 teaspoons artists' acrylic paint

Stiff-bristled brush

Matching fabric

Scissors

Masking tape

Gold tape

Varnish & brush

1 Paint the frame on each side and allow to dry. Then mix a glaze using the scumble glaze and artists' acrylic paint. Stipple the glaze onto the frame with sharp, stabbing motions, which help to create a mottled effect.

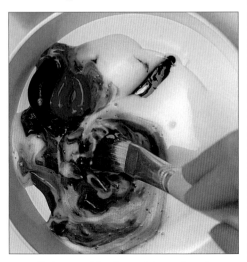
▲ Mix the scumble glaze with acrylic paint

▲ Cut out fabric pieces for templates

2 While the glaze is drying, cut out some of the designs from the fabric. Position these on the frame, creating templates for the final pattern. Remember that some pieces will have to be turned upside down, in order to create a balanced, symmetrical design around the frame.

▲ Stipple on the glaze with jabbing motions

▲ Use the fabric as templates for masking

3 Position masking tape around the pieces of fabric, following each angle as closely as possible. Then remove the fabric – your shapes will be outlined by the remaining masking tape. (Although it is possible to proceed without masking tape, especially as gold tape has straight edges, these temporary borders provide useful guides for ensuring a perfect finish.)

4 Apply size to a couple of the areas bordered by masking tape. Then apply strips of gold tape to the size and press in place. Remove the backing paper from the tape, brush away any residue on the surface and remove the masking tape. Repeat these steps on each section, working on two or three masked-off areas at a time. Once dry, you may varnish the surface for additional protection. However, picture frames are not usually subjected to heavy handling so this is not vital.

▲ Apply the gold tape to the size

HINTS & TIPS

• Cheap masking tape is ideal for this kind of work because it tends to have little adhesive gum and so will not lift the acrylic paint from the frame when it is removed.

• Use a good quality brush to apply size as this will help to ensure the medium is laid in a thin, even coat.

• Only decant small amounts of gold size at a time. More can be added if it is needed, but unused size should never be put back in the original container, as it is likely to have picked up some dirt and dust from the atmosphere.

• Patterns need not be geometric – any design could be used, including motifs from curtains or other soft furnishings.

For further projects using gold see:
Calligraphy Lampshades pp92–94; Traveller's Writing Desk pp106–107; Verdigris Chandelier pp118–120; Gold Leaf Tray pp138–139; Storage Trunk pp172–174

Distressed Frame

❖ YOU WILL NEED ❖

Frame 32 x 25cm (13 x 10in) internal, 50 x 43cm (20 x 17in) external

Medium and fine grade abrasive papers

Tack rag

Oyster pearl and blush acrylic gouache paints

2.5cm (1in) brush

Wet-and-dry paper

Cork sanding block

Varnish and brush

▲ Corners should show greater wear and distress

1 Rub down the frame with medium and then fine grade abrasive papers, and wipe off the dust residue with the tack rag. Then apply the oyster pearl acrylic paint with the 2.5cm (1in) brush to one side of the frame and leave to dry. Repeat on the other side. Then apply two rough coats of blush to the frame, over the oyster pearl, in the same way.

2 Wrap the wet-and-dry paper around the cork block and immerse it in water. Sand the frame with the block, gently removing the top coat of blush so that the frame acquires an aged, distressed appearance. Remember to sand in the same direction, following the grain of the wood. For extra effect, apply additional pressure to corners and other areas of the frame that are likely to show wear.

3 Allow the frame to dry and then wipe away any residue with the tack rag. Apply two or three coats of acrylic varnish, sanding between each coat with abrasive paper.

HINTS & TIPS

Wire wool can be used for a very worn effect, but choose a fine grade and avoid exerting too much pressure, otherwise the paint will appear scratched, rather than worn.

For further ageing projects see:
Verdigris Chandelier pp118–120; Granite Effect Fireplace pp136–137; Pine Panelled Cupboard pp144–146; Scandinavian Scroll Chair pp147–149; Antiqued Cupboard pp158–160; Folk Art Chair pp161–163; Carved Linen Chest pp168–169; Seashore Cabinet pp192–194; Chequered Table & Chairs pp204–206; Verdigris Table pp224–226

Beads & Pearls Frame

❖ YOU WILL NEED ❖

Frame 32 x 25cm (13 x 10in) internal,
50 x 43cm (20 x 17in) external

Blue acrylic paint

Chalk pencil

Adhesive glue & paste brush

Various beads

▲ Use an assortment of trinkets

1 Apply a coat of blue acrylic paint to one side of the frame. Allow to dry before painting the other side. (Balance the frame on paint tins, to maximize air flow around the frame.)

2 Use the chalk pencil to roughly mark out your design and the positions of each piece on the frame. These marks will be covered, or can be rubbed away, later.

3 Use the adhesive to fix the beads to the frame, starting with the inside border. For strings of pearls or beads, cut the lengths to the correct size and seal the thread at each end with adhesive.

4 For tiny beads and pearls, spread glue onto the frame with a paste brush and then sprinkle the trinkets over the wet adhesive.

HINTS & TIPS

• It may be worth working out a rough design for your pattern on a piece of paper, cut to the size of the frame. That way, you avoid putting experimental marks on the wood, and can cut and arrange the beads and trinkets into their desired positions, before transferring them to the frame.

• Experiment with all different kinds of objects. Montage can involve shells, cones, or even dried chillies – whatever you have lying around the house.

For further projects using beads see:
Verdigris Chandelier pp118–120

Mosaic Frame

❖ YOU WILL NEED ❖

Frame 32 x 25cm (13 x 10in) internal,
50 x 43cm (20 x 17in) external

Pencil

Ruler

Mosaic tiles

Tile adhesive

Tile cutters

Goggles

Rubber gloves

Grout

Sponge

Cloth

1 Use the pencil and ruler to mark out the design on the surface of the frame. Remember that cutting mosaic tiles does take practice and soft, rounded edges can be difficult to achieve so aim for large curves instead.

2 Use the tile cutters to cut out the mosaic tiles into squares, rectangles and triangles. Do not worry about slight irregularities in shape and size – these will help to create the final fragmentary effect.

3 First, use the adhesive to apply the red tiles that form the diagonal lines. Then glue diagonal tiles to the inside border of the frame, creating a triangular effect.

4 Apply the mosaic tiles to the rest of the frame, working from one side to the next. Remember also to add tiles to the outside edges. Allow to dry for at least 24 hours.

5 Using the rubber gloves, spread grout over the frame, ensuring that all areas between the mosaic tiles are filled. Sponge off the excess grout and allow to dry for 24 hours. Polish the tiles with a dry cloth.

HINTS & TIPS

• If using coloured grout, be sure to mix enough quantity for the whole project. Otherwise, it will be difficult to match the exact colour for a second mix.

• It is a good idea to use a mask, as well as gloves and goggles, when cutting and grouting tiles. This is because the dust generated can be allergenic.

For further mosaic projects see:
Mosaic Vase pp227–229

▲ Use diagonal lines on the frame corners

Traveller's Writing Desk

THIS ELABORATE WRITING DESK was originally one of those cheap, flat-packed tables designed for kitchen use. Despite several years of work as a dining surface, it was in remarkably good condition and required very little sanding or preparation before being coated with generous amounts of yew-coloured wood stain. A single sheet of wrapping paper depicting an old map of the world, the seven wonders of the world, and other interesting historical and mythical images were used for the decoupage finish. Of course, any theme can be used but these images suit the new role of this desk as a place to write memoirs and travel correspondence. It now makes an interesting centrepiece for any living room or even a study.

❖ YOU WILL NEED ❖

Yew-coloured wood stain

Household paintbrush

Pencil

Steel rule

Craft knife and cutting mat

Manicure scissors

Wrapping paper

Adhesive paste

Large cloth

Varnish

Fine grade abrasive paper

Tack rag

Gold marker pen

1 Apply the wood stain following the instructions on the tin. Leave to dry thoroughly and apply further coats if required, allowing sufficient drying time between coats. Then, lightly measure and mark out the position of each design with a pencil on the surface of the table.

2 Cut out the various designs for the decoupage. Use the steel rule to help with straight edges and cut onto a cutting mat to protect the surface beneath. For intricate shapes, use manicure scissors.

3 Apply adhesive to the back of each cut-out and, if necessary, the desired position on the table surface. Once positioned, gently push down on the paper cut-out, ensuring that all the edges are fully stuck down. For the large design use the cloth, folded into a flat pad, for pressing the map into place. Take care not to apply too much pressure as the dampened paper may tear. Any minor wrinkles should disappear when the glue dries.

4 Use a gold pen to rule off square edges and add any intricate borders. For the gold lines around the edge of the table, simply rest the marker pen on its side with the nib on the table and the plastic surround of the nib resting against the table's edge. Then run the pen along the table, keeping the plastic on the edge, to produce a straight line. Once dry, apply several layers of varnish to the table, rubbing down with abrasive paper and a tack rag between coats.

HINTS & TIPS

Use the ruler upside down when drawing straight edges with the gold pen. This will help to reduce the likelihood of smudging.

For further table projects see:
Round Coffee Table pp95–97; Vine Leaf Table pp114–117; Table & Chair pp154–157; Chequered Table & Chairs pp204–206; Verdigris Table pp224–226

▲ Measure and mark out the pattern

▲ Outline the map with a gold pen

▲ Use smaller cut-outs for a decorative border

Decorated Lloyd Loom Chair

LLOYD LOOM FURNITURE is made from a special type of strong brown paper that is woven around steel wire. Versatile and elegant, it was remarkably popular in the 1920s and 1930s, and remains a classic style of furniture for modern times. This chair was not old enough to class as an antique, although it had acquired several years' worth of different paint layers. Stripping woven furniture is not practical, so the chair was cleaned down as much as possible before being redecorated with a new paint finish. Cane and wicker furniture can be similarly treated.

❖ YOU WILL NEED ❖

Wire brush

Wire wool

Medium and fine grade abrasive papers

Tack rag

Vacuum cleaner

Base paint

Selection of household brushes

Top paint

Masking tape

Tape measure

Paintbrushes

Varnish, mixed with a small quantity of artists' acrylic paint (raw umber) if required

Lloyd Loom chairs can easily be given a new lease of life

1 Use the wire brush to vigorously brush over the whole surface of the chair and remove flaking paint. Then rub down with fine grade abrasive paper to key the surface. Use a tack rag and vacuum cleaner to make sure the weave is totally free of dust. Clean the brass feet with wire wool.

▲ Remove flaking paint with a wire brush

2 Apply the base paint to the whole of the chair, and leave to dry. Then use masking tape to make a criss-cross pattern across the inside of the chair and over the seat. Measure the centre of the back of the chair and work outwards on either side, making sure the tape sticks well.

▲ Apply the base coat and leave to dry

▲ Use masking tape for the criss-cross pattern

3 Apply the top colour paint to the whole chair. Leave to dry and then carefully remove the masking tape. Apply a protective coat of varnish to all the surfaces – for an aged effect, add a little raw umber artists' acrylic paint to the varnish.

▲ Apply the top coat to the chair surface

HINTS & TIPS

Use a soft-bristled brush with the vacuum cleaner to help free dust and dirt.

For further paint technique projects see:
Round Coffee Table pp95–97; Shaker Chair pp126–128; Granite Effect Fireplace pp136–137; Scandinavian Scroll Chair pp147–149; Chequered Table & Chairs pp204–206

Stamped Mirror

STAMPED DESIGNS are an excellent way of creating individual patterns and may be as simple or as complex as you like. Wooden stamping blocks can be bought or made and are ideal for repeating patterns on various objects around the home. However, for a simpler variation, why not try cutting designs into vegetables, such as a potato or carrot (see below) and printing from that? The secret of effective stamping lies in keeping the design as simple as possible. If necessary, repeat the same shape several times using chalk markings to help ensure accuracy.

❖ YOU WILL NEED ❖

Paint for the frame surface

2.5cm (1in) brush

Fine abrasive paper

Tack rag

Chalk

Stamp

Artists' acrylic paint

Smooth sponge

Cotton bud

1 Repair any damage to the mirror frame and rub down with fine grade abrasive paper and a tack rag before applying at least two coats of the chosen final surface colour. Remember also to rub down the wooden surface between each coat.

2 Use the chalk to mark where the design is to appear on the mirror border. It is also adviseable to measure and mark the back of the stamping block, to indicate the centre of the design. This will help to ensure symmetry as the block is reapplied.

▲ Apply the base paint to the frame

3 Use the sponge to dab artists' acrylic paint to the design on the stamp, covering the whole design evenly. If you wish to use more than one colour on the stamp, apply these at the same time. This will prevent the difficulty of trying to re-position the stamp in the exact place a second time.

▲ Test the stamp on scrap paper

4 Align the stamp with the chalked marks on the frame, taking care not to touch the painted surface until you are confident the stamp is in its correct position. Press the stamp firmly into place and gently rock it. Use both hands for large designs, to ensure even pressure.

▲ Mark guidelines for the stamp with chalk

▲ Apply even pressure to the stamp

5 Lift the stamp cleanly upwards, taking care not to smudge the paint. Remove any stray paint by carefully lifting it off with a cotton bud. Leave to dry for several hours.

HINTS & TIPS

Simple relief designs can be made by cutting into the surface of half a potato.

1 First, wash the potato and then cut it in half with a sharp knife. Let the potato stand for a while and then wipe off any excess moisture which might make the print watery.

2 Carve the relief design into the potato with a sharp knife – taking care with your hands. Try to make the cuts as deep and clean as possible. Remember that whatever is cut away will remain blue (or whatever colour the mirror border has been painted).

3 Dry the potato on a paper towel and paint with a water-based paint. Press firmly on to the surface, as before. Remember that potato blocks are likely to become watery and lose their crisp shape quite quickly, so use designs that can be simply recut. To do this, make a print from the potato on to some spare paper, cut out the shape and then position this on a new potato.

For further stamping projects see:
Folding Filigree Screen pp90–91

BOTH FUNCTIONAL AND SOCIABLE,
DINING ROOMS SHOULD PROVIDE
THE PERFECT ENVIRONMENT FOR
LIGHT LUNCHES AND ELABORATE
ENTERTAINING. SO WHETHER YOU
ARE PLANNING TO TRANSFORM THE
DINING FURNITURE, OR SIMPLY ADD
A FINISHING TOUCH TO THE ROOM,
THESE PROJECTS SHOULD HELP
CREATE THE IDEAL ATMOSPHERE
FOR A TASTE SENSATION!

Dining Room Projects

Vine Leaf Table

BASIC AND FUNCTIONAL, the round table below simply needed a touch of finesse. Lightening the colour and adding a stencilled grape pattern has created a flexible piece of furniture, suitable for quick morning coffees, lunch with friends or elaborate evening meals. The design even allows for a middle leaf extension, ensuring the table is both attractive and adaptable.

After stripping the varnish, several coats of acrylic glaze or varnish should be applied to help preserve the painted design and to give a durable finish. The swirling patterns were created by first coating the table with a cream eggshell base, and then applying butterscotch glaze. Large bunches of leafy grapes were then stencilled on as the centrepiece, with a twining vine leaf pattern around the edge.

❖ YOU WILL NEED ❖

Various paintbrushes

Varnish remover

Medium and fine
grade abrasive papers

Fine wire wool

Tack rag

Cream eggshell paint

Fine glasspaper or finishing paper

Radiator roller with sleeve for
oil-based paint

Artists' oil paints in burnt umber
and yellow ochre

Paint kettle

Large spoon

Transparent oil glaze

White spirit

Stipple brush

Clingfilm

Tape measure

Permanent fine-tip pen

Plastic stencil film

Scalpel, blade and cutting mat

Adhesive spray

Stencil oil sticks in wine red, deep blue,
leaf green and dark emerald green

Acrylic glaze, satin or gloss

1 Remove the old varnish and dirt with a good varnish remover, and sand down with medium and then fine grade abrasive papers. Rub gently with fine wire wool soaked in white spirit and leave to dry. Wipe down with a tack rag.

2 Turn the table upside down and paint the underside and legs in cream eggshell. Allow to dry and gently sand with fine glasspaper. Wipe with a tack rag to remove any dirt and apply a second coat.

Apply the paint to the top surface with a radiator roller. This will help to ensure a really smooth surface for the final decorative finish. As before, gently sand the surface with very fine glasspaper and wipe with a tack rag to remove hairs and any paint particles. Apply a second coat in the same way.

If a good cover has not been obtained with two coats, try applying a third layer. Always sand and clean the painted surface before coating with another layer of paint.

This simple table provides a good base for a beautiful stencilled design

3 Add a tube width of yellow ochre and half this amount of burnt umber, to a spoon of transparent oil glaze. Stir until smooth. Keep adding small amounts of paint, in this ratio, until a butterscotch colour is achieved. Then add transparent oil glaze and white spirit in the ratio of two parts glaze to one part white spirit. Stir in a spoon of cream eggshell paint. When there is enough mixture, the final consistency should be like single cream.

▲ Paints and equipment for glazing

▲ Stir the oil paint into the oil glaze

4 Choose a discreet section, such as the table legs, to begin applying the glaze. This will enable you to practise the technique. Apply the butterscotch glaze to the eggshell base with the paintbrush. Then stipple the glaze immediately, using a moderate, up-and-down stabbing motion to

▲ Apply the butterscotch glaze

remove the brush strokes. Repeat the process on remaining sections, including the top. Once complete, move immediately on to the next step.

5 Cut pieces of clingfilm approximately 30cm (12in) square. Take one of the squares between the thumb and forefingers of each hand, and hold it 30cm (12in) above the surface. Lean over the table and blow into the centre of the clingfilm, allowing it to float down on to the table. Blow over all the areas of the clingfilm while it is stuck

▲ Stipple over the butterscotch glaze

to the glaze. Gently peel up one corner and then pull the whole piece off in one movement.

Repeat this process evenly over the whole table, overlapping slightly so that parts are not missed and no hard edges are left. Whenever the clingfilm becomes loaded with glaze, replace it with a new square. Leave the table to dry.

6 Place the stencil film over the template on page 242 and draw around the outlines with the permanent pen. Carefully cut around the lines with a sharp scalpel (a new blade is best). There are five pattern pieces: two vine twists, leaves with two grapes and two separate grapes. Trace and cut the single grapes on a separate piece of 15cm (6in) stencil film so that they can be used at the same time as the leafy grape stencils.

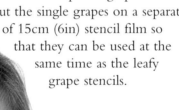

▼ Use clingfilm to create a swirling effect on the table

7 Measure a circle in the centre of the table and position the stencil. The pattern piece of leaves with two grapes will be used to make the large bunches. These large configurations should be alternated with smaller bunches, created by using the pattern piece of two separate grapes.

▲ Draw around the outline of the template

8 Spray a light coating of the adhesive spray on to the back of the stencil and position it. Cut a small square section of plastic and rub all of the stencil oil sticks in their own corners to break the transparent seal covering the stick. This leaves paint on the plastic, creating a palette.

Work the stencil brush into the leaf green colour and stipple with a circular motion into the leaf part of the design. Work into the brush a small amount of the dark green and stipple around some edges for contrast shading. With a separate brush, use the wine red colour to create bunches of grapes (see step 9). Proceed around the table, using the pattern pieces until the circle of grapes and leaves is complete.

▲ Create bunches by overlapping the stencil

9 To create the bunch of grapes effect, practise the technique on a separate piece of paper, perhaps with a real bunch in front of you. Remember that odd half grapes give the bunch a good shape at the edges, so that the bunch tapers to the end. The red and blue mixed together make purple to shade the darker grapes and edges.

Starting at the top of the bunch, with the two top grapes as a guide, stencil the large grape on the outside and then slightly below to create a cluster effect. Keep the colour transparent and light at this stage, so you can layer over existing grapes for a 3-D effect. After stencilling approximately five large grapes downwards, change to the smaller grape and stencil four or five irregularly to create the tail of the bunch. Mix a darker purple and shade the top surface grapes to bring them into the foreground.

Remember that oil paints can be very slow to dry and harden, so leave the painted design for at least 48 hours

▲ Stencil the vine leaf border

in a well-ventilated room. Depending on the shape of the table, you may want to create additional bunches, perhaps of different sizes, but remember that much of the design's charm comes from its simplicity. The size of the table should also influence the size of the bunch of grapes – small tables need smaller designs, whereas large tables can incorporate larger, more elaborate flourishes.

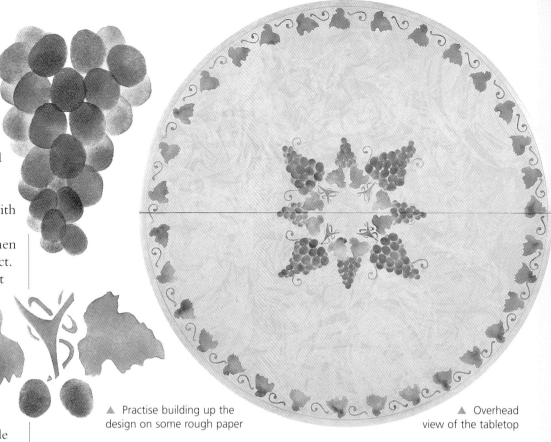

▲ Practise building up the design on some rough paper

▲ Overhead view of the tabletop

10 Using adhesive spray, stick a small piece of protective plastic over the grapes and vine stalk on the main stencil. This is because you will be using only the leaves for the border. Then stencil one leaf next to the outside edge, creating an outward leaf with an inward twine. Repeat in reverse, creating an inward leaf with an outward twine (see photograph).

11 For the protective glaze, avoid using an oil-based varnish as this will create a yellowed appearance and spoil the colours of the design. Instead, take the time to apply

▲ Varnish the table with acrylic glaze

several layers of acrylic clear-glaze varnish. This can be bought in matt, satin or gloss finishes, creating a variety of different potential sheens. Using an acrylic glazing brush, apply a coat over the entire table, including the legs and decorated surface. When wet, the varnish has a milky appearance but this will dry to a clear finish. Allow plenty of time for the varnish to dry between coats and avoid overbrushing as this tends to cause brush marks.

HINTS & TIPS

- Paint the legs of the table first as this will enable you to practise the technique.

- Stipple the wet glaze immediately to make sure any brush marks are removed.

- Have clingfilm squares ready. This will allow you to move straight on to creating the swirling effect, before the glaze has a chance to dry.

- Experiment with the grape design on paper to calculate the number of different bunches you will need.

- Always allow plenty of drying time between coats of paint or varnish.

For further stencilling projects see:
Decorated Lloyd Loom Chair pp108–109; Bedside Chest pp175–177; Cherub Wardrobe pp182–185

Verdigris Chandelier

VERDIGRIS IS A TERM for the green, natural patina which forms on old metals such as brass and copper. Plain metal, plaster and any hard carved or figured surface can be transformed very easily into a beautiful verdigris finish. The technique is particularly effective on very ornate pieces such as this brass five-armed ceiling hanging light with raised

patterns and fine filigree. Crystal droplets are ideal for decorating the light fitting, especially if the attachments are made of brass-coloured metal, which can also be given the same verdigris effect. Many antique street markets sell oddments of beads, crystal strands and glass droplets, often remnants from other old chandeliers. Alternatively, children's discarded dressing up toys may present some ideas.

❖ YOU WILL NEED ❖

Warm soapy water

Wire wool

Old toothbrush

Tack rag

Clean rags

Small artists' brush
or fitch brush

Mid-brown emulsion

Stencil brush

Verdigris kit or pale
and dark jade shades
of green emulsion

Gold oil stencil stick
or gilding cream

Round stencil brush
size 2 or larger

Coloured glass paint

Card of fuse wire

Tape measure

Small pliers

Kitchen paper

Selection of glass
or crystal beads

Ruler

Be sure to check the wiring on old light fittings

1 With warm soapy water and a small wad of wire wool, clean the fitting thoroughly, taking care to remove all the dirt and dust from between the grooves. Use an old toothbrush to brush down all the fine crevices and corners. Then wipe off the whole surface with a wet cloth. Allow the fitting to dry thoroughly and rub with a tack rag to remove any remaining particles or dust.

2 Use the fitch brush to stipple a generous coat of the mid-brown emulsion over the entire surface of the fitting. Take care to coat all of the corners and crevices, perhaps using a small artists' brush to paint the difficult areas. Leave the chandelier to dry, following the paint manufacturer's recommended guidelines. If necessary, apply a second coat to areas where the paint did not adhere.

3 Pour a small amount of light green emulsion into the lid of the can, and firmly dip in the tip of the stencil brush. Work off any excess paint on to a rag or piece of paper kitchen towel. Stipple the paint on to the surface of the fitting over the brown coat, blending carefully so that a fine mottled effect is created. Again, leave the paint to dry following the manufacturer's recommendations.

▲ Apply the brown base coat

▲ Apply light green emulsion over the brown

▲ Apply the dark green emulsion

4 Use the fitch brush to apply a very small amount of dark green paint to the tip of the chandelier, wiping off any excess paint. Using light, feathery strokes, highlight the raised patterns and some of the recesses of the chandelier with this dark contrast. The paint should accentuate the line and pattern of the piece, contrasting with areas of exposed light green and helping to create an aged effect.

5 Using the gold oil stencil stick or gilding wax cream, rub a small amount of gold colour on to your thumb and forefinger, then rub this into some of the edges, curves and ends of the fitting.

6 Use the same verdigris techniques on any decorative pieces you wish to attach, such as beads or even leaves. Glass pieces can be coloured with glass paint before fixing. For the swag of glass beads, measure the distance between the arms of the fitting and allow an extra 5cm (2in) of strand so that the beads drop in a loop effect. Attach these to the main droplet loops and then attach them to the arms in the required position. If necessary, use a small piece of fuse wire to make a fixing loop for the strands. The wire can be discreetly disguised with a quick coat of green emulsion, or possibly even gold paint for a finishing touch.

▲ Highlight the edges and curves in gold

HINTS & TIPS

• Light fittings have often been stripped of their electrical fittings for safety reasons, or rewired and labelled accordingly. If the fitting is intact, but not labelled, it's important to have the wiring checked by a qualified electrician.

• Such chandeliers look particularly effective with seasonal decoration, such as holly or gold leaf at Christmas.

• Remember to adjust the length of the chandelier chain according to the height of the room. Many modern houses have low ceilings which are not suitable for full length, hanging chandeliers.

For further paint effect projects see:
Round Coffee Table pp95–97; Display Decanter & Glasses pp124–125; Shaker Chair pp126–128; Granite Effect Fireplace pp136–137; Gold Leaf Tray pp138–139; Antiqued Cupboard pp158–160; Folk Art Chair pp161–163; Carved Linen Chest pp168–169; Shutters & Louvre Doors pp198–199; Chequered Table & Chairs pp204–206; Sponged Cot pp218–219; Verdigris Table pp224–226

▲ Attach the crystal beads and droplets to the chandelier

Oriental Chair

Simple church chairs with ladder backs, flat tops and sometimes even book shelves at the back, can be obtained fairly easily from antique shops. They are usually inexpensive but, once the dealer has stripped and waxed them, the cost increases enormously. Be on the look out for untreated chairs, particularly individual items that tend to be more of a bargain than sets of four or six. Such furniture is very adaptable and can be decorated to suit the decor of virtually any room. The inspiration for this chair was the children's book and pantomime 'Aladdin'. Decoupage cut-outs of dragons and oriental calligraphy decorate the main struts, while the bright, festive red paint works alongside the black and gold to suggest traditional oriental lacquering.

❖ YOU WILL NEED ❖

Warm soapy water
and cloth

Medium and fine grade
abrasive papers

Tack rag

Bright red eggshell
paint or gloss

Small paintbrush

Photocopier

Various oriental
paper patterns

Craft knife and
cutting mat

Fixing spray
Soft cloth

Tube of black artists'
oil paint

Small
sharp-pointed scissors

Adhesive tack

Craft glue

Lacquer

Varnish brush

1 Wash the chair with warm, soapy water. Once dry, rub down with medium and fine grade abrasive papers. When the loose and flaking paint or varnish have been removed, and the surface has a suitable 'key', wipe down with a tack rag.

2 Turn the chair upside down and paint the underside and legs. Then stand the chair the right way up and paint the remaining surfaces. Allow for the manufacturer's recommended drying time and then apply a second coat of paint.

3 Photocopy the chosen design several times. Remember to reverse some of the dragons (see p244) so that the pattern will be symmetrical. For a finishing touch, copy an assortment of characters and small pieces for the narrow sides of the chair. Cut out all the designs carefully.

Salvaged from a church, this old chair needed little preparation other than basic cleaning

▲ Apply a coat of bright red paint

▲ Experiment with the position of the cut-outs

121

▲ Glue the final design into place

4 Experiment with the position of each cut-out, using adhesive tack until you are happy with the arrangement. Then apply the craft glue to the back of each piece and stick them in place. Dab over with a clean cloth to remove any surplus glue and press firmly to ensure full adhesion to the chair. When dry, spray one good coat of fixative spray over each design to prevent the ink bleeding.

5 To burnish the edges of the chair, squeeze a small amount of black artists' oil paint on to your thumb and rub this with your index finger. Then smudge the paint along the edges and in the joins of the chair to create

an aged, burnished appearance. For further authenticity, add some smudging to the edges of the seat and any other areas that are likely to have become very worn. For example, the bottom of the chair legs, where scuffing will have occurred, should be coated. Similarly, highlight any indentation or ridges in the seat.

6 For the laquer finish, apply two coats of lacquer to the chair, allowing the surface to dry between coats. However, remember that cellulose lacquers cause damage to oil-based paints, so check that your lacquer is compatible with the paints used on the chair surface.

▲ Burnish the edges with black oil paint

HINTS & TIPS

• When painting chairs, always turn them upside down first and paint the underside, legs, and spindles before moving on to the rest of the chair.

• For furniture that has been rubbed down to the original wooden surface, use primer and undercoat to seal the wood, before painting in gloss.

• Specialist coloured or clear lacquer can be used to create the oriental lacquerware finish. Alternatively, a high gloss varnish or acrylic glaze can be used to produce a similar effect.

For further chair projects see:
Decorated Lloyd Loom Chair pp108–109; Shaker Chair pp126–128; Scandinavian Scroll Chair pp147–149; Table & Chair pp154–157; Folk Art Chair pp161–163; Rocking Chair pp214–217; Deck Chair pp232–233

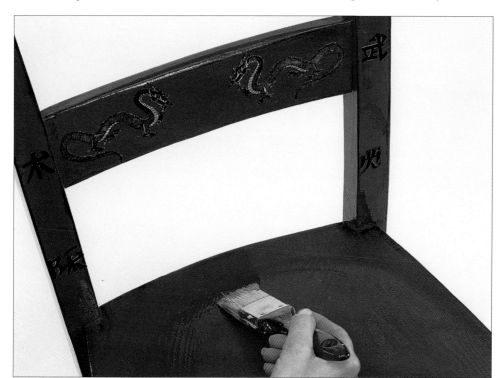

▲ Apply one or two coats of protective lacquer

Display Decanter & Glasses

AN ATTRACTIVE FOCUS on any table or cabinet shelf, this decanter and glass set is decorated with spray enamel paint, gold pens and glitter glue. However, special glass paints and tubes of water-resistant colour are also available, which means that glassware can be highly decorated and still used as functional objects. The frosted effect on these pieces was created with a pearl and vanilla high-gloss spray that is fast drying and ideal for craft projects. For repeating patterns, it's a good idea to use a template which you can draw around (see below) or make a stencil which can be enlarged or reduced accordingly on the photocopier. Templates are provided at the back of the book, but it may be interesting to try out your own designs.

❖ YOU WILL NEED ❖

Warm soapy water

Cloths

Methylated spirit

Wet-and-dry paper

Protective sheeting

Protective mask

Enamel spray paint

Stencil film

Permanent pen

Scalpel

Cutting mat

Glitter glue

Gold medium-tipped metallic flow pens

Newspaper

Coloured glass paint (if required)

Small art brush

1 Wash the glass thoroughly in warm soapy water and dry well. Wipe over with a damp cloth and methylated spirit to remove any excess dirt and allow to dry. Rub over all the surfaces with wet-and-dry paper and wipe down with a dry cloth.

2 Cover the surrounding area with protective sheeting. Then, holding the can of spray paint approximately 30cm (12in) from the object, spray the glass with a thin coat covering all areas. Allow to dry before applying a second, thin coat.

3 Position the stencil film over the large and small stars and the 'fleur-de-lys' pattern templates (p242) or your chosen design, and trace around the outlines with a permanent pen. Cut out with the scalpel and cutting mat, keeping the centre of the stars in one complete piece (these will be used as templates to outline the pattern). The small 'fleur-de-lys', however, can be cut in fragments.

Simple glassware can be easily transformed with colour

4 Very carefully hold the star shape in place and draw around it with the gold pen. Then remove the template and fill in the shape with colour. To outline the 'fleur-de-lys', draw around the inside of the design with the pen. Fill in with silver glitter glue.

5 To make a continuous line around the top of the decanter and rims of the glasses, squeeze the tube of glitter glue carefully around the rim in one continuous line. To finish, swirl around the stopper with the glitter and then follow the line with paint.

HINTS & TIPS

• Use two thin coats, rather than one heavy coat, of enamel spray paint to help create an even surface.

• The same gold metallic pens as those used for the calligraphy lampshades can be used for this project.

For further glass-related projects see:
Potichomanie Glass Jar pp188–189;
Glass Cupboard pp195–197

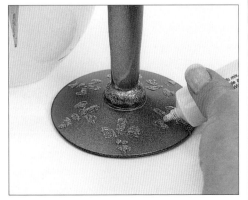

▲ Fill in the design with silver glitter glue

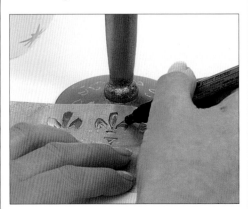

▲ Outline the design with a metallic pen

Shaker Chair

SHAKER STYLE FURNITURE originates from the early American settlers and has become extremely popular. Its simplicity is appealing and the furniture is now produced commercially by large companies, in pale, natural, and muted colours such as linen, jute and duck-egg blue. Originally, the chairs were hung up on the walls when not in use. Simple flower and heart motifs were cut out of the woodwork, creating a basic, uncluttered décor that blended in with a plain and simple environment. The minimalist style of Shaker decoration is ideal for furniture that needs to be subtle, stylish and able to blend with different rooms. This church chair is coated in duck-egg blue with a very simple hand-painted flower motif that anyone can achieve.

❖ YOU WILL NEED ❖

Warm, soapy water and cloth

Furniture cleaner

Medium and fine grade abrasive papers

Tack rag

'Old white' pigment paint

'Dark blue' pigment paint

Paint kettle and stirring stick

Household paintbrush

Prussian blue artists' acrylic paint

White artists' acrylic paint

Fine line art brush

Fine artists' brush

Neutral furniture wax

Clean soft cloth

1 Wash the chair with warm, soapy water and a cloth or a good furniture cleaner. Once dry, rub down with medium, then fine grade abrasive papers to remove loose and flaking paint or varnish and provide a key to the surface. Be gentle – rubbing too roughly can permanently scratch and damage the wood. Wipe down with a tack rag.

2 Pour half the 'old white' paint into the paint kettle and add a very small amount of the dark blue traditional paint. Stir thoroughly and gradually add more blue until you obtain the pale blue you require.

3 Apply two coats of the blue paint over all the surfaces of the chair, turning the chair upside down and painting the underside and legs first. Allow the manufacturer's recommended drying time between coats.

Simply designed church chairs are ideal for basic patterns

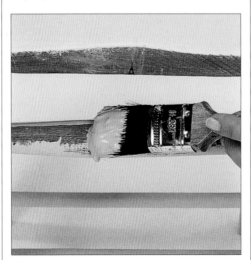

▲ Apply an even coat of the base blue

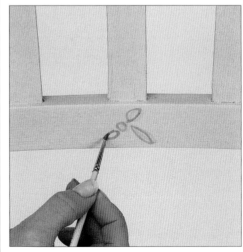

▲ Carefully outline the petal shapes

4 Squeeze two small separate amounts of prussian blue and white artists' acrylics on to a palette. Use the liner brush to mix some of these together so that there is a third colour; pale blue. Use the pale blue paint to create a small circle for the middle of the flower and five petal shapes around the centre. Then use the fine art brush to outline the edge of each petal with prussian blue.

5 Once the chair is completely dry, fold a soft clean cloth into a wad and rub it well into the neutral furniture wax. Using a circular movement, gently apply the wax to all surfaces of the chair and buff.

HINTS & TIPS

• When choosing the main paint colour, bear in mind that the final waxing will tone down the colour to a slightly darker shade. To gauge the final colour, lick your finger and press it on to the painted surface before waxing; this will show the approximate finished hue.

• Use neutral wax on duck-egg blue as the slightly grey tone of the wax complements the blue-grey shades of the paint.

• When mixing paint, always add dark colours a little at a time. This is because it is far harder to re-lighten a colour than it is to make one darker by adding more shade,

For further chair projects see:
Decorated Lloyd Loom Chair pp108–109; Oriental Chair pp121–123; Scandinavian Scroll Chair pp147–149; Table & Chair pp154–157; Folk Art Chair pp161–163

The simple motif can be replicated on the higher strut

▲ Apply the wax with a soft cloth

▲ Buff the waxed surface for an even sheen

Lacquered Butler Tray

THE PAINT TECHNIQUE used for this tray is meant to give the impression of oriental lacquer-work, particularly by the choice of colour. Truly authentic lacquer-work involves craftsmen applying dozens of layers of coloured lacquer, traditionally made from the sap of a type of gum tree, although modern practitioners use shellac over a gesso base. The surface is then decorated or carved to reveal the lower layers. Here however, a layer of varnish was applied over the black paint to ensure that when the red paint is distressed, none of the white primer shows through. Then acrylic goldsize was painted over the transferred design, before carefully applying the bronze powder with a fine brush. The Chinese motifs were sourced from an old reference book.

❖ YOU WILL NEED ❖

Coarse grade abrasive paper

Sanding block

Tack rag

Acrylic wood primer

Paintbrushes

Black traditional paint

Water-based varnish

Varnish brush

Lacquer-red traditional paint

000 grade wire wool

Methylated spirit or water

Shellac or spray varnish

Brush for applying shellac

Ruler

Pencil

Masking tape

Tracing paper

Talcum powder

Acrylic goldsize

Bronzing powder

Cotton wool

Clear wax

Oil-based varnish (optional)

1 Roughen the highly varnished surface of the tray by sanding it with a coarse grade abrasive paper wrapped around a sanding block. Rub the tray in a circular motion, applying even pressure to remove as much of the shine as possible. Wipe down the sanded surface with a tack rag to remove dust.

2 Paint the tray with a coat of acrylic wood primer and leave to dry. Then apply two coats of black paint, allowing the first coat to dry thoroughly before applying the second. Once complete, apply a coat of water-based varnish over the surface to help seal it. Leave the varnish to dry for several hours, and paint two coats of red paint over the tray top and legs. Again, ensure that there is sufficient drying time between each coat. If the stand is collapsable, remember to paint any areas of wood that are exposed when the legs are folded.

This butler's tray was rather plain and uniform

3 Using a circular motion, rub down the surface of the red paint with fine wire wool dipped in methylated spirit. (If you have used traditional chalky paints, wire wool and water are sufficient.) Then seal the tray with a coat of clear shellac.

▲ Roughen the surface with coarse paper

▲ Paint the tray with a coat of acrylic primer

▲ Seal the black paint with a coat of varnish

4 Measure the sides of the tray and mark the centre of each with a pencil dot. Place a ruler on the pairs of opposite dots to find the centre of the tray and also mark this with a dot. Trace over the circular design on page 247 and cut it out. Position the shape in the centre of the

▲ Apply two coats of strong red paint

tray and secure it with masking tape. Trace over the design with a hard pencil, pressing firmly so that the pattern is transferred to the wood, and remove the tracing paper. Calculate the number of key segments needed to fit around the border of the tray, by measuring from the centre of each side towards each corner. The corner key adds a nice touch but doesn't have to be used. Transfer the border (p247) on to the tray with a pencil in the same way. Dust the tray with talcum powder and spread it over the tray with a soft brush. This makes the pencil marks visible and prevents the possibility of the gold powder sticking to any area other than the one that has been coated in size.

5 Carefully paint the centre of the design with acrylic goldsize, using a fine paintbrush, and leave for 15–20 minutes for the size to become tacky. Using a fine soft brush, dust bronzing powder over the size. Do so more heavily in some areas than others. Continue in this way until you have completed all the decoration on the tray. Stick two rows of masking tape on the top edging of the tray. Brush the acrylic goldsize between the lines of tape; when this has dried clear, dust with bronzing powder.

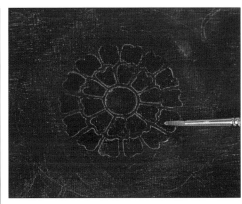

▲ Paint the centre of the design with size

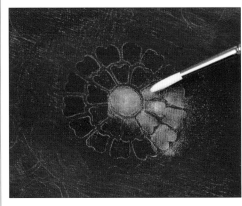

▲ Gently dust bronzing powder over the size

6 Gently remove all the excess gold and talcum powder from the tray with a damp cotton wool pad, taking care not to damage the design. Then seal the decorated surfaces with a coat of shellac or spray varnish, but avoid overbrushing any area. Apply two protective coats of matt water-based varnish and finish with a clear wax polish and buff. For a more heat-resistant finish, use an oil-based varnish instead of water-based.

HINTS & TIPS

• If you paint the size over too large an area at once, it is likely to get marked. In particular, take care not to smudge the talcum powder over the size because this will prevent the bronzing powder from adhering.

• If you prefer, the design can be applied with gold paint, particularly with the use of a stencil. However, although this will provide an effective finish, the surface design will lack some of the subtlety and shading provided by the bronzing powders.

For further ageing projects see:
Verdigris Chandelier pp118–120; Gold Leaf Tray pp138–139; Pine Panelled Cupboard pp144–146; Antiqued Cupboard pp158–160; Folk Art Chair pp161–163; Verdigris Table pp224–226

▲ Rub down the painted surface with wire wool

Enamel Jug

THIS OLD JUG was found at an antiques market, dotted with rust but in generally good shape. Once cleaned up, it revealed an elegant shape suitable for decoupage design. Here, cut-outs of rampaging anemones have been used, making the jug an ideal vase for dry or freshly cut flowers. The decoupage design was a little too large for the handle, however, so this was decorated with a thin line of magenta paint. The same colour was also used around the rim of the jug, helping to pull the total design of decoupage and paint together.

❖ YOU WILL NEED ❖

Wire wool

Brushes

Rust-inhibiting primer

Fine grade abrasive paper

Tack rag

Emulsion paint

Acrylic sealant

Paper design

Large scissors

Manicure scissors

Adhesive tack

PVA glue

Roller

Soft cloth

Acrylic craft paint and brush

Polyurethane varnish

Wax

Soft cloth

▲ Rub down rust with wire wool

1 Use wire wool to rub off any rust patches and then coat the surface with two coats of rust-inhibiting primer, both inside and out. Once dry, lightly rub down the jug with fine grade abrasive paper and a tack rag, before applying two or three coats of thinned-down emulsion paint. Then apply a coat of acrylic sealant.

2 Cut out the chosen design, using the large scissors to make the pattern more manageable, before following the intricate lines with the manicure scissors. Use adhesive tack to temporarily position the cut-outs as you arrange the design. Make sure that trailing ends don't interfere with any other part of the design as they wind around the jug. Position the butterflies last, between the stems, so that they add balance to the otherwise rambling design.

3 When the final pattern has been arranged, glue each piece into position and use a roller and cloth to squeeze out and remove any excess glue. Check that each edge is totally stuck down and wipe off any glue residue with a cloth wrung out in warm water. Paint a magenta line down the middle of the handle and

▲ Apply thin emulsion to the rust-inhibitor

around the rim of the jug, making sure that the colour complements the colours used in the main design. If necessary, use two or more colours for implements with large handles.

4 Once dry, apply two coats of polyurethane varnish, leaving 24 hours between each coat. Rub down the jug very gently with fine grade abrasive paper and go over it with the tack rag. Give the jug six more coats of varnish, rubbing down and tack ragging between each coat. Finally, apply a coat of wax with a soft cloth. Buff this surface to reveal a gleaming decorative finish.

▲ Use manicure scissors for intricate shapes

HINTS & TIPS

Be persistent when rubbing down rusted surfaces. Although it is time consuming, eventually the metal beneath can be found.

For further decoupage projects see:
Needlecraft Workbox pp98–99; Floral Cutlery Box pp134–135; Floral Place Mats pp140–141; Writing Desk pp170–171; Freestanding Cupboard pp186–187; Potichomanie Glass Jar pp188–189; Seashore Cabinet pp192–194; Toy Soldier Bedstead pp207–209; Nursery Mirror pp210–211; Wooden Trug pp230–231

Floral Cutlery Box

OLD CUTLERY BOXES such as this one turn up everywhere, usually with no insides and the veneer chipped and lifting. Decoupage is ideal for this kind of project because the designs stick easily to flat surfaces and help to conceal knocks and grazes in the wood. This particular box was given a new lease of life with some mother-of-pearl insets and a tumbling, Victorian-style flower design which helps to soften the rather hard edges. A luxurious, watered silk lining also provides that finishing touch.

❖ YOU WILL NEED ❖

Palette knife

Wood glue

Wood filler

Fine grade abrasive paper

Tack rag

Black emulsion paint

Brushes

Paper cut-outs

Adhesive tack

Drawing paper and pencil

Thin mother-of-pearl nacre strips

Bowl of very hot water

Small sharp scissors

White chalk

PVA glue

Soft cloth

Cotton buds

Acrylic sealant

Polyurethane varnish

Fine wire wool

White spirit

▲ Sketch out the position of the cut-outs

▲ Use sharp scissors to cut the mother-of-pearl

1 Stick down the veneer by using the palette knife to insert glue between the wood and surface covering. Stand a heavy object on top while the glue dries. Then fill any small holes or chips with wood filler, allow to dry and rub down the whole surface with fine grade abrasive paper. Wipe over the box with a tack rag before applying several coats of slightly thinned-down emulsion paint.

2 Arrange the design on the box with adhesive tack, then make a rough drawing of the box and the positions of each piece. Remove the mother-of-pearl pieces and soak them in very hot water. The water will help to soften the nacre and make them less brittle for cutting.

3 Once the mother-of-pearl has softened, use scissors to refine the final shapes. Reposition them on the cutlery box with adhesive tack to ensure that the pattern still forms your chosen design. It can be useful at this stage to mark numbers on the back of each cut-out and their corresponding positions on the drawing.

▲ Remove unwanted paint with a cotton bud

4 Draw around each mother-of-pearl piece on the box with a piece of chalk. Then remove them, glue their backs, and stick them into position. Press each one down firmly with a clean fingertip and wipe off any excess glue, and the chalk marks, with a warm cloth.

5 When the glue has completely dried, give the box another coat of black emulsion paint. Quickly remove any paint marks on the mother-of-pearl with a cotton bud dipped in warm water. Then glue on the paper designs, around the mother-of-pearl, using the sketch for reference.

HINTS & TIPS

Fragments of mother-of pearl often turn up at antique stalls and markets. Small, mis-shapen pieces are normally quite cheap and are ideal for this kind of decoration.

For further decoupage projects see:
Needlecraft Workbox pp98–99; Enamel Jug pp132–133; Floral Place Mats pp140–141; Writing Desk pp170–171; Freestanding Cabinet pp186–187; Potichomanie Glass Jar pp188–189; Toy Soldier Bedstead pp207–209; Nursery Mirror pp210–211; Wooden Trug pp230–231

Granite Effect Fireplace

PREVIOUSLY RIPPED OUT and carelessly discarded in favour of modern-day heating, fireplaces are now coming back as a popular feature of many people's homes. They provide a useful focus for any dining or living room, even if there is no working fire or chimney in place. This particular old fireplace was salvaged from a skip with the kind permission of its owners. The granite effect creates a good rustic feel and disguises pits and digs, although a smoother paint finish could be used. However, seek professional advice before restoring a fireplace that you want to have properly installed. Specialist, heat-resistant paint must be used to avoid harmful fumes and fixings should obviously be secure. Similarly, chimneys must be professionally checked before a fire is lit.

❖ YOU WILL NEED ❖

Cloth & bowl

Sugar soap solution

Medium and fine grade abrasive papers

Tack rag

Spoon

Eggshell paint

Various household paintbrushes

Paint kettle

Acrylic scumble-glaze

Monestial green and viridian artists' acrylic tube colours

Stirring stick

Dark green glitter

Fine silver glitter

Fine black glitter

Paper

1 Wash the fireplace outside with sugar soap solution. Then gently sand the surface using medium and then fine grade abrasive papers, before wiping with a tack rag.

2 Apply the eggshell colour (this should be paler than the chosen granite colour) and leave to dry. Gently sand with fine grade abrasive paper and wipe off the dust with the tack rag. Apply a second coat and allow to dry.

3 Put a spoon of the acrylic scumble glaze into the paint kettle and add two tube widths of the monestial green and viridian artists' colours. Mix until smooth and keep adding small amounts of colours in this ratio until you achieve the desired colour. Then add more acrylic scumble glaze until there is sufficient mixture – remember it is better to have too much than too little. Continue stirring until the consistency is like single cream.

4 Stirring all the time, gently tap in the small containers of silver, black and green glitters. Continue stirring until the glitters have been completely worked into the paint mixture.

5 Apply the glaze to the fireplace, taking care to cover all ridges, curves and corners. Leave the coat to dry and then apply a second coat. To increase the glittery effect, put some fine glitter onto a piece of paper and gently blow this over the surface while the glaze is still wet.

HINTS & TIPS

• Granite paint can be made in any number of colours. The fireplace here has been designed to have a two-tone look (using contrasting silver and green) but you can be as adventurous (or reserved!) as you like.

• Use an old brush which can be thrown away for the granite paint as the bristles may be difficult to clean.

• Glitter travels easily and can find its way into carpets, rugs and corners. For this reason, it is better to work outside – when the weather is fine and there is little breeze.

For further painting projects see:
Round Coffee Table pp95–97; Picture Frames pp100–105; Decorated Lloyd Loom Chair pp108–109; Verdigris Chandelier pp118–120; Display Decanter & Glasses pp124–125; Shaker Chair pp126–128; Scandinavian Scroll Chair pp147–149; Ironware Barge Pot pp164–165; Sponged Cot pp218–219; Verdigris Table pp224–226

▲ Apply the base eggshell paint

▲ Mix glitter with paint for the granite effect

Gold Leaf Tray

SMALL, PORTABLE and cheap to replace, trays are excellent items on which to practise decorative techniques. Wooden trays are normally quite easy to pick up at garage sales or boot fairs, and can be painted, stencilled or even covered in decoupage cut-outs.

This tray has been brightened up using three different techniques. After painting on a green marble base, gold leaf was applied to create the classical, antique effect. A stencil was then used to produce the elaborate motif in the centre. For different pattern ideas, see the template section on page 242.

❖ YOU WILL NEED ❖

Wooden tray

2.5cm (1in) brush

Leaf green, white pearl, gold and storm blue gouache paints

Ruler and pencil

Masking tape

Medium

Clingfilm

Goldsize and brush

Gold leaf sheets

Cotton gloves

Old silk scarf

Shellac and brush

Stencil blank & brush

Fine-point permanent marker

Scalpel and cutting knife

Paper towel

Acrylic varnish and brush

1 Use the brush to apply a coat of leaf green to the inside and outside of the tray. Leave to dry before applying a second coat. Then find the centre of the inside surface and mark out a rectangle in the middle of the tray and mask with masking tape. Paint the inside base and sides with medium but avoid the centre rectangle or top edges of the sides.

2 Mix all four paints together and then dab the clingfilm into the paint. Use the clingfilm to apply the paint, in swirling motions, on to the wet medium. Remove the tape and leave to dry for 24 hours.

3 Apply the gold leaf size medium to the rectangle and allow it to 'set'. Test the size by running your finger along it. If the finger glides as it would along sticky tape, the size is ready for the gold leaf. Then put on the gloves and carefully lift a sheet of gold leaf. Gently place the sheet in the desired position on the tray's surface.

Pat it lightly with your fingertips. Any section of gold that comes into contact with the size will set almost straight away, so perform this step slowly. Repeat until the rectangle is complete.

4 Screw the scarf into a tight ball and rub over the sheets of gold leaf so that they are flattened. Then apply gold leaf in the same way to the top of the edges and to the bottom of the handle cut-outs. This provides a nice finishing touch and completes the matching gold effect.

5 Coat the gold leaf with shellac following the manufacturer's instructions and leave to dry. Then position your stencil on the tray but do not use adhesive to keep it in place, as this will damage the gold leaf. Dip the dry stencil brush in the leaf green paint, dab it on the kitchen paper to remove any excess, and apply over the stencil, working in a circular motion. Carefully remove the stencil and leave the tray to dry for about 24 hours.

HINTS & TIPS

- Always wear cotton gloves when handling gold leaf. Otherwise, oils from your hands will cause it to discolour.

- Try to apply gold leaf in one smooth action to avoid unwanted tears or damage.

- Don't worry if the shellac appears cloudy when it is first applied over the gold leaf. It should dry to give a clear, smooth finish.

For further gilding or stencilling projects see:
Vine Leaf Table pp114–117; Lacquered Butler Tray pp129–131; Bedside Chest pp175–177; Glass Cupboard pp195–197

▲ Stencil the motif on to the gold leaf

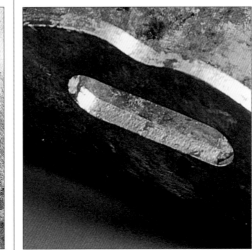

▲ Add gold trim detail to the handles

Floral Place Mats

STYLISH DINING TABLE MATS can be remarkably expensive and are often only available in packs of six or eight. This can be inconvenient for many people, particularly those who want additional mats for table candles and condiments, or matching coasters to protect surfaces from hot drinks. The solution is to find a cheap assortment of old mats and decorate them according to your personal needs and taste. Here, decoupage flowers have been used with a craquelure finish, to create a simple yet stylish set of mats, each with their own floral design.

❖ YOU WILL NEED ❖

Old place mats

Medium and fine grade abrasive papers

Undercoat

Base coat

Paper design

Scissors

Adhesive tack

Roller

Clean, damp cloth

Paper glue

PVA sealer

Water-based varnish

Craquelure glaze

Artists' oil paints in raw umber or gold paint/powder, linseed oil and driers

Clear gloss varnish

Various household brushes

Tack rag

1 Rub down the mats with the abrasive papers to help roughen the existing laminate. Then apply undercoat and two coats of base colour.

2 Carefully cut out the chosen design and experiment with the position of the cut-outs with adhesive tack. Once happy with the arrangement, stick the pieces to the mat, carefully squeezing out any excess glue with a roller and wiping away with a soft, dampened cloth.

3 Protect the applied design by brushing on a ready-mixed sealer, or PVA glue diluted in the ratio of two parts glue to one part water. Use firm, quick strokes, allow to dry and then apply a second coat. Once this coat has completely dried, apply two coats of protective varnish, following the manufacturer's directions.

4 For the aged, cracked effect, carefully apply a coat of craquelure glaze to the surface. Remember that the thicker the application of glaze, the larger the size of the cracks. So for tiny hairline cracks dilute the glaze slightly, following the manufacturer's instructions. Leave the glaze to dry or, to help the cracks develop, hold a warm hairdryer over the surface for a while.

▲ Apply several coats of varnish

5 To highlight the cracks, apply diluted raw umber artists' colour, gold oil paint or gold powder mixed with a drop of linseed oil and a little driers. Drive the colour into the cracks with a stiff-bristled artists' brush before immediately wiping the surface clean. Paint will remain in the cracks.

6 Apply several layers of gloss varnish, allowing for drying time between each coat. Alternate the direction of the brush for each application and rub down the surface with very fine grade abrasive paper and a tack rag between some of the later coats. Repeat at least six times.

HINTS & TIPS

• If bubbles that appear during the sealing process do not disappear after a day, it is probable that an area of the cut-out was not fully stuck down. To rectify the situation, try injecting glue into the bubble with a syringe.

• Use raw umber to give the cracks an aged appearance or gold for an ornate look.

For further gold ageing projects see:
Verdigris Chandelier pp118–120

▲ Seal the paper cut-outs with diluted PVA

▲ Brush on the colour and quickly wipe away

Busy, creative kitchens need plenty of storage and surface space. They should also be comfortable and homely, offering an informal setting for a quick coffee or a culinary creation. This chapter provides plenty of ideas for transforming old but favourite furniture – giving tables, chairs and cupboards a brand new lease of life.

Kitchen Projects

Pine Panelled Cupboard

THIS CUPBOARD was bought in good condition and had already been stripped, although it was not waxed. Original old pine furniture is much sought after, and quite expensive, so it was important not to change the look of the natural wood. To add interest and complement the antique pine, the doors of the cupboard were decorated with prints of old pictures, which were then aged with crackle varnish to make them look authentic. Two 18th-century French prints with a kitchen theme were chosen, part of a set called 'Tradesmen in Costume': *Le jardinier* ('the gardener') and *La confiseuse* ('the confectioner'). Finally, four wooden doorknobs were attached to the bottom of the cupboard to make it floor standing.

❖ YOU WILL NEED ❖

Cleaning materials:
bowl of water and vinegar,
nailbrush or soft scouring pad,
clean soft cloth

Sanding sealer

Print or paper designs

Metal-edged ruler

Scalpel and cutting mat

Adhesive tack

Paper paste and brush

Fixing spray (optional)

Rabbit skin glue

Two-part crackle varnish

Small jar of black patina
or charcoal oil paint

1 Mix equal parts of warm water and vinegar in a bowl and wash the cupboard with the solution, using a nailbrush or soft scouring pad in order to remove any stains and surface dirt. Wipe off with a soft cloth and clean water and leave to dry.

2 Paint a coat of sanding sealer on the surfaces to which the pictures will be pasted. This will prevent seepage from the wood penetrating the paper and provide a good surface for the glue. Then leave the sealer to dry for the length of time recommended by the manufacturer.

3 Using a metal-edged ruler, scalpel and a cutting mat, cut the prints to the size of the panels. Fix the prints into position using adhesive tack so that you can adjust them. Once they are in the correct place, lightly mark the position on the cupboard in pencil.

A well-made but plain antique pine cupboard can be transformed without losing the beauty of the wood

Then remove and trim off any excess paper around the edges. Mix the paper paste and apply it evenly to the back of the prints. Position the cut-outs, then use a dry paste brush or soft cloth to smooth them, working from the middle to the outer edges. Wipe off the excess paste and allow to dry.

▲ A range of materials will be needed

▲ Apply sanding sealer to the panels

▲ Measure the pictures before cutting to size

Habit de Jardinier

La Confiseuse

Habit de Jardinier

La Confiseuse

4 To prevent the ink bleeding from photocopied prints, apply a coat of fixing spray (make sure that the spraying area is well ventilated and wear a protective face mask). Then mix 16 parts rabbit skin glue to 1 part of moderately hot water, stirring the mixture until all the pieces are dissolved. While still warm, paint a generous coat of glue over the print and leave to dry. This will stop the varnish penetrating the paper.

5 Apply the oil-based crackle varnish. Leave to dry until tacky, and then apply a coat of the water-based crackle varnish. (For large cracks, allow about 1–1½ hours between the two varnishes. For very fine cracks, allow about 3 hours.) To encourage the crackling, gently blow a hairdryer over the surface but do not continue with this additional heat once the cracks have started to appear.

6 To emphasize the cracks, rub a small amount of black patina or thinned charcoal artists' oil paint over the dry varnish with a clean cloth and wipe off straight away. Apply a final coat of oil-based varnish.

▲ Apply rabbit skin glue

▲ Apply the crackle varnish

For further ageing and decoupage projects see:
Writing Desk pp170–171; Freestanding Cabinet pp186–187; Seashore Cabinet pp192–194; Laundry Box pp200–201

▲ The panels should appear cracked and aged

Scandinavian Scroll Chair

THIS OLD CHURCH CHAIR, one of a set used in a restaurant, was given a Scandinavian look with the addition of a carved scroll back, cream paint with a crackle-glazed finish, hand-painted design and gilded highlights. The finished result looks unusual, stylish and expensive. Old church chairs are often available from antique dealers, and are generally inexpensive unless they have already been stripped and waxed. Any good timber merchant or carpenter could cut out the scroll in medium density fibreboard (MDF); there are also companies that specialize in cutting designs from customers' templates. MDF provides an excellent surface for painting. The chair was given a padded cushion with tassel ties made of jute, natural raffia and gold coloured yarn.

❖ YOU WILL NEED ❖

Cleaning materials: bowl of water and detergent, nailbrush or soft scouring pad, clean soft cloth

Medium and fine grade abrasive papers

Tack rag

Pencil and ruler

Thick card

MDF cut-out scroll

Drill

2 screws and screwdriver

Wood glue

Traditional furniture paint or emulsion in deep red, old white and yellow

Decorators' paintbrushes: 2.5cm (1in) and 4cm (1½in)

Crackle and peel medium

Tracing paper

Carbon paper

Fixing spray

Tubes of acrylic artists' colours in yellow ochre, cadmium yellow, white, black, prussian blue, and burnt sienna

Artists' brushes: flat brush (size 1), round brush (size 1 or 2) and a fine liner

Tube of artists' oil paint in burnt umber

Small jar of gilding wax cream

Soft rags

Neutral furniture wax

▲ The scroll top for the chair is cut from MDF

▲ Paint over the crackle and peel medium

1 Clean the chair thoroughly before rubbing down with medium and then fine grade abrasive papers. Wipe off with a tack rag.

2 To make the scroll top, measure the width at the top of the chair and draw the scroll design to size on thick card. When getting the scroll cut to shape, remember to specify all dimensions, including the width of the MDF. Drill a hole for a countersunk screw at each end of the scroll and screw it into place to the top back of the chair. It's a good idea to use wood glue as well for the adjoining surfaces.

3 Make sure any rough edges are rubbed down with the fine grade abrasive paper after attaching the scroll, then wipe the chair thoroughly with a tack rag to remove any remaining dust.
Paint one coat of rich dark red traditional furniture paint over the entire chair and leave to dry for the manufacturer's recommended time.

4 Working in sections, paint the chair with the crackle and peel medium, taking care not to apply too thick a coat or allow any runs. Leave the areas that are to be painted and a small surrounding margin free of the medium. Be sure to cover the flat top and scroll edges. All the areas that are coated with the medium will crackle and peel slightly when you apply the next coat of paint.

5 Mix the old white traditional furniture paint with a small amount of yellow ochre (stainer or acrylic) until you obtain an old cream colour. (Remember that the final waxing will slightly darken the tone.)
Using a well-loaded brush, apply the paint with quick even strokes, taking care not to overbrush on areas treated with crackle varnish or you will lose the aged effect. Any paint build-up or runs that occur at this stage should simply be left to dry, because they can be dealt with when sanding down the chair in the next step.

▲ Trace the design on to the chair back

▲ Add fine detail to the painted design

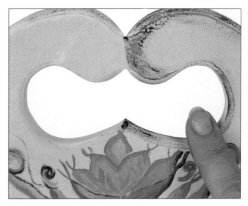

▲ Apply gold to the edges of the chair

6 With a fine grade abrasive paper or fine wet-and-dry abrasive paper, very gently rub down rough areas and any paint build-up or runs. If there are thin, patchy areas, or poor joins between the crackle and main colour, touch them up at this stage with old cream paint. When dry, repeat the sanding process. The wet-and-dry paper will create distressed areas and make visible some of the deep red colour underneath.

7 Using the template on page 243, copy the design on to tracing paper with a heavy pencil. Place a piece of carbon paper, carbon side down, on the furniture. Then holding the paper pattern on top, trace the patterns lightly on to the painted furniture surface. Spray over with a fine coat of fixing spray.

8 Use the size 1 flat brush to mix small amounts of yellow ochre, cadmium yellow and white on the palette to create a pale yellow, then mix grey (mix black and white for this), prussian blue and white to create a pale blue-grey.

Dip the flat artists' brush into water and side-load the paint on to the brush, floating it inside the patterns. Use yellow for flowers and contrasting blue for the scrolls.

Using the round artists' brush, shade the flower patterns with yellow ochre and burnt sienna to outline the edges. With the same brush and a slightly darker mixture of grey, prussian blue and white, outline one side of the scroll slopes. Then, with the fine liner brush, paint the finest scroll lines, outlines, swirls and details.

9 For the aged effect, use your thumb and forefinger to apply the burnt umber paint randomly to the edges, joins, corners and scroll top. At the top front centre of the scroll, use both thumbs, taking them from the centre outwards to make two adjoining semi-circles, giving the effect of two separate carved pieces.

Repeat the process with the gilding wax cream. Do not apply it meticulously – smudging enhances the aged effect. This technique looks especially effective when used in parts over the burnt umber, giving an old gold leaf effect. Finally, use a clean rag to apply neutral wax evenly over the entire surface of the chair. Leave for the desired time before buffing to a soft sheen.

HINTS & TIPS

• When painting furniture, it's not necessary to remove all the old colour or varnish, so long as you obtain a clean, matt surface to which the new paint can adhere.

• For ideas on repeating decorative motifs, see the templates section on page 242.

For further ageing paint effects projects see:
Verdigris Chandelier pp118–119; Antiqued Cupboard pp158–160; Folk Art Chair pp161–163; Chequered Table & Chairs pp204–206

This workaday sturdy church chair was given an air of sophistication with a Scandinavian feel

Freestanding Cabinet

MANY UNWANTED pieces of furniture are functional but rather plain, often made from MDF (medium density fibreboard) and covered in some kind of laminate. Lacking the appeal of genuine wood or a stylish shape, such basic items have little intrinsic charm and are not immediately obvious candidates for being successfully transformed.

Yet a fresh look at this plain unit, with its harsh, blank surfaces turned it into a highly individual cabinet with the help of some decorative colour, ornate aluminium panelling and attractive door handles. Various materials could be used for the new panels, and there is a wide choice of handles available, made from wood, ceramic, brass or even glass, to add that individual touch.

❖ YOU WILL NEED ❖

Filler and spatula

Medium and fine grade abrasive papers

Ruler

Pencil

Tinted scumble glaze

Household paintbrushes, including a broad flat brush for dragging

Tack rag

24 gauge (0.6mm) aluminium sheeting (available from engineering suppliers)

Coloured pencil

Pointed and flat nail punches

Hammer

Sheet of hardboard to protect table (optional)

Half-round beading

Mitre box, tenon saw and G-clamps

Primer undercoat

New handles (optional)

Top coat paint

Bradawl

Panel pins

Drill

Screwdriver and screws for handles

Polyurethane satin finish varnish

Masking tape

1 Remove the handles and doors from the unit so that you can work on a flat surface. Fill the holes left by the handles and, using medium and fine grade abrasive papers, thoroughly rub down all of the surfaces that are to be decorated. Remove any remaining dust residue with a tack rag.

2 Use a ruler and pencil to mark out the area of the doors to be panelled. Then apply the background colour or glaze, using even brush strokes. Drag a broad flat brush through the glaze, working sections in different directions to create the impression of separate pieces of timber. Wipe off clean straight edges at the 'joins' and

This unpromising kitchen unit was revamped with imaginative use of colour and new panels to add interest

paint the edges of the cabinet. Leave to dry. (The colour used here was ready mixed and added to the scumble glaze with a little water.)

▲ Drag the glaze for the desired texture

▲ Draw the pattern on to the aluminium

3 Work out the design for the panels on paper and, when you are satisfied with the results, mark it out on the back of the aluminium sheets using a coloured pencil. Then, still working from the back, hold the pointed nail punch vertically over the panel, and tap the head with the hammer to 'punch' the pattern. Work along the pencilled guidelines, leaving approximately a nail-punch distance between each punch mark. This can be varied according to your design. For instance, you could make the punches further apart for long, straight lines and closer together for more detailed areas.

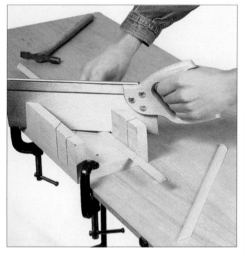

▲ Saw lengths of beading in the mitre box

4 If possible screw the mitre box to the work surface, or use G-clamps to secure it. Mark off the lengths of beading with a pencil and cut them to length with the saw. (If you are working with very long pieces of beading, cut them roughly to length first before sawing the mitred ends.)

▲ Apply the top coat to the beading

▲ Use a pointed nail punch to hammer out the the design for the aluminium panels

5 Paint the lengths of beading and any new wooden handles with primer undercoat, making sure no area is left unpainted. Leave to dry for the recommended time before applying the top colour. If necessary, apply a second coat of top colour.

6 Use a bradawl to make holes in the aluminium panels to attach them to the doors: one hole at each corner and one or two along the outer edges. They should be close enough to the edge to be concealed by the beading when it is in place.

▲ Make holes to attach the panels

▲ Pin the aluminium panels to the doors

▲ Attach the new door handles

For further paint effects projects see:
Round Coffee Table pp95–97; Shaker Chair pp126–128;
Bedside Chest pp175–177; Cherub Wardrobe
pp182–185; Glass Cupboard pp198–199;
Multipurpose Chest pp212–213

HINTS & TIPS

• Always cover the surface with a protective board when punching metal. It can be useful to clamp the aluminium and protective board to the surface, to avoid anything slipping as you work.

• Some paint manufacturers have ranges of ready-made glaze colours. These can be applied over a coat of emulsion in a different shade for a more colourful effect.

7 Carefully place the aluminium panels in position on the doors, lining them up with the pencil positioning marks. Then secure them in place with the panel pins.

In order to avoid marking the aluminium with the hammer, use the flat nail punch to drive the pins home.

8 Place the wooden beading in position around the panels. It should be positioned so that it overlaps the edges of the panels just enough to conceal the panel pins, but enough space should be allowed for the beading pins to be driven into the door itself. Fix the beading in place with panel pins, making sure that the mitred ends are tightly butted together. (Do not place the panel pins too close to the end of the pieces of beading, because the wood may split.)

Mark the positions for the new door handles. Drill holes for the handles and secure them in place.

9 Apply a coat of polyurethane varnish to the painted surfaces, (If you don't have a steady hand, mask off the aluminium panels to protect them while varnishing the beading.) Allow to dry, then apply a second coat of varnish. When fully dry, reassemble the whole unit and move carefully into place.

▲ Pin the beading into place

▲ Apply a final coat of varnish

Table & Chair

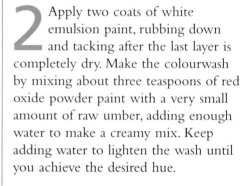

THIS OLD TABLE AND CHAIR were acquired on separate occasions and seemed like an unlikely match. The chair came from a church clear-out and had a plain, simple charm whereas the pine table was purchased as part of a job lot in a house clearance sale. The table had, at different times, been covered in linoleum, stripped and re-covered with a laminate top only to be re-stripped and given a coat of gleaming white paint. Here, both pieces have been covered with a rustic, cream colourwash and then decorated with a simple, hand-painted design.

❖ YOU WILL NEED ❖

Fine wire wool

Methylated spirit

Cleaning materials: bowl of water and vinegar, nailbrush or soft scouring pad, clean soft cloth

Medium and fine grade abrasive paper

Tack rag

2 x 4cm (1½in) household paintbrushes

White emulsion paint

Red oxide powder paint

Raw umber powder paint

Clean, dry cloths

Polyurethane spray varnish

Tracing paper

Pencil

Acrylic paints

Artists' fine paintbrush

Old newspaper

Scissors

1m (40in) suitable fabric

1m (40in) contrasting fabric

Approximately 25cm (10in) thick polyester wadding

Cotton

Needle

Pins

Approximately 3m (10ft) No.3 piping cord

Tape measure

25cm (10in) touch-and-close fastening

1 If the furniture has been polished, use fine wire wool dipped in methylated spirit to remove the polish. Once dry, then rub down with medium grade abrasive paper. If not, simply wash the furniture well with vinegar and water, wipe down with a clean wet cloth and allow to dry. Then rub down with medium and fine grade abrasive papers to remove any loose paint or varnish and provide a key to the surface so the paint will adhere. Use a tack rag to dust off the surfaces after using abrasive paper.

2 Apply two coats of white emulsion paint, rubbing down and tacking after the last layer is completely dry. Make the colourwash by mixing about three teaspoons of red oxide powder paint with a very small amount of raw umber, adding enough water to make a creamy mix. Keep adding water to lighten the wash until you achieve the desired hue.

3 Coat the table and chair in the wash – turn them over and deal with the legs and undersides first. Allow a few minutes for the wash to begin to dry, then go over it with a clean, dry brush, working the wash into the grain and taking off any surplus. Keep cleaning the brush on a dry rag as you work to avoid reapplying the wash. Finally, gently buff all of the surfaces with a clean, dry cloth. Turn the table and chair right-side up and treat the top surfaces in the same way.

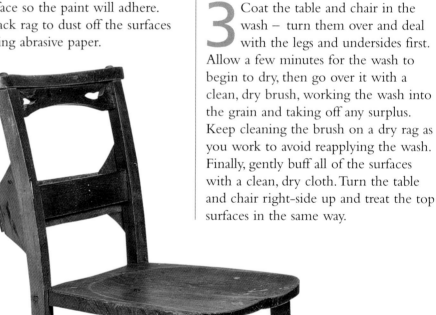

Old church chairs are solidly made and make an interesting alternative to plain kitchen chairs

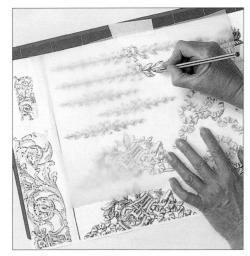

▲ Trace the pattern from a photocopy

▲ Transfer the pattern to the chair

▲ Colour the pattern with acrylic paints

4 Apply a protective layer of spray varnish to the colourwash as soon as possible after it has dried – give it several light coats. This is because a colourwash of this kind is extremely fragile and can easily be rubbed off or dripped upon. Tinned varnish is not suitable for the job because additional brushwork on the surface may move the wash and make it streaky.

5 If you are copying a design, it's a good idea to photocopy the pattern several times to the correct size and experiment by positioning cut-outs on the table surface. The same pattern can then be reduced to the appropriate size for the border motif on the chair. Trace the chosen pattern and transfer it to the furniture. Use acrylic paints with a fine artists' brush to colour the design and then leave to dry. For additional protection, apply one or two more coats of varnish.

▲ Position the design on the table top

6 To make a cushion for the chair, tape a large sheet of newspaper to the seat and carefully trace around the edge with the side of a pencil, drawing a curved indentation where the back struts cut into the seat. Cut out the pattern. To make sure that it is completely symmetrical, fold it in two and trim off any excess.

7 Use the newspaper pattern to cut out one thickness of the main fabric, one of the contrasting fabric, and one of the wadding. Sandwich the wadding between the two pieces of fabric, right sides outwards, and baste across the middle from top to bottom and from side to side to hold the pieces in place.

Cut a strip of contrasting fabric on the cross, approximately 25cm x 4cm (10in x 1½in). Fold in half lengthwise and press, then fold both the raw edges into the middle and press again. Cut this strip of binding in half. Use each piece to bind the curves for the back struts, first basting and then machining them in place.

Next, measure around the front three sides of the chair and add on 20cm (8in) for the fixing tabs. Cut a strip of the main material to this combined length, 7.5cm (3in) deep.

Lay the strip right side up and, starting and finishing 10cm (4in) from either end, pin on a length of piping so that all the raw edges are together. Baste the pieces together.

Measure the space between the two struts at the back of the chair and add 2.5cm (1in) on to the length for hemming. Cut another piece of material

to this length, again 7.5cm (3in) deep. Using the same method as before, sew piping cord along the sides.

8 To make the frill, cut more 7.5cm (3in) deep strips of material and join them together until you have two long strips, each about three times as long as the two piped strips. Hem each along one long side and two short sides. Gather the unhemmed sides until they are as long as the piped sections of the strips. With right sides and raw edges together, baste and machine the long frill to the piped section of the longest strip and the short one to the short strip.

Pin the unattached, piped side of the long frill around the front three sides of the seat cover and the shorter one to the back, between the curves cut for the back struts. Baste and machine them in place. Finally, hem the fixing tabs at either end of both frilled bands. Attaching the fastener so that the tabs will fasten around the back struts of the chair.

HINTS & TIPS

- If available, use a pestle and mortar to help grind colour pigment. This will make it more water-soluble and easier to mix.

- Fill the box at the back of some church chairs with magazines, cookery books or dried flowers for an added finishing touch.

For further decorative paint projects see:
Shaker Chair pp126–128; Lacquered Butler Tray pp129–131; Gold Leaf Tray pp138–139; Folk Art Chair pp161–163

Antiqued Cupboard

THIS OLD CUPBOARD was covered in badly chipped paint, and it would have taken an enormous amount of filling and rubbing down to create a smooth surface for a refined paint finish. To minimize time and effort, it was decided to opt instead for an aged and worn paint technique, using a wax resist over the existing areas of wear. The cupboard has an ideal shape for kitchen use, and lends itself to stencilling or decoupage decoration. However, the narrow panels do restrict the range of pattern size that can be used, so a contrasting band of colour was chosen to give the surrounding edges an interesting focus. The same colour has also been used to paint the inside of the cupboard, which was then distressed without the use of wax resist.

❖ YOU WILL NEED ❖

Cleaning materials: Bowl of water and detergent, nailbrush or soft scouring pad, clean soft cloth

Coarse and medium grade abrasive paper

Wood filler

Filling knife

Clear liquid wax

Small brush for applying wax

Paintbrushes

Emulsion or traditional paint in 3 colours

000 grade wire wool

Masking tape

Kitchen paper

Brown wax

Soft cloth

1 Clean the cupboard thoroughly by washing it with detergent, water, a soft cloth and, if necessary, a nail brush. When it is dry, rub down the surfaces with a coarse grade abrasive paper to roughen the surface and remove all loose and flaking paint. Fill any large holes with wood filler, leave to set and then rub down with medium abrasive paper. Brush on the liquid wax where you want to reveal the base coat, paying attention to the areas where the cupboard would naturally wear and the paint has chipped. Leave the wax to dry for about half an hour.

2 Give the cupboard two base coats of paint. Then paint the door panels in a top colour and the sides, ends and panel surrounds in a different paint. Then use masking tape to create a straight line for the inner red border.

This battered kitchen cupboard was decorated with an antiqued paint effect

3 Use wire wool or medium grade abrasive paper – or a combination of both – to rub the painted surface until the original colour beneath is revealed and you have achieved the desired antiqued effect. The paint should come off quite easily where the wax has been applied.

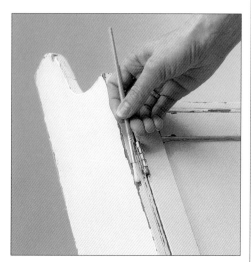

▲ Apply wax resist to areas of wear

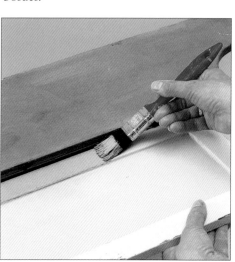

▲ Paint the cupboard in its new colours

▲ Use wire wool for an aged effect

4 Stick masking tape inside the door panel, about 6mm (¼in) in from the edge, to prevent any of the paint accidentally being applied to the panel. Paint a border around the panel in the third paint colour. Once dry, rub lightly with abrasive paper to create a distressed effect.

5 To complete the aged effect, apply a brown or antique wax to all the surfaces of the cupboard with a pad of kitchen paper. Leave the wax to dry for about half an hour, then buff to a shine with a soft cloth.

▲ Add a contrasting border to the panels

HINTS & TIPS

• A distressed effect using wax relief can also be obtained on newer surfaces. Simply repeat steps 2 and 3 twice in contrasting colours, so that a second paint colour is revealed beneath the top coat. To further the illusion of age, bash a set of keys against the surface to produce dent marks.

• The inside area of the cabinet is rarely seen and, to save time, needen't be waxed or distressed. However, protect any paint on the inside with two coats of varnish.

• There are no rules restricting the use of paint combinations. A light colour on a dark base or a dark colour on a light base can be used to equal effect.

For further accessory projects see:
Picture Frames pp100–105; Stamped Mirror pp110–111; Gold Leaf Tray pp138–139; Ironware Barge Pot pp164–165; Potichomanie Glass Jar pp188–189; Laundry Box pp200–201; Mosaic Vase pp227–229; Decorative Pots pp236–238

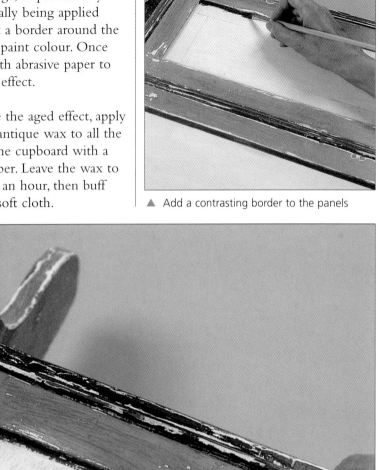

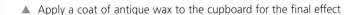

▲ Apply a coat of antique wax to the cupboard for the final effect

Folk Art Chair

IT'S SURPRISINGLY SIMPLE to give a plain old chair the appearance of German or Old American origin, by applying bold, colourful paintings in rich, earthy colours. (German settlers took their folk art to Pennsylvania in the late 1700s, with its traditional motifs including flowers, leaves and animals intermingled with geometric designs.) This chair has been given a basic folk pattern and then aged with a simple technique using crackle and peel medium. To enhance the lines of the chair, wooden doorknobs were attached to the ends of the flat top.

▲ Screw the knobs into the top of the chair

▲ Use a template as a guide when painting

1 Clean the chair thoroughly and then rub down with medium and fine grade abrasive papers. Wipe off with a tack cloth. Fix a small wooden doorknob at each end of the flat chair top, in line with the sides of the chair back, by drilling a hole and screwing in a double-ended screw with pliers. (Alternatively, use a knob with a screw already in place.) Use wood glue for extra adhesion and wipe off any excess with a cloth. Sand any rough edges with fine abrasive paper and dust down with a tack rag.

2 Apply a coat of deep red paint over the entire chair and leave to dry for the recommended time. Apply a second coat if necessary.

3 Paint the chair with the crackle and peel medium, working in sections and following the manufacturer's instructions carefully. The areas intended for the design should be left clear, but be sure to coat around the flat top and on parts of the knobs. All the areas coated with the medium will crackle and peel slightly when the next coat of paint is applied.

4 Mix a small amount of yellow ochre acrylic paint with the white furniture paint to attain an old cream colour. Using a small, well-loaded brush, apply the paint in quick even strokes, taking care not to over-brush the crackle areas or you will lose the effect. If there are any runs or paint build-up, leave these to dry and deal with them in the next step.

5 With fine wet-and-dry abrasive paper, gently rub down rough areas and any paint build-up or runs. The wet-and-dry paper will create distressed areas, as well as making some of the red paint beneath visible.

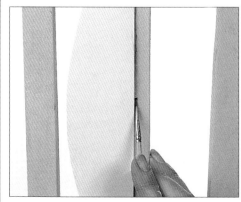

▲ Paint along the edges of the struts

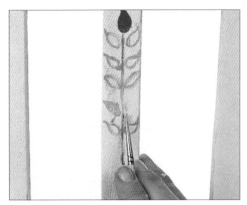

▲ Paint the outlines of the leaves

▲ Distress the paint with wet-and-dry paper

▲ Use neutral furniture wax to finish the chair

6 For the hand-painted decoration, cut a semi-circular piece of card to fit between the knobs on the flat top of the chair, leaving a clearance distance of about 2.5cm (1in). Hold this in place and, using the fine artists' liner brush, paint a line of prussian blue around the curved edge of the template. Then paint blue lines down the edges of the back slats of the chair, using the straight edge of the template as a guide. On one slat, paint the outline of three pairs of coloured leaf-shaped patterns, alternating the colours between the prussian blue and yellow ochre. At each end of the pattern, add the outline of a small red bud with blue leaves.

7 Use a small amount of water to mix some white with the paints and create paler tones. Then fill in the pattern. Side-load the brush, without water, with the original darker shade and apply a bold stroke around one section of the outside edge over the paler colour, to make a contrasting shaded effect. Leave to dry for the manufacturer's recommended time. Repeat the design as desired on the other back slats and top of the chair, adapting the template accordingly.

8 To create the aged effect, squeeze a small amount of prussian blue acrylic paint into a small lid or container and, using thumb and forefinger, apply this at random to the corners, edges, wood joins and knobs of the chair. Allow to dry, then repeat the process with the gilding wax cream. Make sure the paint is completely dry, then, using fine wet-and-dry abrasive paper, very gently sand off small sections of the pattern with careful up-and-down movements to create a distressed look.

9 With a clean rag, apply neutral furniture wax evenly over the entire surface of the chair and leave for the length of time recommended by the manufacturer, before buffing to a soft sheen. Alternatively, using a small varnish brush, apply two coats of matt polyurethane varnish, allowing drying time between coats.

HINTS & TIPS

• Paint the underside and legs of chairs first. This makes painting the top surfaces easier and allows you to practise techniques in unseen areas.

• When applying crackle glaze, try not to apply too thick a coat or allow any runs.

• If there are patchy areas or poor joins between the crackle and colour, touch up with more cream paint, allow to dry and sand again before starting the motifs.

For further chair projects see:
Decorated Lloyd Loom Chair pp108–109; Oriental Chair pp121–123; Shaker Chair pp126–128; Scandinavian Scroll Chair pp147–149; Rocking Chair pp214–217

▲ Mixing white with the colours for paler hues

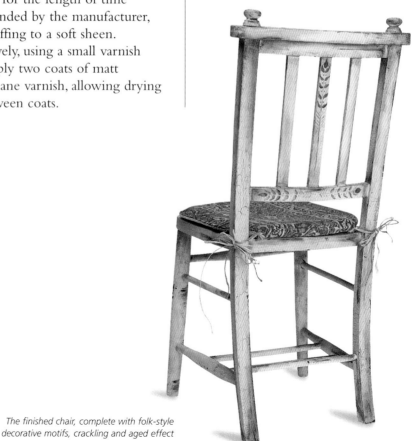

The finished chair, complete with folk-style decorative motifs, crackling and aged effect

Ironware Barge Pot

THIS POT WAS DISCOVERED at an antiques market. Although rusty and in need of repair, it was an ideal shape for barge painting. Once painted it can no longer be used for cooking but it does make a perfect kitchen container, such as a bread bin.

The exuberant roses are a traditional barge-painting design although you could choose a kitchen-related theme. Flowers, in particular, are ideal designs because they can be separated for simple borders, or painted in clusters to form the main motif. A dark colour definitely sets them off to best advantage.

❖ YOU WILL NEED ❖

Rubber gloves

Rust remover

Fine wire wool

Wet-and-dry abrasive paper

Damp cloth

Rust-inhibiting primer

3 x 2.5cm (1in) household paintbrushes

Very fine abrasive paper

Enamel paint in midnight blue or similar dark colour

Pencil and paper

Piece of chalk

Small pots of enamel paint in crimson, bright red, yellow, white, lime green, tan, black

White spirit

Artists' paintbrush (size 3 sable or synthetic mixture)

Polyurethane gloss varnish

1 Wearing rubber gloves, remove the rust with rust remover and wire wool. Rub down the pot with wet-and-dry abrasive paper until it is as smooth as possible, wipe down with a damp cloth and allow to dry. Apply two coats of rust-inhibiting primer to prevent further rust, then rub down lightly with very fine abrasive paper.

2 Paint the surface of the pot with the dark-coloured enamels. Allow to dry before applying a second coat and leaving this to dry.

3 Before starting the decoration, roughly work out the shape of the design on a piece of paper. Then chalk circles on to the pot to act as a guide to where the roses are going to appear. There is no need to worry about the circles being mathematically accurate – minor discrepancies enhance the spontaneous effect of true barge painting. However, do make sure that the base circles for the roses are sufficiently distanced to allow space for the petals, yet not so far apart that they will look isolated. The same goes for the leaves and the daisies.

4 Use the artists' paintbrush and a selection of bright enamel colours to paint the circles and shadows for the rose design (see the section on 'Barge Painting' on page 68) on both pot and lid. While these are drying, carefully paint in the leaves and the centres for the daisies.

While this paint dries, add the top petals to the roses. Return to the daisies and add a few filling strokes, stamens and trimmings. Once finished, clean the brush with white spirit.

5 Leave the pot to dry overnight and then give it a coat of varnish. Leave it for another 24 hours before applying a final coat of varnish.

HINTS & TIPS

Iron pots make useful kitchen containers for everything from sugar and teabags, to pasta and flour. However, use a separate inner container, such as a plastic tub, inside the pot for storing loose foods.

For further storage projects see:
Needlecraft Workbox pp98–99; Cutlery Box pp134–135; Storage Trunk pp172–174; Glass Cupboard pp195–197

Although rusty and in need of cleaning up, this pot was a perfect candidate for barge painting

▲ Apply rust remover to the rusty areas

▲ Give the pot a coat of rust-inhibiting primer

A PLACE OF REST AND RETREAT, THE BEDROOM SHOULD HAVE A PERSONAL STYLE, OFFERING PLENTY OF COMFORT AND LUXURY. THIS CHAPTER TRANSFORMS MANY TIRED BUT USEFUL PIECES OF FURNITURE, ENSURING THAT RESTYLING YOUR ROOM DOESN'T HAVE TO MEAN SACRIFICING STORAGE OR SPACE.

Bedroom Projects

Carved Linen Chest

HIS ATTRACTIVE CUPBOARD had parts of the door frame missing when it was found in a junk shop. It had been partly cleaned and stripped, but desperately needed some proper attention to bring it back to its former glory. The back of one of the drawers, which were made from the same wood as the carcass, was used to replace the missing panel on the door. The chest was stripped back to the bare wood then liming wax was used to enhance the beautiful carved panels and edgings while a rub with fine wire wool brightened up the hinges.

❖ YOU WILL NEED ❖

Electric sander

Medium and fine grade abrasive papers

Wire brush

Tack rag

Liming wax

Artists' brush

Clean lint-free cloth

Neutral and cream furniture wax

1 Sand the surfaces of the chest with the electric sander and medium grade paper. Use a forward and backward motion following the grain of the wood – movement across the grain will damage the surface. When the surface dirt and old finish have been removed, change to fine paper and continue until the surface is smooth.

2 Sweep the wire brush in one direction along the grain on the carved areas to open up the grain. This will enable the liming wax to penetrate the wood. Wipe down the whole unit thoroughly with the tack rag to remove any dust.

3 Use the artists' brush to apply the liming wax – the intricate pattern on the chest makes the usual technique of applying it with a cloth inappropriate. Paint the wax into, and all over, the carved areas of the chest, working it well into the grooves. Leave for no more than ten minutes before moving on to the next step.

▲ Open up the grain with a wire brush

4 With the clean lint-free cloth, wipe off the excess liming wax on the flat surface areas of the raised patterns but leave any build-up of wax in the grooves, pattern niches and edges, to create the limed effect. Leave to harden thoroughly overnight.

5 Using a wad of clean soft cloth, apply neutral furniture wax to the limed areas. Leave the wax for approximately 20 minutes and then buff to a sheen with a clean lint-free cloth. If the limed areas look too white against the natural tones of the chest, repeat the procedure in order to tone it down and create a more aged effect.

6 Apply cream furniture wax to the rest of the cupboard and leave to soak in for at least an hour, before buffing to a sheen. This process needs to be repeated over a period of time to obtain a really good finish.

HINTS & TIPS

- It is advisable to wear a dust mask when using an electric sander over large areas.

- When applying the cream furniture wax, avoid getting it on the limed areas as this will create an undesirable yellowing effect.

For further cupboard projects see:
Pine Panelled Cupboard pp144–146; Freestanding Kitchen Cabinet pp150–153; Antiqued Cupboard pp158–160; Freestanding Cabinet pp186–187; Glass Cupboard pp198–199

▲ Use an electric sander to strip the chest

▲ Apply liming wax with an artists' brush

▲ Remove the excess wax with a cloth

Writing Desk

T HIS OLD DESK WAS found at the back of a stable, and carried much of the dirt and smell associated with livery! However, after a thorough cleaning, scrubbing it first with bleach then detergent, some filling to even out irregularities in the wood and a few coats of white emulsion paint, it eventually provided an ideal surface for elaborate floral decoupage decoration. It also makes a useful bedroom writing desk, although it would also make an effective dressing table, with its range of handy storage drawers and recess for a stool.

❖ YOU WILL NEED ❖

Cleaning materials: Bowl of water and detergent, nailbrush or soft scouring pad, clean soft cloth

Wood filler

Filling knife

Medium and fine grade abrasive paper

Tack rag

Water-based undercoat

Cream emulsion paint

Household paintbrushes

Sealant

Paper cut-outs

Adhesive tack

PVA glue

Roller

Soft lint-free cloth

Acrylic varnish

---

1 Wash thoroughly, wipe down and leave to dry. Fill holes or cracks with wood filler and leave to dry, then rub down the surface with medium and then fine grade abrasive paper. Wipe down with a tack rag.

2 Apply two coats of the undercoat and leave to dry for the recommended time. Apply up to eight thinned-down coats of emulsion paint, rubbing down lightly and tacking after the third and subsequent coats. When a smooth, silky finish has been achieved, give the desk a coat of sealant.

3 Arrange the cut-outs on the desk, using adhesive tack while trying out the design. When it is finalized, remove the pieces one by one, coat the backs with glue and stick down. Squeeze out any bubbles with a roller and remove excess glue with a damp cloth. Check the edges of each piece and re-stick any that have lifted. Allow to dry and then check for shiny patches of dried glue. Clean these off with a cloth wrung out in warm water and leave everything to dry out again.

4 Apply three coats of acrylic varnish, allowing to dry between coats. When the third coat is dry, very gently rub down with fine abrasive paper and tack. Continue applying varnish, rubbing down and tacking until the edges of the design are undetectable. Finish with two coats of yacht varnish, rubbing down and tacking after the first.

This sturdy pine desk was transformed into a piece fit for the bedroom

---

HINTS & TIPS

For an antique effect, try applying two coats of crackle varnish.

For further decoupage projects see:
Pine Panelled Cupboard pp144–146; Folding Collage Screen pp178–181; Potichomanie Glass Jar pp188–189

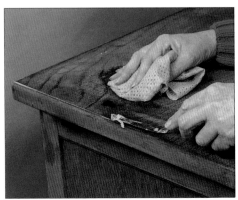

▲ Fill any cracks in the wood

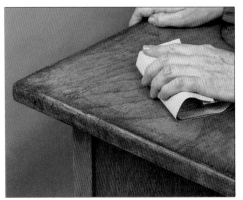

▲ Sand the desk to prepare for painting

▲ Apply a water-based undercoat

Storage Trunk

TRUNKS CAN BE FOUND in many junk shops, although their condition varies – some are fine, lacquered timber, others basic pine. Travelling trunks often had brass corners and fittings to provide reinforcement and protection, which can easily be polished to a renewed sheen. The old trunk used for this project had a broken lid but has been fully renovated and given a decorative finish with scumble-glaze. Decorating all four sides means that it could be used for a coffee table as well as handy bedroom storage.

❖ YOU WILL NEED ❖

Screwdriver

Medium and fine grade abrasive
paper and a sanding block

Tape measure

Timber for repairs

Saw

Drill

PVA glue

Bradawl

Screws

Two-part resin wood filler

Spatula

Various paintbrushes

All-in-one primer

Undercoat paint

Paint for top colour

Scumble glaze
(available from an art suppliers)

Pigments or artists' acrylic paints –
for example, red ochre or red oxide,
olive green, burnt umber, yellow ochre

Items to make glaze patterns,
such as card, combs (available from
specialist decorators' merchants),
corks, potatoes or cloth

Jars for mixing paints and glazes

Varnish

Fine wire wool

This solid and spacious trunk was transformed into a show piece with a smart scumble glaze finish

1 Remove the hinges from the broken pieces of lid, then rub down the edges of each plank with medium grade abrasive paper. This removes any old glue as well as giving a clean, sharp edge to the pieces.

2 Measure and cut two pieces of timber for reinforcing the lid and drill three or four holes in each. Apply glue to the long edges of the lid pieces and push them together carefully. Use a bradawl through the holes in the reinforcing pieces, to mark out the position of the screws on the lid. Apply glue to the underside of the reinforcing pieces and fix immediately in place with screws, making sure that all sections fit together properly. Put aside and leave to dry.

3 Fill any holes and gaps with a two-part resin wood filler. Pay particular attention to where the lid has been glued. When the wood filler is dry, use a sanding block with medium and then fine grade abrasive papers to rub down the whole trunk.

▲ Apply glue to the edges of the lid pieces

▲ Fill any holes with a resin wood filler

▲ Apply a coat of all-in-one primer

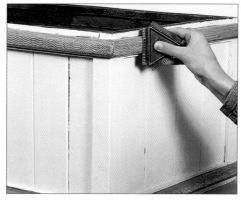

▲ Use a decorators' comb to make a pattern

▲ Use half a potato to apply the glaze

4 Apply a coat of all-in-one primer to the trunk and allow it to dry. Then add a layer of undercoat. Once this has dried, add the top colour paint – this will be the base for the glaze work.

5 Mix the glaze with your chosen pigments. Brush the mixed glaze and pigment on to the top and bottom edges of the trunk first, and use a decorators' comb to make the pattern. Then apply the glaze and decoration in stages, for example, one panel at a time. This pattern was created using half a potato, dipped in the glaze, as a stamp.

6 Apply the final colour glaze with even brush strokes. Remember to wipe off the edges as you go along, before the glaze dries. Then leave the trunk to dry.

Fix the lid of the trunk securely back into position. Apply a coat of varnish to all the surfaces, then leave to dry completely.

Once the varnish has dried, the surface can be distressed to give a slightly aged and worn look, by gently rubbing fine wire wool over the panels. Pay particular attention to the edges as they would be more likely to show the effects of wear and tear than the side panels.

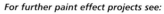

HINTS & TIPS

• Always mix plenty of glaze so that there will be enough in one batch for the whole project (otherwise colours will vary). Store excess amounts in a jar with a tight lid for retouching chipped areas at a later date.

• To make glazes, first mix up the required concentrated colour. Add about half of this colour to the acrylic scumble glaze and blend thoroughly before adding a little water to 'loosen' it. Try out this mixture on a piece of paper or card, adding more glaze or water until the right tone is achieved. Too much water will cause the paint to run, and too little will make the glaze too thick and it will dry in ridges.

For further paint effect projects see:
Folding Filigree Screen pp90–91; Ironware Barge Pot pp 164–165; Cherub Wardrobe pp182–185; Laundry Box pp200–201; Multipurpose Chest pp212–213; Sponged Cot pp218–219

▲ Brush on the final colour

Bedside Chest

THIS CHEAP PINE CHEST did not need any repair work although it was a little lacking in character. However, with some new paint and distress work, together with a simple stencilled design, it now presents an imposing piece of furniture, earning the right to be noticed for its style, as much as for its function. The beauty of stencil designs is that they can incorporate any pattern you choose, and they are particularly suited to creating matching effects in rooms. For example, to create a pattern on a piece of furniture to complement your bedroom curtains, simply photocopy a section of the fabric, enlarging or reducing as required, trace the appropriate elements and turn these into a matching stencil design.

❖ YOU WILL NEED ❖

Medium and fine grade abrasive papers and sanding block

Tack rag

White acrylic wood primer

Household paint brushes

Pink and green traditional or emulsion paint

00 grade wire wool

Photocopies of stencils (see pp245–246)

Stencil film and pencil or acetate and pen

Scalpel

Cutting mat or thick cardboard

Masking tape

Acrylic paint in 2 shades each of pink and green

Paint palette or plate

Stencil brush

Liming wax

Kitchen paper

Soft cloth

This pine bedside chest was practical and useful but a little dull and benefited from some individual decoration

▲ Apply one coat of pale pink paint

1 Rub down the chest using medium then fine grade abrasive papers and a sanding block. Then wipe off any dust with a tack rag.

▲ Paint the edges of the drawers green

2 Apply a coat of white acrylic primer to all of the surfaces and leave it to dry thoroughly.

Once the primer is dry, paint the whole chest, including all three drawers, with one coat of pale pink traditional paint and leave to dry overnight.

When the pink paint is dry, apply one coat of green traditional paint around the edges of each drawer. Hold the paint brush steady to make sure that you do not get paint on the front of the drawers. Alternatively, mask off the edges with tape. Next, paint the chest top and then the rest of the unit. Leave overnight to dry completely.

3 Rub wire wool gently over the painted surfaces. Remove just enough paint so that a hint of white primer shows through the pink paint, and a hint of pink shows through the green.

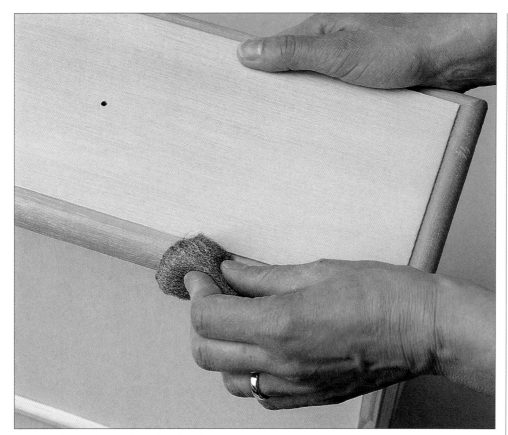

▲ Rub wire wool over the painted surface

• A variety of paint types can be used for stencilling but acrylics were used for this project because they are particularly vibrant and so will not disappear under the liming wax.

• When stencilling, do not use too much paint and dab off excess amounts on to kitchen paper. This will prevent paint from 'bleeding' under the stencil edge.

• Use two shades of pink for the roses and two greens for the stems and leaves, in order to give a shaded effect to the colour and to add some depth.

• Traditional chalky paints were used for the background colour on the chest. These colours would normally darken when varnished or waxed, but by applying liming wax to the paint, the pale chalky quality is retained.

For further stencilling projects see:
Vine Leaf Table pp114–117; Display Decanter & Glasses pp124–125; Gold Leaf Tray pp138–139; Bedside Chest pp175–177; Cherub Wardrobe pp182–185; Glass Cabinet pp195–197; Shutters & Louvre Doors pp198–199

4 Trace the rose stencil designs on to stencil film with a pencil, or with a suitable pen if you use acetate. Place the tracing on a cutting mat or a piece of thick cardboard to protect the work surface. Carefully cut out the design using a scalpel (always cut away from you and keep your hand out of the path of the blade).

5 Experiment with the design until you are happy with the final arrangement. Then secure the stencil to the chest with masking tape.
   Apply the paler pink acrylic paint through the stencil with the stencil brush using a stippling motion. Next, fill in with the lighter green and then, more sparingly, the darker colours. Continue until you have completed all of your design. (Alternatively, use spray paint but remember to also mask the surrounding areas, to prevent spray drifting to other areas of the surface.)

6 Apply liming wax all over the chest with a wad of kitchen paper and leave to dry for half an hour. The wax will subdue the colour of the paint. Finally, polish the chest to a shine with a soft cloth.

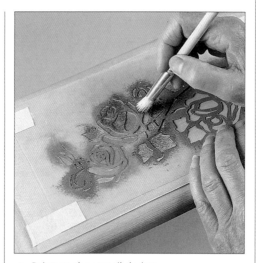

▲ Paint on the stencil design

▲ Apply liming wax with kitchen paper

Folding Collage Screen

SCREENS HAVE BEEN IN USE since at least the 17th century, providing useful concealment and private space for activities such as dressing. The Victorians, in particular, were fond of these pieces, decorating the panels with 'scraps' such as coloured paper images of fruit, flowers and quaintly dressed children. Screens are currently enjoying a renaissance, but now they conceal unattractive features, such as computers or work areas, as well as providing simple decoration. Old pieces, such as this one, are often badly damaged, but a few simple repairs can transform them into screens that are as good as new. Furthermore, decoration can include virtually anything, from painting a continuous scene between panels, to decoupage, stencilling or stamped designs.

❖ YOU WILL NEED ❖

Tack extractors (pliers, scissors and a small hammer)

Tape measure

Pencil

Calico (canvas)

Sewing scissors

Staple gun

Water sprayer

Paintbrushes

White emulsion

PVA glue

Paint for background colour

Coloured paper pieces

Plain coloured paper (for example, wrapping paper)

Plain paper for templates

Strong paper glue (for example, border adhesive)

Varnish

Braid

Rubber solution glue

Jars for mixing paint and glue

1 Carefully remove the old canvas from the screen, and extract all old nails and tacks. The tools required for this task will depend on the state of the screen, but pliers, scissors and a small hammer can all be useful.

2 Measure and cut new calico for each panel. Lay the panels flat and position the pieces of calico, making sure the weave is straight vertically and horizontally. Begin by stapling the centre of the top and bottom edges, then repeat this on the sides, which will make a diamond-like shape of the canvas.

Then proceed from the centre outwards along the long sides. Pull the canvas tight as you staple it in place, but do not pull it so tight that it wrinkles around the edges. Do not staple into the corners. Next, staple the top and bottom, again from the centre fixing outwards. Finally, fix down the corners.

This will help to ensure that the canvas is adequately stretched taut across the whole panel frame.

This Victorian screen has been given a new lease of life with a collage of cut-outs from magazines

▲ Remove the old canvas and nails

▲ Attach the new canvas to the frame

▲ Spray water over the new canvas

▲ Mark out the position of the frames

▲ Glue the 'frames' in place

3 Spray a mist of water over the new canvas and leave to dry. This 'stretches' the calico taut across the screen, because the material will shrink slightly and tighten as it dries out again.

6 Cut out several strips of plain coloured paper which will make the 'frames'. Glue them into position on the screen using a strong paper adhesive, such as border adhesive or PVA glue.

7 Work out the design for each decorative panel on tracing paper, then transfer it on to plain paper. Cut around the outline to provide a paper template. Then make a template for each panel of the screen.

▲ Seal the canvas with size

4 Seal the canvas by applying a size mixture. This is made by combining emulsion paint and PVA glue. Use approximately one tablespoon of PVA to 2.5 litres (4½ pints) of emulsion paint, diluted to a thin, creamy consistency with water. Leave to dry thoroughly, then apply another coat of the size mixture.

5 Apply two or three coats of the background paint in the chosen colour for the frame, leaving the screen to dry thoroughly between each coat. When the background paint is dry, measure up and mark out where the picture 'frames' will be positioned on the screen.

▲ Cut out a paper template

▲ Glue coloured paper on to the templates

▲ Cut away excess paper

▲ Glue the designs in place

8 Glue pieces of coloured paper on to the side of the templates. Make sure that the paper pieces will be visible once they have been pasted into position on the screen, using border adhesive or PVA glue.

9 Turn to the reverse side of the designs and use a scalpel to cut away the excess paper. Leave the designs to dry pressed between some books to help flatten them out and prevent wrinkling.

10 Mark out the position of each design on the panels with pencil. Then glue the designs and leave to dry. Varnish all the panels and surfaces and leave to dry.

Attach braid to the edges of the screen, using a rubber solution glue. Use thumbtacks to hold the folded mitred corners together until dry.

HINTS & TIPS

• An alternative way to achieve a similar look for this screen, but without using collage, is to photocopy botanical prints. Tint the black and white photocopies by hand, cut the designs out and glue them into place.

• Upholstery studs, which come in a variety of shapes and sizes and are available from upholstery suppliers, could be used instead of glue to attach the braid to the frame. This will create an extra dimension to the decoration on the border.

For further decoupage projects see:
Writing Desk pp170–171; Potichomanie Glass Jar pp188–189; Seashore Cabinet pp192–194; Toy Soldier Bedstead pp207–209; Picnic Hamper pp234–235

▲ Attach the braid to the edges with rubber solution glue

Cherub Wardrobe

THIS WARDROBE, which has been rag-rolled and stencilled with a light, bright, whimsical cherub theme, was originally a gentleman's wardrobe, but modern children's wardrobes are made to a similar design. Because it is made from good, solid wood, with shelving up one side and a hanging rail, the wardrobe would be ideal for a child's bedroom or a small guest room. The flat doors lend themselves perfectly to both the paint techniques of stencilling and rag rolling. If the door handles are unsuitable for painting, or do not blend in with the final effect, replace them with silver or glass knobs. Two inexpensive silver tassels purchased from a soft furnishing department of a store were used here to add a stylish finishing touch.

❖ YOU WILL NEED ❖

Screwdriver

Wood filler

Palette knife

Medium and fine grade abrasive papers

Tack rag

Primer

Household paintbrushes

Paint tray

Radiator roller with sleeve for oil-based paint

Eggshell base coat

Transparent oil glaze or acrylic or ready-made acrylic mix

Paint kettle

Black artists' oil paint

White spirit

Pink flesh-tone eggshell

Stippling brush

Stencil film and permanent pen

Cherub stencil (see page 243)

Black and white stencil sticks

Medium-sized stencil brush

Clean lint-free cotton rags

Scalpel and cutting mat

Spray adhesive

Two silver tassels

Two glass knobs

Acrylic paintbrush

A dark solid piece of wooden furniture can easily be made more cheerful

1 Remove the handles from the wardrobe in order to make sanding and painting easier. Fill any unwanted holes with a good wood filler. Allow the filler to dry and then rub down the entire surface of the wardrobe with medium grade abrasive paper, following the grain of the wood. Wipe off any dust with a tack rag, then apply a coat of primer and allow to dry completely overnight.

2 Pour the eggshell paint into the tray. Then use the radiator roller, fitted with a sleeve for oil-based paint, to apply the paint to the entire wardrobe. Finish edges with a small paintbrush before leaving the paint to dry for the manufacturer's recommended time. Apply a second coat in the same way. Rub down any runs or paint build-up with fine grade abrasive paper and wipe off with a tack rag.

3 To mix the rag-rolling glaze, place a tablespoon of transparent glaze into the paint kettle, then squeeze into it a tube width of black artists' oil paint and stir into the glaze until smooth. Continue to add more transparent oil glaze plus white spirit in the ratio of two parts glaze to one part of white spirit, finally adding one spoon of pink flesh-tone eggshell, until you have a sufficient quantity of glaze to cover the piece of furniture. (Eight tablespoons of glaze were used for this wardrobe.) The consistency of the final mix should be similar to single cream.

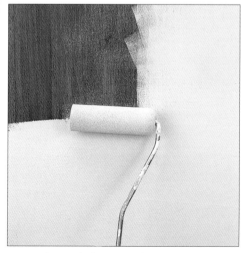

▲ Apply eggshell paint with a radiator roller

▲ Use a stippling brush over the glaze

4 With a well-loaded, stippling brush, apply the glaze over one section of the wardrobe. Work quickly and do not overbrush.

While the glaze is still wet, apply the stippling brush with a moderate up-and-down stabbing motion to remove the brush strokes and create a fine speckle-effect finish. Move on to the next step immediately.

5 Cut up the cotton material into large rag pieces. Screw up a piece of rag, twisting it into a sausage shape. Place the rag at a top corner and roll it down to the bottom of the wardrobe, using your fingertips and applying even pressure. Return to the top of the wardrobe door and position the rag to the side of the last section. Repat the movement, making sure that you overlap the last 'run' slightly, in order to avoid hard edges. Then repeat steps 4 and 5 on the next panel, and gradually work around the wardrobe.

6 To make the cherub stencil, position the film over the template for part 1 of the cherub stencil on page 243, and trace the outline with a fine-tip permanent pen. Allow a surplus of plastic stencil film around the edges to mix colours, and for the positioning marks. Cut along the lines with a scalpel and cut out the circular line-up dots, which will enable you to position the second stencil cut-out in the correct place. Use a cutting mat and always cut away from yourself. On a separate piece of film repeat the same for part 2 of the stencil.

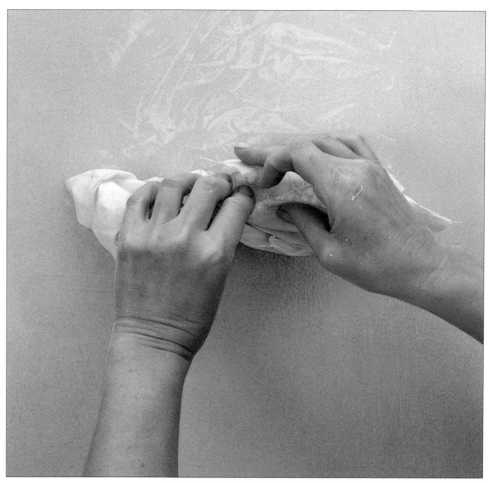

▲ Roll a rag down the glaze

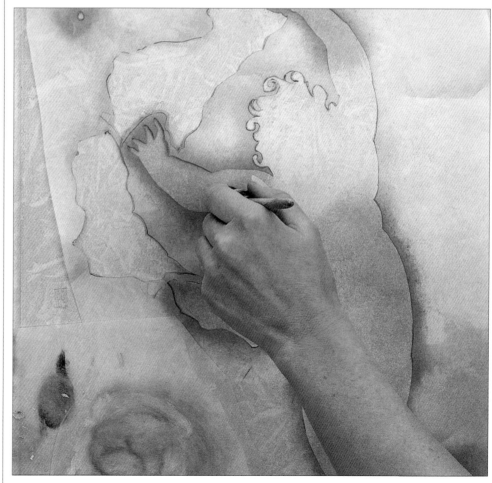

▲ Stencil part 1 of the design in pale grey

▲ Stencil part 2 of the design in dark grey

▲ Detail of the darker parts of the stencil

- Do not be tempted to overload colour on to the brush, because heavy paint will cause smudging and the stencil design will lack the required soft texture.

- If a stippling brush is not available, place a clean sleeve for oil-based paint on the radiator roller and very gently roll over the glaze to smooth out the brush stokes.

- During the stencilling process, it can be common to feel that not enough paint has been applied but, when the stencil is removed the design will be much heavier than you imagined.

- Keep a small dish or saucer of water and lots of cleaning fluids to hand, to remove any smudges or dribbles immediately.

7 Apply spray adhesive to the reverse side of the part 1 stencil and stick it into place on the wardrobe door. Stand back to check the position and adjust if necessary before applying the colour.

Break the seals of the stencil sticks (manufacturers' instructions are given on the packaging) and work an amount of black and white on to the spare area of the film. Mix the colours together to produce a pale grey shade. Working the stencil brush into this mix, cover all of the cut-out areas of part 1, using a circular and stippling motion.

Add positioning marks to the surface for lining up the next stencil, before carefully peeling the stencil away.

8 Apply spray adhesive to the reverse side of part 2 of the stencil, then position it correctly over part 1 of the stencil by aligning with the position marks.

Mix the stencil sticks as before but make a darker grey colour, and keep some neat black beside this to use for highlighting small areas. Colour all the cut-out areas of part 2 with dark grey, accentuating some intricate parts and features by stippling with a small amount of black.

Peel the stencil off and wipe away the line-up marks. Then clean the stencil with a clean rag moistened in white spirit, and allow to dry. Repeat the stencilling process on the other door by reversing the stencil.

Wipe off the marker lines and leave both doors for at least 24 hours to dry thoroughly.

9 With the acrylic brush, finish the wardrobe by applying two coats of acrylic satin glaze. This initially gives the appearance of a milky finish but it will dry clear, so do not overwork the medium. Allow the manufacturer's recommended drying time between coats.

For further stencilling projects see:
Vine Leaf Table pp114–117; Display Decanter & Glasses pp124–125; Gold Leaf Tray pp138–139; Bedside Chest pp175–177; Glass Cupboard pp195–197; Shutters & Louvre Doors pp198–199

▲ Detail of a finished cherub

Freestanding Cupboard

THIS CHUNKY OLD CUPBOARD was quite heavy-looking and unattractive, but would provide valuable storage for any room in the house. The useful drawer and top surface area could make it particularly suitable for a bedroom. By replacing the handles, applying a couple of coats of cream paint, some garlands of decoupage roses and an antique finish, the cupboard has been transformed into a light, bright decorative piece which can enhance any bedroom. Of course, the roses could be replaced with any design to suit the room.

❖ YOU WILL NEED ❖

White spirit

Fine wire wool and abrasive paper

Wood filler

Wooden handles

Tack rag

Wood primer

Cream oil-based eggshell paint

Brushes

Paper cut-outs

Adhesive tack

PVA glue

Roller

Polyurethane clear varnish

Crackle varnish

Wax

Soft lint-free cloth

The cupboard was in good condition and simply required a rub down before it could be decorated

1 Wipe the surface with white spirit and fine wire wool to remove any grease and dirt. Remove the handles and fill the holes with wood filler. When dry rub down with fine abrasive paper and wipe with a tack rag.

2 Insert new wooden handles and coat with primer. Apply three coats of eggshell paint, rubbing down and tacking off between coats.

▲ Paint the new handles with primer

3 Cut out the patterns and arrange them on the cupboard, fixing them temporarily with adhesive tack. Then paste them with glue and stick them in position. Use a roller to

▲ Cut out designs from wrapping paper

smooth them out and remove any bubbles. Then use a cloth wrung out in warm water to remove any excess glue.

4 Apply two coats of varnish, allowing sufficient drying time between each coat. Lightly rub down the second coat with fine grade abrasive paper and wipe with a tack rag. Apply coats of varnish, rubbing down and tacking between each, until the design is completely submerged.

5 To give the unit an antiqued effect, apply crackle varnish. When this is dry, apply a protective coat of polyurethane varnish and finish off with wax.

HINTS & TIPS

To avoid runs and drips do not overload the brush when applying varnish. Use several thin coats rather than one thick one.

For further decoupage projects see:
Pine Panelled Cupboard pp144–146; Writing Desk pp170–171; Seashore Cabinet pp192–194; Toy Soldier Bedstead pp207–209; Doll's Cradle pp220–221; Picnic Hamper pp234–235

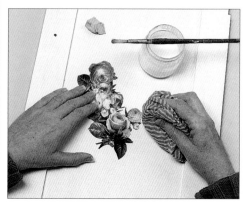

▲ Clean off the excess glue

Potichomanie Glass Jar

OTICHOMANIE is a traditional variation of decoupage applied to glass that dates back to Victorian times. (Elegant jars were in vogue in the 19th century.) The jar used here is a simple container, which is wide enough to allow access for the hand. It is a type commonly available at most jumbles sales or second-hand shops, although more elegant varieties could also be used. For a totally authentic look, try decorating the surface with antique oriental figures but, if these prove illusive, Victorian-style cut-outs such as flowers and birds, are just as effective.

❖ YOU WILL NEED ❖

Soft lint-free cloth

Small paper cut-outs

Adhesive tack

PVA glue

Small piece of sponge

Oil-based eggshell paint

Medium-sized artists' sable brush

The jar that you choose need not be of a particularly elaborate design

1 Ensure that the inside of the glass jar is free of any dust, dirt or grease by polishing it with a soft, lint-free cloth. This will make sure that the glue will stick properly.

2 Try out different designs, arranging the paper cut-outs on the outside of the jar, using adhesive tack to hold them in place temporarily. When you are happy with the design, remove the cut-outs and paste the patterned side of each with glue. Then stick them back in position, but this time on the inside of the jar. Press each piece firmly into place with your fingertips, making sure that all the edges are completely stuck down and smooth out any wrinkles or bubbles.

3 When the completed design has been stuck into position on the inside of the glass jar and lid, clean off any surplus glue from the backs of the prints and the glass using a piece of damp sponge wrung out in hot water.

4 When the jar is completely dry, paint the inside with the sable artists' brush. Work in short strokes, spiralling out from the bottom. Paint over the paper cut-outs so that the brush only travels outwards over the edges. Use the paint sparingly to reduce the risk of it dribbling down the sides. Leave the jar aside to dry for 24 hours, then apply a second coat of paint.

HINTS & TIPS

Containers such as these can be useful in any room of the house. Buy several matching pots and decorate accordingly to create a useful bathroom or kitchen set. You could incorporate a permanent label such as 'tea', 'coffee' and 'sugar' into the decoupage design.

For further decoupage projects see:
Needlecraft Workbox pp98–99; Writing Desk pp170–171; Seashore Cabinet pp192–194; Toy Soldier Bedstead pp207–209; Picnic Hamper pp234–235

▲ Try out different designs

▲ Glue the cut-outs inside the jar

▲ Paint the inside of the jar

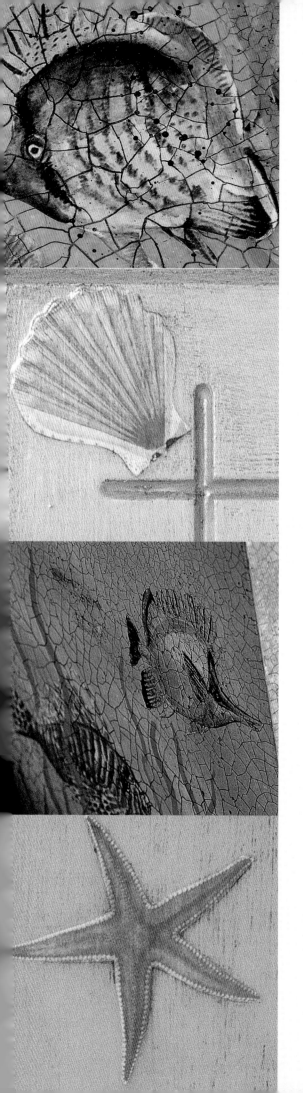

Even the smallest of bathrooms can be given a cheery atmosphere with a little careful planning. Ugly old laundry baskets, cabinets or cupboard doors can easily be transformed into bright, decorative pieces, helping to create a bathroom that's both functional and fun.

Bathroom Projects

Seashore Cabinet

THIS RATHER DULL bathroom cabinet has been enlivened with a decoupage decoration by sticking on paper cut-outs from wrapping paper and some 18th-century shell prints cut from a book. The layers of varnish give a durable finish; ideal for a bathroom cabinet. Test the acrylic primer's adhesion by applying a small patch to the surface, allowing it to dry, and then scratching it. If the layer comes off easily with a fingernail, don't use it. A general-purpose oil-based primer is a good alternative although it will take longer to dry. Antiquing paint highlights the brushmarks left in the primer, giving a rougher, wood-like texture. By painting the cabinet in shades of blue and by adding an ammonite-shaped knob, the sea theme is complete.

❖ YOU WILL NEED ❖

Coarse-grade sandpaper and sanding block

Tack rag

General-purpose acrylic or oil-based primer

Paint brushes

Emulsion or traditional paint in 2 colours

Masking tape (optional)

Paper images of fish and shells

Manicure scissors

Adhesive tack

Glue brush

Paper glue

Sponge

Satin water-based varnish

Varnish brush

White emulsion paint

Raw umber powder pigment

Water

Kitchen paper

Medium grade finishing paper

1 First, roughen the surface of the cupboard using a coarse grade sandpaper wrapped around a sanding block. This will ensure that the paint adheres more readily.

Wipe off the dust with a tack rag. Apply a coat of the general-purpose acrylic primer and leave it to dry completely. Then paint over the primer with your chosen base coat.

2 When the base coat paint is dry, use a fine paintbrush to pick out the indented line with a contrasting colour of paint.

If your cabinet does not have an indented line, create the same effect with paint. To keep the lines sharp, mark out a border between two strips of masking tape and paint carefully between the rows.

3 Choose some suitably sized fish and shell images from books then cut out, or photocopy, a number of them using a sharp pair of manicure scissors. Colour them in if necessary.

Even a very plain and cheap piece of furniture can be transformed

Start experimenting with the design, arranging and re-arranging the images on the cabinet. Fix them into position with temporary adhesive tack and cut out any further prints if they are needed. Avoid over-cluttering the unit, and aim for corner decoration, such as the starfish used here.

▲ Paint over the primer with the base coat

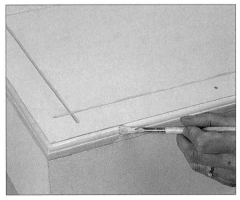

▲ Pick out the indented line with a fine brush

▲ Try out different arrangements of images

▲ Glue the cut-outs in place

4 Brush the glue on to the cupboard, place a paper cut-out over this and press it firmly into position and smooth it flat. Look at the cupboard under a good light to make sure there are no bubbles of trapped air under the cut-outs to spoil the finished appearance. Continue to stick all the remaining fish and shell cut-outs down, then wash off the excess glue with a damp sponge and leave the cupboard to dry for at least two hours.

Check that all the edges are well stuck down, then varnish over the

painted areas with two coats of satin varnish. Leave at least two hours between each coat of varnish and lightly sand between coats. The first two coats must be applied thinly, or the paper might lift and bubble.

5 Mix together 1 teaspoon of white emulsion paint and 3 teaspoons of raw umber pigment and dilute this with water to make a thin, dark brown paint. Brush it over one side of the cupboard and leave it for a minute or two before wiping it off with a piece of kitchen paper. Repeat the process on each of the other sides.

6 Varnish all the painted surfaces of the cupboard to seal the antiquing paint. Then continue to varnish the decoupaged door, with eight or ten more coats, depending on the thickness of the paper you have used and the finish you require. Sand the varnished surface with a medium grade finishing paper, then apply a final coat of varnish. Leave to dry.

HINTS & TIPS

• Do not be tempted to overload the paintbrush. Remember that several thin coats of paint or varnish will create a much more professional final effect.

• If you have to store paintbrushes overnight, suspend them in white spirit or water in a jam jar, but make sure that the metal parts of the brush are kept clear of the liquid.

• Sanding between coats of varnish or paint is essential for a smooth, attractive finish, but do not forget to wipe the surface clean of the sanding dust before applying the next coat.

For further decoupage and paint effect projects see:
Pine Panelled Cupboard pp144–146; Table & Chair pp154–157; Writing Desk pp170–171; Freestanding Cabinet pp186–187; Laundry Box pp200–201

▲ Rub off the antiquing paint

Glass Cupboard

THE WOOD ON THIS small glass cupboard had already been stripped but the finish was poor and there were many cracks that needed filling. By using a thin woodwash over the pine, the overall appearance was improved while visibly retaining the natural grain of the wood. The finish was then distressed using wet-and-dry paper. It's possible to use any motif for this kind of project but the choice of sea horses here helps to create the bathroom atmosphere. The number of shelves installed in the unit can also vary according to your needs.

❖ YOU WILL NEED ❖

Medium and fine grade
abrasive papers

Tack rag

Pale jade emulsion paint

Paint brush

Wet-and-dry paper

Neutral furniture wax

Clean rags

Methylated spirit and
white spirit

Plastic stencil film and
permanent pen

Scalpel and cutting mat

Tape measure

Adhesive spray

Paper and masking tape

Can of spray paint

1 Rub down the surface with medium and then fine grade abrasive papers and wipe with a tack rag. Water down the pale jade emulsion with equal parts of water to paint and paint this on to all of the wooden surfaces as a woodwash (you should be able to see the grain of the wood clearly through the wash). Allow the emulsion to dry.

2 Use the wet-and-dry paper to gently rub over the painted surface so that areas of pine shine through in their natural state and the surface is smooth. When completely dry, apply a coat of neutral furniture wax and buff to a soft sheen.

3 Clean the glass by gently brushing off any loose dust and dirt. Then, use a clean lint-free rag with methylated spirit to wipe off the surface and lift any sticky residue. Once the dirt has been removed, wash off the glass with hot water and detergent, then polish and allow to dry.

This glass cabinet, with its tarnished mirror at the back, was enlivened with a sea horse stencil design

4 Place the plastic stencil film over the templates on page 244 and trace the outlines with a permanent pen. On separate pieces of film, cut out the sea horse and fish using a scalpel

▲ Apply the pale jade base coat

▲ Rub back the paint with wet-and-dry paper

195

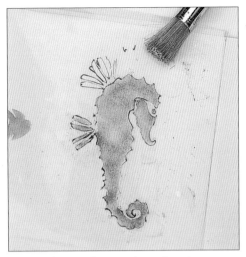

▲ Test the stencils on a piece of card

5 Carefully plan and measure the distances between the stencils, alternating patterns of the sea horse and fish, with equal spacing. (Remember to try and keep the

designs spaced between the shelves, so that the full effect can be seen.) Spray the front of the stencil with adhesive spray and stick it in place on the glass. Mask off the rest of the surrounding area with paper and adhesive tape.

6 Holding the spray can 30cm (1ft) away from the surface, spray the paint as a fine mist in one sweeping left-to-right motion. Avoid heavy bursts as this will cause runs of paint and prevent the stencil from peeling off easily.

7 Remove the stencil and wipe off any excess paint with a clean cloth and small amount of white spirit. Any smudged paint on the cupboard can be removed using a scalpel, when it is dry.

HINTS & TIPS

• Transform ugly shelf brackets by painting them in a metallic colour such as gold.

• You can re-use the stencil to create matching effects on other pieces of furniture or even on the bathroom wall.

• Make sure that there is plenty of ventilation when you are using spray paints, and practise the technique on some paper first.

• Use the scalpel on a cutting mat and always cut away from your body.

For further stencilling projects see:
Display Decanter & Glasses pp124–125; Bedside Chest pp175–177; Shutters & Louvre Doors pp198–199; Decorative Pots pp236–238

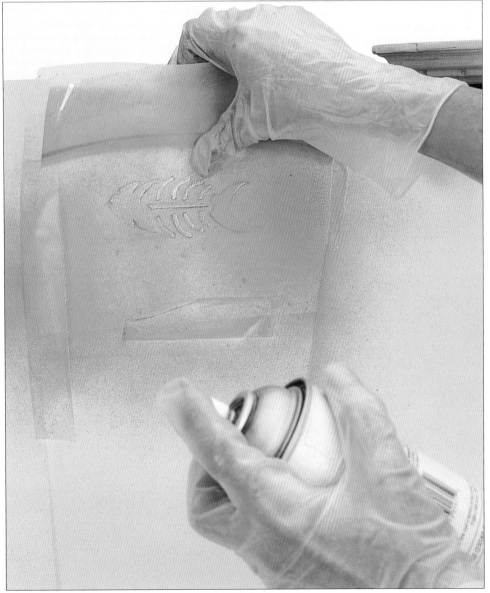

▲ Spray painting the stencil

Shutters & Louvre Doors

PLAIN WHITE LOUVRE DOORS are a common, but often uninspiring, feature of many bathrooms and cupboard units. Rather than replacing such pieces, however, a quick decorative finish can transform them instead into an attractive feature.

Louvre doors can be fiddly and time-consuming to paint by brush, so a spray paint was used. Then a spattered finish was added using burnt sienna for a speckled effect. Brass sea horse handles complete the aquatic theme. The effect can be further enhanced, as shown here, with some matching wall stencilling.

❖ YOU WILL NEED ❖

Hot soapy water and cloth

Medium and fine grade abrasive papers

Tack rag

3 cans of turquoise-blue acrylic spray paint

Protective mask

Burnt sienna artists' acrylic paint

Large, long-bristled artists' brush

Stick or old brush

Spare paper

Spray polyurethane varnish in satin finish

Louvre doors can be fiddly to paint by hand so spray paint is ideal for getting into all of the slots

1 Wash the doors with warm soapy water and leave to dry. Then rub down thoroughly with the medium and fine grade abrasive papers, and remove paint and dust residues with the tack rag.

▲ Spray turquoise paint onto the door

2 Working in a well-ventilated area, apply an even coat of spray paint to one side of the door. Hold the can about 30cm (1ft) away from the surface and move it across the door in long, even strokes. When dry, turn the door horizontally and spray all uncoated edges, then turn again and repeat. Continue this process on the other side of the door. Both sides will probably need 2–3 thin coats applied.

3 For the spattering effect, water down the burnt sienna, and then dip the tip of the art brush into the solution. Knock the handle against a stick or old brush so the paint flicks

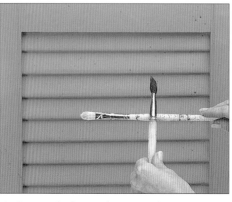

▲ Spatter the burnt sienna evenly

▲ Spray varnish over the painted door

away. Practise on a piece of card, then move on to the louvre doors. Try to apply a fairly even amount of spattering over the entire surface. Leave to dry.

4 Spray a coat of polyurethane varnish over the entire surface. Allow to dry and repeat the process. Add any finishing touches such as handles or stencilled patterns.

HINTS & TIPS

• When using spray paint, a better finish is always achieved by applying several thin coats, rather than one heavy layer which tends to cause paint build-up and runs. It is not necessary to wait until each coat is completely dry to add the next layer.

• Always use a protective mask when spraying paint or varnish and work with as much ventilation as possible. However, if working outside, try to avoid windy days because this will cause the paint to drift. Dust is also more likely to settle in the wet finish before it has time to dry.

For further decorative paint projects see:
Folding Filligree Screen pp90–91; Shaker Chair pp126–128; Scandinavian Scroll Chair pp147–149; Bedside Chest pp175–177; Seashore Cabinet pp192–194

Laundry Box

THIS BASIC, PLYWOOD rubbish bin has been turned into an attractive bathroom laundry box. The decoration comprises of simple stippling, paper cut-outs and craquelure glaze. This project is ideal for people new to using glaze effects because any resulting bubbles will only add to the final decoration! The fish were all cut from a sheet of wrapping paper and stuck onto the box at random, along with some of the shells from the border of the paper. Of course, any pattern or design could be used, but this aquarium effect seems especially suitable for bathroom storage.

❖ YOU WILL NEED ❖

Medium and fine grade
abrasive papers

Tack rag

Primer

Stiff brush for stippling

Small soft brush

Artists' acrylic paint
in shades of blue,
green and orange

PVA glue

Paper cut-outs

Scissors

Wallpaper paste

Craquelure glaze

Small foam roller

Varnish and brush

1 Rub down the box with medium and fine grade abrasive papers before wiping down with a tack rag. Then apply a coat of primer and leave the box to dry completely.

Following a general diagonal flow, stipple artists' acrylic paint straight from the tube onto the surface. Use two or three different shades of blue, mixing and blending the paint with firm jabbing motions. Leave the box aside for several hours to dry completely.

2 Cut out a selection of images following an aquatic theme. Then experiment with the position of the fish on the box before gluing them into place with paper paste.

Once the images are dry, paint on the green and orange water plants design using a small soft paintbrush and acrylic paint.

To create the illusion that the fish are swimming through the plant life at the bottom of a pond or lake, paint bits of plant over the fish images, as well as up to and above them.

3 Once the paint is dry, apply a coat of craquelure glaze using a small foam roller to give a thick and even coat. If you wish to create bubbles, avoid applying the craquelure too evenly, but remember that such features tend to appear at random!

Once the glaze is dry, go over the surface with a coat of dark blue paint and quickly wipe off – the darker paint should seep into and remain in the cracks and bubbles caused by the glaze. For a final, protective finish, apply a coat of neutral varnish.

HINTS & TIPS

If you paint the inside of the box, make sure that you use water-resistant paint to avoid staining damp clothes.

For further paint effects projects see:
Seashore Cabinet pp192–194; Doll's Cradle pp220–221; Wooden Trug pp230–231; Picnic Hamper pp234–235

▲ Stipple the surface with acrylic paint

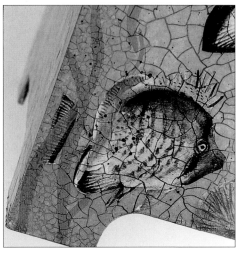
▲ Dark blue paint accentuates the crackle effect

Just like their toys, children's rooms should be bright, fun and durable. They also need to change with the times, matching the different needs of growing infants. Transforming pieces of old junk provides the perfect solution, helping to create inexpensive, handy furniture that can be passed between generations.

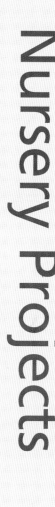

Nursery Projects

Chequered Table & Chairs

THIS DISCARDED NURSERY school table, with matching chairs, was remarkably cheap and makes an ideal surface for children's play. The colourful design is popular with young infants, but should retain appeal for several years as children grow older. The colours used for the chairs were incorporated into the table by painting the occasional diamond shape here and there. Getting the design to fit accurately took time but, for a less complicated approach, simply mark a chequered pattern in line with the table, rather than creating the harlequin effect.

❖ YOU WILL NEED ❖

Cleaning materials:
Bowl of warm water and
detergent, clean soft cloth

Medium and fine
grade abrasive papers

Tack rag

Wood filler

Filling knife

Primer

White emulsion paint

Paintbrushes

Masking tape

Water-soluble pencil

Ruler

Emulsion or traditional
paint in 3 colours

Satin or matt
water-based varnish

Varnish brush

1 Wash and rub down the surfaces before filling any holes with wood filler. Then rub down again with medium and fine grade abrasive papers, before wiping off with a tack rag. Apply a coat of primer and leave to dry completely.

2 Paint each surface with three coats of white emulsion. Allow each coat to dry thoroughly before applying the next. Make sure the final coat is smooth by sanding it with a fine grade abrasive paper, then stick masking tape around the edges of the table and the seat and the back of each chair.

3 Plan out the design by deciding on the approximate size of the diamonds you require and work out how many will fit along the top and down the sides of the table. This one needed six complete diamond

▲ Fill any cracks with wood filler

shapes running across the width of the table. Mark the width of the table with a series of dots where the points of the diamond will go and the length of the table in the same way. Join up the first dot along the width with the first dot along the length, using a water-soluble pencil and a ruler.

Continue in this way until you have covered the full length of the table. Repeat this process starting from the

Serviceable but worn, this table and chair can be turned into a colourful and exciting nursery set

▲ Mark out the design on the table

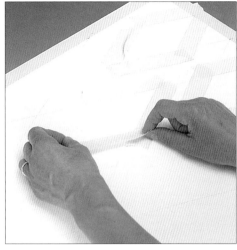

▲ Mask around alternate diamonds

▲ Paint the diamonds the chosen colour

For further table and chair projects see:
Round Coffee Table pp95–97; Vine Leaf Table pp114–117; Table & Chair pp154–157; Folk Art Chair pp161–163

opposite side and so forming a diamond pattern. Mark the design on the chairs. This time you only need to decide how many diamonds you want across the width of the chair back, making sure the design is centred.

Use strips of masking tape around the edges to separate alternate diamond shapes on the tabletop.

4 Paint the diamonds in the colour of your choice, brushing in the direction of the grain of the wood. When these are dry, mask the remaining diamonds and fill with more colour, this time incorporating the colours in the chairs in a random way.

5 Place a second row of masking tape just inside the first, then remove the tape next to the edge of the table. Paint this in the main colour of the table. Fill in the diamond shapes on the chairs and paint the border around the edges.

6 Wipe off all the pencil marks with a damp cloth then, using a medium grade abrasive paper, rub lightly over the painted surface to soften the effect. Finally, protect the furniture with two coats of satin or matt water-based varnish, allowing the first coat to dry completely before applying the second.

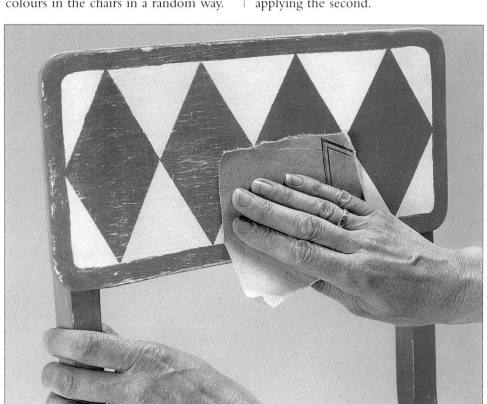

▲ Rub down lightly with abrasive paper

Toy Soldier Bedstead

As this child's bedstead demonstrates, decoupage needn't be restricted to conventional patterns with flowers and butterflies. Popular cartoon or nursery characters can be just as effective and provide an unusual technique of decoration for children's rooms. Here, the theme is the nursery rhyme the 'Grand Old Duke of York', partly inspired by the shape of the bedhead which literally provides a hill for the soldiers to march up and down. To continue the nursery rhyme theme, old sheets of music were also cut up and used, but these can easily be photocopied or drawn out if there are none to hand. Choose a bright background colour for the decoupage technique because the many coats of varnish tend to yellow it slightly.

❖ YOU WILL NEED ❖

Medium and fine grade abrasive papers

Tack rag

Sanding sealer/primer

Blue and red eggshell or emulsion paint

Paintbrushes

Sheet music

Small craft scissors

Tea bag

Adhesive tack

Craft glue and brush

Soft clean cloth

Varnish

Varnish brush

The rounded shape of the bedhead provided a hill for the decoupage soldiers to march up

▲ Apply the base coat

1 Rub down the bedhead with medium and fine grade abrasive papers, before wiping down with a tack rag. Apply a coat of sanding sealer or primer and leave to dry.

▲ Cut out the paper soldiers

2 Paint two coats of blue paint over the headboard, end board and legs, allowing the length of drying time recommended by the manufacturer between coats. Use a fine brush to paint a rim of bright red around the outside edge moulding.

3 Draw or paint soldiers on to white paper and make several colour photocopies to the correct size until you have sufficient different figures to create an army.

Also draw or make some black and white copies of sheet music.

4 Carefully cut out the various soldiers, including the horseman and an assortment of drummers and riflemen.

With a sweeping motion, use the scissors to round off the edges of the music and make them look like old-fashioned manuscripts.

207

▲ Wipe a tea bag along the edges of the music

▲ Paste the soldiers into position

• Always use non-toxic paints and varnishes for children's furniture.

• Pick a really bright base colour paint, because the several layers of varnish needed for decoupage will tend to dull the vibrancy of the hue.

For further decoupage projects see:
Needlecraft Workbox pp98–99; Enamel Jug pp132–133; Writing Desk pp170–171; Seashore Cabinet pp192–194; Doll's Cradle pp220–221

5 To age the music, wipe wet, warm, tea bags around the edges of the sheets of music and randomly across them in places to create an old, well-used appearance. Leave the paper to dry thoroughly.

6 Experiment with the design by positioning the cut-outs on the bedstead with temporary adhesive tack. Stand back to check the overall view and ensure the design works when viewed from all angles. When working out the design, remember to take into account the width of the mattress and pillows, otherwise a great deal of decoration may be hidden when the bed is made up.

When you are happy with the overall effect, paste the reverse side of the figures with glue, making sure you cover all the edges. Place them into position and smooth down with a clean cloth, removing any excess glue immediately. Leave to dry.

7 Apply a coat of varnish, leave to dry and repeat. After the first three coats, gently sand the surface with fine grade abrasive paper, wipe with the tack rag, and apply another coat of varnish. Continue in this way until the paper and varnish levels are smooth to the touch. Always allow plenty of drying time between each coat of varnish.

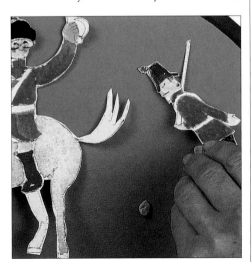

▲ Plan the position of the soldiers

▲ Varnish the decoupage design

Nursery Mirror

THIS OLD MIRROR was coated in thick, uneven paint that had to be stripped professionally. After this, a number of cracks and holes were revealed, but a simple bit of filling and rubbing down soon took the wood back to a flat, even surface. Some charming illustrations have been used for the attractive decoupage finish, carefully balanced with additional decorative features such as a selection of butterflies, bugs and birds. Such images are ideal for balancing and integrating decoupage designs, or for tying several different elements together.

❖ YOU WILL NEED ❖

Wood filler

Medium and fine grade abrasive papers

Tack rag

Wood primer

Brushes

Oil-based eggshell paint

Paper cut-outs

Adhesive tack

PVA glue

Soft lint-free cloth

Roller

Polyurethane clear varnish

Antiquing fluid

Piece of nylon cloth

Wax polish

Wooden knob for the drawer

Wood glue

Thick, badly applied paint needed commercial stripping before the mirror could be decorated

1 After stripping the paint, fill any cracks and holes with wood filler and allow to dry. Rub the surfaces down, with the abrasive papers before wiping off with a tack rag.

▲ Fill cracks and holes with wood filler

2 Taking care to rub down and tack between each coat, give the mirror two coats of primer followed by three coats of paint, leaving 24 hours between each application.

3 Arrange the paper cut-outs on the mirror frame with temporary adhesive tack until you are happy with the design. Remove each piece individually, paste it with glue and return it to its place. Press the small pieces in place with a clean fingertip and a cloth wrung out in warm water. Go over the larger pieces with the roller to squeeze out any excess glue. When everything is dry, re-stick any loose corners and wipe off any spots of dried glue with the warm damp cloth.

4 Give the frame eight coats of varnish. After the first two, gently rub down and wipe with a tack rag between the remaining coats.

▲ Paint on a generous coat of antiquing fluid

5 To age the mirror, apply a coat of antiquing fluid, brushing it into all the ridges and crevices. When the fluid has dulled, work it into the wood with a clean paintbrush, especially where real dirt would have gathered over the years. Finally, make a smooth ball from a piece of nylon and begin to rub off the antiquing a little, taking off more in places where there would have been a lot of wear.

▲ Rub off the antiquing with a nylon cloth

6 Leave to dry for a few hours before applying a final coat of varnish. Finally, apply a coat of wax polish, following the manufacturer's instructions.

Multipurpose Chest

COMBINING STORAGE and activity space can be a common problem in many children's rooms. This chest helps to relieve at least some of the clutter by offering a play unit as well as vital drawer storage. On one side, corkboard provides the perfect place for sticking pictures and postcards. On the other, a blackboard offers fun drawing and writing space that can simply be washed down again and again. Using a bright range of colours helps to increase the unit's appeal – but remember to use paints that are lead-free and non-toxic.

❖ YOU WILL NEED ❖

Coarse, medium and fine abrasive papers

Tack rag

Primer paint

2.5cm (1in) brush

Undercoat paint

Ruler

Masonite

Cutting equipment

Nails and hammer

Blackboard paint

Corkboard

PVA wood glue

Beading

Range of colours in gloss/enamel paint

1 Remove any knobs or handles and sand the chest thoroughly, using coarse, medium then fine grade abrasive papers. Wipe with a tack rag to remove the dust residue. Apply primer and undercoat to the unit, following the manufacturer's instructions.

2 Measure the right-hand side of the chest and mark out the dimensions on the masonite. Cut the masonite to size and fix it to the side using the nails and hammer. Paint with blackboard paint. Measure the cork for the lefthand side, cut out the cork and nail it into place.

3 Cut the beading to fit like a frame around the blackboard and corkboard. Apply primer, undercoat, then top coats of paint. Once dry, fix around the black- and corkboards using panel nails.

4 Coat the unit, drawers and handles with your chosen paint colours. To ensure durability (which is essential in a child's bedroom), apply three or four applications, lightly sanding and wiping with the tack rag between coats.

5 When the paint is fully dry, replace the handles on the drawers and put them back into place on the chest.

HINTS & TIPS

• To avoid a build-up of paint on the inside, which could inhibit the smooth movement of the drawer in its runners, consider painting only the visible fronts.

• Always remove drawers from a unit before painting – otherwise they may end up being painted shut.

• Try the technique on larger pieces of furniture, such as wardrobes, but remember that the 'activity' areas need to be within reaching distance for a child.

For further children's painted projects see:
Chequered Table & Chairs pp204–206

▲ Five glossy colours will appeal to children

▲ A blackboard gives the opportunity for play

Rocking Chair

A POPULAR FEATURE of many nurseries, rocking chairs provide both comfortable seating for rocking a baby to sleep and a decorative room feature. They can often be found at garage sales or antique shops. Yet many tend to acquire layers of paint over the years, which need to be stripped back before applying a fresh decorative finish. This chair has been given quite a strong two-tone ageing effect, but other shades could be used in order to achieve a more subtle finish. The box-seat cushion features a separate strip to make up the depth of the cushion, which is highlighted by contrasting piping. The headrest is made in a similar way, providing additional comfort when feeding a baby as well as making the chair feel more luxurious.

❖ YOU WILL NEED ❖

Brown paper for making templates

Pen

Scissors

Fabric for cushion and headrest

Two zips – the length required is the width of the cushions less 5cm (2in)

Piping cord

Approximately 1m (1yd) of contrast fabric for ties and piping

5cm (2in) thick foam for inside the cushions

Fine grade abrasive paper

Tack rag

White quick-drying primer

Two contrasting colours of matt emulsion paint

Paintbrush

Liquid varnishing wax

1 To make the templates for the seat and head cushions, lay some brown paper on the chair, draw the exact shape required and cut the paper out. Do the same for the headrest.

2 Draw around the template, on the reverse side of the fabric, with a 2cm (¾in) seam allowance all around. Fold the fabric double, to obtain two of each piece. Then cut them out.

3 Make the seat and head cushions in the same way. Cut out the fabric for the depth of the cushions. Take the depth of the foam, 5cm (2in), plus 1.5cm (½in) seam allowance each side, making it 8cm (3in) deep. For the length, calculate how much is needed to go around the two sides and the front of the cushion. Calculate the back depth by dividing the foam depth in two, and adding 3cm (1¼in) seam allowance on each side. Cut two pieces to this depth, in this case 5.5cm (2¼in), and as long as the

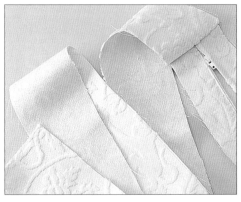

▲ Cut out the fabric for the cushions' depth

width of the back of the cushion, plus an additional 2cm (¾in) for seam allowances. Machine the zip into the two back depth pieces, joining them together, and then machine one end of this piece to the rest of the depth piece.

4 To make piping, cut the fabric strips on the cross. Cut them as long as possible and about 5cm (2in) wide. Place the piping cord in the centre of the fabric strip and machine stitch the two edges together, using a piping foot, close to the cord.

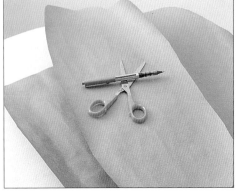

▲ Make the templates for the cushions

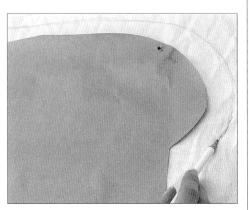

▲ Draw around the template

▲ Cut fabric strips for the piping

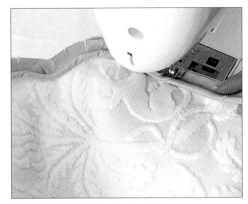

▲ Machine stitch the piping in place

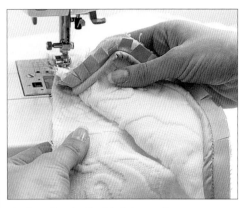

▲ Sew the depth strip into position

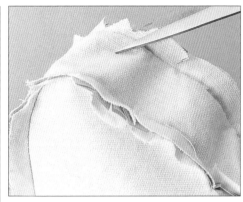

▲ Cut V-shape nicks into the seam allowance

5 Next, pin the piping around the top and bottom piece of the cushion fabric. Once positioned, machine stitch the piping into place. However, bear in mind that when you are sewing around corners the piping will sit better if you snip the fabric from the edge up to the seam of the piping cord.

8 Mitre all the corners by cutting little 'V' snips or nick into the seam allowance wherever there are any bends in the material.

9 Cut a piece of foam to size from the original paper templates for both the seat cushion and head pad. Insert into the cushion covers.

10 Rub down the chair with abrasive paper and wipe off any dust with a tack rag. Apply a coat of quick-drying primer (if the wood is bare, otherwise proceed to step 11) and leave to dry. When this is completely dry, lightly rub down the chair again, then wipe with a tack rag to remove all traces of dust.

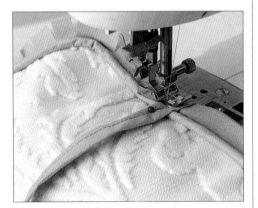

▲ Machine stitch the ties in place

6 Cut and make the cushion ties; four for each cushion. For each tie, cut a piece of fabric measuring 40 x 5cm (16 x 2in). Fold both of the long edges into the centre and press. Then fold the whole length of the tie in half again and machine stitch along the edges.

Machine two of these, equally spaced across the back, on to the rear of the cushion, then repeat for both the top and bottom piece of the cushion.

7 Starting with the zip piece centrally placed at the back of the cushion, pin the depth strip to the top cushion piece along the existing seam line. Then machine stitch the depth strip into place. Open the zip, pin and machine the bottom cushion piece to the depth strip.

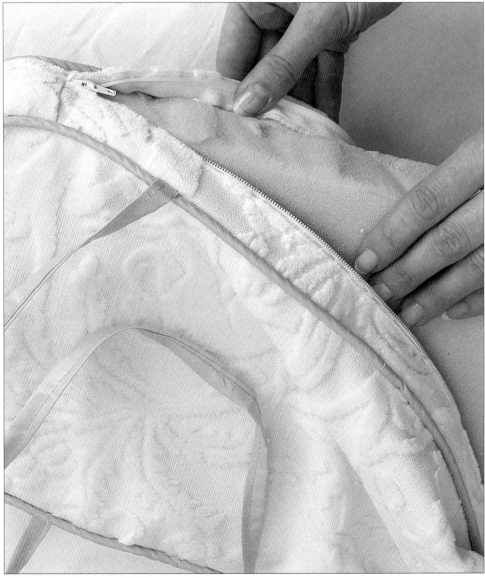

▲ Insert the foam in the cushion covers

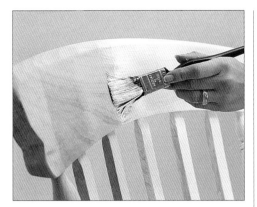

▲ Apply a coat of primer to bare wood

11 Apply a coat of the chosen base colour, in this case lime-green. Once the paint is dry, lightly rub down and wipe off with the tack rag. Then apply the top coat.

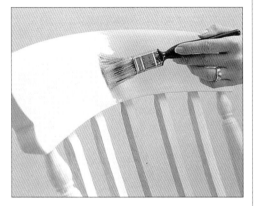

▲ Apply the base coat of your chosen colour

12 Gently rub down the surface, following the direction of the grain, with fine grade abrasive paper. Focus particularly on areas that are likely to show wear – such as along the edges, the main ridge of the seat and around joins – to reveal the base colour of lime-green. Continue sanding until you are happy with the distressed look. Once you have finished, wipe the chair down well with a tack rag to remove the dust.

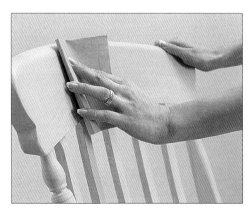

▲ Lightly sand the chair for a smooth finish

▲ Apply the chosen top coat of paint

13 Apply a final, protective coat of varnishing wax. Leave to dry and then buff up the whole chair with a soft cloth. Tie the cushions into place.

▲ Sand in the direction of the grain

▲ Apply a layer of liquid varnishing wax

HINTS & TIPS

• Existing cushions can be used, but these box cushions are particularly comfortable because of the separate strip that makes up the depth of the cushion

• Box cushions also use blocks of foam to pad them out, making for a smarter look especially where piping has been used.

For further chair projects see:
Decorated Lloyd Loom Chair pp108–109; Scandinavian Scroll Chair pp147–149; Table & Chair pp154–157; Folk Art Chair pp161–163; Deck Chair pp232–233

Sponged Cot

CHILDREN'S COTS are often passed between families, acquiring years' of wear and tear. However, most sturdy wooden cots will last for several generations and can be transformed for each new arrival; looking as good as new with only a little time, work and imagination. Cots are particularly fun to decorate, and can involve a whole range of characters or pictures. The sponge printing technique used here is very simple and almost any motif can be used – from simple geometric designs to animals, boats, or whole stories in printed shapes.

❖ YOU WILL NEED ❖

Medium and fine grade abrasive papers

Wood filler

Tack rag

Brushes

All-in-one primer and undercoat

Artists' acrylic colours – yellow ochre, black

Top coat (or scumble glaze mixed with various artists' colours)

Tracing paper

Felt-tip pen

Kitchen sponges

Scalpel

Paintbrushes, including a wide flat one for 'dragging'

Jars for mixing paint

Flat dish for printing

Matchstick

Non-toxic varnish

1 Clean and sand all surfaces, using medium, then fine grade abrasive papers. Fill any holes with wood filler, and rub down again before wiping with a tack rag. Apply an all-in-one primer and undercoat to any raw wood. When dry, apply a second coat of all-in-one primer and undercoat, tinted with a small quantity of yellow ochre and a touch of black to make a soft 'off white'. Apply a coat of dilute paint or artists' colour in glaze. Then 'drag' the brush through the paint to create a textured effect.

2 Apply the top colour in sections, allowing drying time between sections and wiping off overlaps on the edges. While you are waiting for the paint to dry, work out the design for your sponge on tracing paper. Apply the design to the sponge by cutting around the paper and marking the outline on the sponge. Cut around the design with a scalpel.

3 Cut away the area of sponge around the outline so that the design stands proud. Mix a colour in a jar and pour out on to a flat dish. Push the sponge design down into the paint and coat it evenly. You may wish to touch up some areas of the sponge with a brush. Then apply the sponge stamp firmly to the head panel.

▲ Use a small sponge cut-out to overprint

4 Re-coat the sponge with paint for each printed motif. Position each print closely to the previous one and keep an even line to make a linked row of elephants. Allow the first colour of printing to dry. Make some smaller sponge cut-outs and overprint onto the elephants in a different colour.

5 When the second colour is dry, add further detail using the end of a matchstick and a third colour. Leave to dry, then varnish all surfaces with a minimum of two coats to protect your handiwork, making sure that the varnish is non-toxic.

▲ Drag the brush through the paint

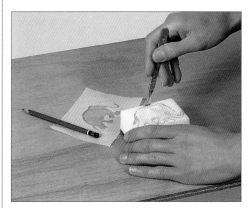
▲ Cut around the design with a scalpel

▲ Use a matchstick to apply the third colour

Doll's Cradle

A DOLL'S CRADLE makes a charming accessory for any playroom. This one was originally covered in a lurid pink paint and heavily studded with round-headed screws. It needed to be stripped professionally before being rubbed down and repainted. The decoupage decoration comprises a collection of nostalgic drawings of Edwardian children at play from an old picture book, which suited the traditional dolly occupant and her crisp white bed linen perfectly. However, cartoon characters or pictures of toys would be just as suitable.

❖ YOU WILL NEED ❖

Coarse, medium and fine abrasive paper

Wood filler

Tack rag

Wood primer

Brushes

Artists' oil paints in ultramarine and raw umber

White spirit

White oil-based eggshell paint

White paper

Small rectangular piece of varnished glass

Paper cut-outs

Adhesive tack

PVA glue

Roller

Soft lint-free cloth

Polyurethane clear varnish

1 Remove the round-headed screws and replace with counter-sunk, flat-headed ones. If stripping causes the grain to lift rub it down a little with coarse grade abrasive paper. Then fill any holes, cracks, and abrasions with wood filler and leave to dry. Rub down the whole cradle with medium and fine grade abrasive papers and wipe with a tack rag.

2 Apply a coat of primer and leave to dry. Lightly rub down again and wipe off with a tack rag.

3 Mix about 2.5cm (1in) of ultramarine artists' oil paint with a touch of raw umber and some white spirit for the soft lavender blue base. Gradually add the white eggshell paint until you arrive at the correct colour, and mix to a creamy consistency. Smear a little of the colour on a piece of white paper and view the result through a piece of varnished glass (see p44) to gauge the final effect and make any necessary adjustments. Apply three or four coats of this base colour to the cradle, rubbing down and tack ragging between each application.

This doll's cradle looked very plain after it had been stripped but a decoupage design brightened it up no end

4 Arrange the cut-outs with adhesive tack. Then glue them in position, squeezing out any excess glue and wipe off with the soft cloth wrung out in warm water. Check each piece is stuck down before going on to the next. When the design is complete, stick down any loose ends.

5 Check for shiny patches of dried, excess glue and wipe them off with a cloth wrung out in hot water. Then apply two coats of polyurethane clear varnish, leaving 24 hours between each coat. Rub down gently and wipe off with a tack rag. Continue to varnish, rub down and wipe with a tack rag, for several coats.

▲ Add white eggshell to coloured paints

▲ View the colour through a piece of glass

▲ Stick down any loose edges

WHETHER YOU WANT NEW
GARDEN FURNITURE OR SIMPLY
SOME DECORATION FOR THE PATIO,
RENOVATING OLD JUNK CAN BE
A CHEAP AND FUN SOLUTION.
THIS CHAPTER PROVIDES LOTS OF
INSPIRING PROJECTS THAT CAN
ALL BE EASILY ADAPTED TO CREATE
THE PERFECT FINAL EFFECT FOR
YOUR GARDEN AND HOME.

Garden Projects

Verdigris Metal Table

R OUND METAL TABLES are quite easy to find and are relatively inexpensive, although they may come complete with a coat of paint or rust! This one was in good condition, but it needed rubbing down to roughen the surface ready for the verdigris effect.

The design for the table top is a simple star, completed in alternate sections of ochre mixed with raw umber, and mint-green mixed with cobalt blue. By using deeper tones of colours similar to those already used for the verdigris legs, the star gives unity to the table design as a whole.

❖ YOU WILL NEED ❖

Methylated spirit

Kitchen paper or rag

Wire brush and wire wool

Rust-inhibiting metal primer

Paintbrushes

Water-based gold paint

Brown shellac or french enamel varnish

Varnish brush

Blue-green emulsion paint

Stencil brush

Mint-green emulsion paint

Mutton cloth

Off-white emulsion paint

Acrylic paint in two shades

Acrylic scumble

Water

Water-soluble pencil

Ruler

Straight edge or long ruler

Masking tape

Satin water-based varnish

This metal table was given a coat of verdigris to soften the modern look

1 De-grease the table by wiping it with methylated spirit using kitchen paper or a rag. Use a wire brush, followed by medium wire wool to work off any flakes of paint or rust and wipe down to a clean, smooth surface. Then coat the table with the rust-inhibiting metal primer.

2 Once dry, apply a coat of gold paint to the table and leave to dry, before applying a layer of brown shellac or french enamel varnish over the top to tone it down. Leave to dry thoroughly.

3 Apply blue-green paint sparingly with a stencil brush, using a stippling motion for a textured effect. Leave to dry. Then, with the stencil brush again, dab mint-green paint slightly more generously over the top, allowing patches of blue-green paint to show through.

4 Dip a piece of the mutton cloth in the methylated spirit and dab this over the stippled paint to blend it. Alternatively, if you prefer, you can dab on a dilute wash of dark green acrylic paint and water to strengthen the colour a little.

5 Paint the table top with two or three coats of off-white emulsion paint, allowing each coat to dry thoroughly before applying the next. This provides a more suitable base than brilliant white.

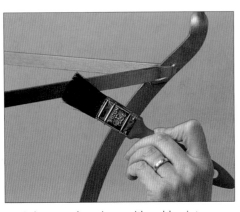

▲ Paint over the primer with gold paint

▲ Apply blue-green paint with a stencil brush

▲ Dab mint-green paint over the blue-green

▲ Blend the colours with mutton cloth

6 Mix two slightly different shades of acrylic paint with acrylic scumble. Add a little water to each so that they both become less jelly-like and are able to hold the brush marks. Brush a thin layer of one colour lightly and in a random way over the table top, so as not to leave obvious brush marks in any particular direction. If you want to eliminate the brush strokes altogether, dab the surface with a clean piece of mutton cloth.

Leave this to dry then brush on the second colour. This process can be repeated until you have the shade you require. Using two colours gives added depth and interest.

7 Mark out the design for the star as shown in the template (p245). Draw a line through the centre

of the circle and a second at right angles. Then add two more lines to divide the circle into eight equal segments. Measure from the centre of each line to about 1.5cm (⅝in) from the edge and mark with a dot. Join the dots with lines as shown. When all the lines are completed, erase those which do not form part of the star.

▲ Apply two or three coats of emulsion

8 Paint the segments of the star with your choice of acrylic colours mixed with acrylic scumble. Mask around each section to be painted, to help guard against runs and spills and keep the edges sharp.

Then dab the surface of the table with a piece of mutton cloth to give a subtle transparent appearance. Protect the table surface with a satin or matt water-based varnish.

HINTS & TIPS

Although this table is ideal for garden lunches, avoid leaving the surface exposed to harsh weather conditions, which will damage the decorative finish.

For further paint effects projects see:
Folding Filigree Screen pp90–91; Picture Frames pp100–105; Stamped Mirror pp110–111; Antiqued Cupboard pp158–160; Ironware Barge Pot pp164–165; Laundry Box pp200–201; Decorative Pots pp236–238

▲ Dab the surface with a mutton cloth

Mosaic Vase

MOSAIC TILES can be used to cheer up many surfaces. Terracotta pots, in particular, make ideal mini projects for mosaic finishes. The jolly, vibrant tiles not only add some colour to the pot, they also conceal knocks and blemishes that are common on old garden containers. Decorated pots are suitable for living plants or even for freshly cut or dried flowers.

This tall container was decorated with a combination of blue and green glass shapes and special mosaic tiles. If preferred, broken pieces of tile or ceramics could be used in place of the mosaic tiles. The vase is completed with some plaster cherubs which are readily available in either gold or verdigris finishes from shops, garden centres and markets or seasonal Christmas stalls.

❖ YOU WILL NEED ❖

Terracotta pot

Damp cloth or sponge

Waterproofing agent

Chalk pencil (optional)

PVA waterproof or tile adhesive

Tile nippers

Goggles

Protective gloves

All-in-one fix and grout

4 plaster verdigris cherubs

Sheet of mosaic tiles

Glass decorative shapes

Clean, lint-free cloth

Adhesive tack

Even a humble terracotta vase can be made into a perfect gift or unusual accessory for a patio or conservatory

▲ Glue the cherubs in place

▲ Cut the mosaic pieces to the correct size

1 Make sure all surfaces of the pot are clean, sound, and free of dust. Then apply two coats of waterproofing agent to the inside of the pot – this will seal the porous terracotta and prevent water seeping out on to the underside of the mosaic and weakening it.

2 If desired, use the PVA adhesive to stick the four cherubs equally spaced around the top rim of the vase. Alternatively, if you plan to create a mosaic pattern, lightly work out the design on the terracotta surface with the chalk pencil.

3 Wearing goggles and protective gloves, use tile nippers to cut the mosaic and glass tiles into the desired shapes. Try to make a variety of shapes, including triangles, small oblongs and squares to increase the interest of the pattern.

▲ Attach the mosaics to the vase

4 Coat a small area of the vase with all-in-one fix and grouting, and place the mosaic pieces into position. The tiles may tend to slide a little until the adhesive sets, so tilt the pot on its side and work in sections. It's a good idea to work from the top down, to ensure the tiles fit evenly.

5 Once the tiles have been positioned on the pot, leave the glue to dry for 24 hours. Then apply grouting over the pot, making sure that all of the small gaps between the tiles are filled. Then wipe down the surface with a damp cloth or sponge to remove any excess grouting and leave to dry overnight.

6 Using PVA adhesive, stick the decorative glass shapes into place around the top rim of the vase (if appropriate) and leave to dry. Buff the mosaic with a clean lint-free cloth to remove any powdery cement film. Allow the pot to dry for a further 48 hours in a warm, dry place before using it outdoors.

HINTS & TIPS

• Sheets of mosaic tiles can be bought from tile stockists or there are mail order companies who specialize in mosaic and mosaic patterns. Alternatively, use any tile or ceramic pieces broken up.

• If you are unsure how to turn the cut mosaic pieces into a design, first experiment with different arrangements, fixing with temporary adhesive tack.

• When using grout on any tiling projects, always wipe off the excess immediately from the surface of the tile. Similarly, any tile repositioning should be completed quickly because adhesive and grouting can be difficult to remove once they have begun to dry.

For further container projects see: Enamel Jug pp132–133; Floral Cutlery Box pp134–135; Ironware Barge Pot pp164–165; Decorative Pots pp236–238

▲ Wipe away excess grouting with a damp sponge

Wooden Trug

THIS ELEGANT TRUG was found at the back of a shed, full of tools and covered in oil. After a scrub down with bleach, the battered remains of a coat of flat paint could be seen over the usual old red ochre primer. This kind of 'distressed' finish is highly coveted, so the outer surfaces were left in their original state but two or three coats of flat emulsion paint were applied to the inner panels. The decoupage Byzantine angels add both an ecclesiastical note and a touch of class.

❖ YOU WILL NEED ❖

Soft cloth and warm water

Tack rag

Coarse, medium and
fine grade abrasive papers

Acrylic sealant

Emulsion paint

Gold poster paint

Paper cut-outs

Adhesive tack

Roller

Matt varnish

Gloss varnish

Varnish brushes

Paintbrush

Glue

Paste brush

1 Although detergents should normally be avoided on ageing wood, they may be necessary for particularly greasy or oily pieces of junk. Once washed off and dry, give the trug a good rub down with coarse, medium and then fine grade abrasive papers. Wipe with a tack rag to remove any dust residue.

2 Apply an acrylic sealant to the outside of the trug and the handle, so that the glue used for the decoupage will not be absorbed by the wood. Paint the inside with two or three coats of green emulsion paint, (this can be mixed at a local paint supplier to match the outer surfaces). Lightly rub down between each coat.

3 When the emulsion paint is fully dry, apply some well-stirred, but undiluted, gold poster paint roughly around the upper rim of the trug and along the edges of the handle. Use your little finger to gently rub into the wood, so that the paint is worn off in places, helping to match the distressed look of the outer panels. Once dry, apply another coat of acrylic sealant to the whole trug, including the rim, inside and outer panels.

4 Cut out the decoupage pieces and experiment with the design by positioning them on the trug with adhesive tack. Then glue the pieces to the outer edges and handle. The angel cut-outs were a little large for the borders so their haloes were folded over the rim of the trug, where they merge well with the gold paint. Use the roller to squeeze out any excess glue and wipe off with a cloth rung out in warm water. Press around the edges once again with a clean fingertip and check for any pieces that are not stuck down. The rim, in particular, may need extra adhesive applied to it.

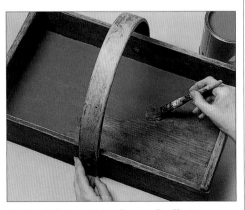
▲ Apply flat emulsion for a soft effect

▲ Wipe off excess glue with a damp cloth

5 For an interesting contrast, apply matt varnish to the inner panels of the trug and gloss varnish on the outer edges. The decoupage will need at least eight coats of varnish to protect the surface whereas the inner panels may only need two or three.

HINTS & TIPS

• Remember to sand down the surface gently between each coat of varnish and to wipe off with a tack rag.

• The decoupage design can be extended to the inside of the trug. However, remember if you do this, the interior will need as many coats of protective varnish as the outer panels.

• Try to choose a design that will suit both the object's environment and fit on the piece comfortably. However, overlapping patterns can create an interesting, repetitive effect on symmetrical objects.

For further decoupage projects see:
Needlecraft Workbox pp98–99; Enamel Jug pp132–133; Floral Cutlery Box pp134–135; Floral Place Mats pp140–141; Freestanding Cabinet pp150–153; Writing Desk pp170–171; Potichomanie Glass Jar pp188–189; Toy Soldier Bedstead pp207–209; Nursery Mirror pp210–211; Doll's cradle pp220–221

Deck Chair

DECK CHAIRS, SUCH AS this one with a useful hood to provide shade, can be given a new lease of life by using some bright, cheerful new canvas. Plain material, stripes, a contemporary pattern or tartan, such as the canvas that was used here, provide an amazing and complete transformation. The old pieces of canvas can be used as a pattern guide for cutting out the new pieces. A dark tinted varnish was applied to the rather tired-looking wood to protect it from the elements and provide a striking contrast to the highly coloured fabric.

❖ YOU WILL NEED ❖

4m (4½yd) deck chair canvas

Pins

Scissors

Strong cotton

Fine grade abrasive paper

Tack rag

Clear, matt polyurethane varnish

Jam jar

Tube of universal stainers (blue)

4cm (1½in) house-painting brush

Round-headed tacks

Glue gun or any strong, colourless glue

2m (2¼yd) cotton tassels

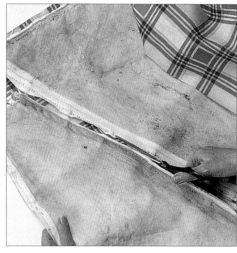
▲ Use the old canvas as a pattern

▲ Tack the new canvas into place

1 Remove the existing canvas very carefully so that the pieces can be used as templates for cutting out the new material. The hood, in particular, must be unstitched and pressed flat. Even the seemingly straight up and down seat has, in fact, been carefully folded so that it tapers towards the front.

2 Pin the old canvas to the new fabric and cut out around the pattern pieces. Then, following the original pattern, pin and tack the various pieces together. Remember to leave an adequate hoop at both ends of the main seat for the wooden cross pieces and to keep checking the hood for a taut fit. Then, using a suitable machine needle, sew the pieces together.

3 Scrub the frame thoroughly to remove the accumulation of dirt. When it is dry, rub it down with some fine grade abrasive paper and wipe over it with the tack rag.

Varnish the frame to protect it from the weather. You can tint the varnish – in this case blue – so that the frame picks up the background colour of the tartan canvas. To do this, decant some of the varnish into a jam jar and mix in a generous squeeze of universal stainers of the right colour.

Give the frame two coats of the coloured varnish, leaving 24 hours' drying time after each application and lightly sanding between coats.

4 When the varnish is fully dry, tack the seat canvas on to the frame with some round-headed tacks and fix the hood on with a tack in each corner.

Finally, using a glue gun (or use another strong glue that dries transparently), fix the yellow tassles around the edge of the hood.

The drab old canvas on this deck chair masked its rather jaunty personality, which is better suited to tartan

Picnic Hamper

THIS BATTERED PICNIC HAMPER was completely covered in dirt and had also been burnt slightly, before it was unearthed in a corner of an old junk store. However, after a good scrub down and couple of coats of paint, it already looked much better. Floral fabric cut-outs were then applied as a variation of the conventional decoupage technique (which usually involves paper). The hamper is now the perfect picnic companion or it can be used as a handy household container. For example, it would make an ideal knitting basket or newspaper tidy.

❖ YOU WILL NEED ❖

Hot soapy water and cloths

Oil-based eggshell paint

House brushes

Scissors

Piece of non-fraying fabric for the decoupage, such as glazed cotton

Adhesive tack

PVA glue

Soft, lint-free cloth

Acrylic craft paint

Artists' paintbrush

Polyurethane clear gloss varnish

1 Scrub the basket thoroughly with hot soapy water, then put it in a warm place and allow to dry thoroughly. Apply two coats of the chosen colour of oil-based eggshell paint, allowing plenty of time to dry between coats.

2 Using small, sharp scissors, cut the design elements from the fabric in exactly the same way as when cutting from paper.
  Arrange the pieces of fabric on the basket and fix them in position with temporary adhesive tack. When you are satisfied with the design, take one piece at a time and paste the back generously with PVA glue.

3 Position the glued cut-out fabric pieces on the basket, pressing them well into the weave with a cloth wrung out in hot water. Take time over this application because the fabric pieces must adhere securely to the basket surface.

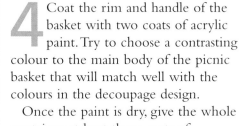

A lick of paint and a floral theme rescued this junk shop discovery

4 Coat the rim and handle of the basket with two coats of acrylic paint. Try to choose a contrasting colour to the main body of the picnic basket that will match well with the colours in the decoupage design.
  Once the paint is dry, give the whole container at least three coats of polyurethane clear gloss varnish. This will protect it from wear and tear and also seal the design in place.

▲ Apply glue to the cut-outs

▲ Wipe a warm damp cloth over the cut-outs

▲ Paint the rim and handle to contrast

Decorative Pots

Brighten up a patio or balcony with these unusual and colourful terracotta flower pots – bold, bright checks in purple and white, a swarm of busy bees stamped on a honey-coloured base coat, an elegant contemporary version of a traditional garlanded pot, and striking, stencilled brilliant red dots on a complementary background. Alternative colour combinations are almost infinite. Always seal the pots inside and out before painting them and protect the decorated surface with two or three coats of varnish before transferring plants to them.

Painted Checks

❖ YOU WILL NEED ❖

24cm (9 in) terracotta pot

All-purpose sealer (water-based)

2.5cm (1in) bristle base-coat brush

Acrylic gouache paints in the following colours: oyster pearl, amethyst, dioxazine purple

Tape measure

Chalk pencil

Masking tape

2cm (½in) flat brush

Satin varnish (water-based)

1 Seal the pot inside and out with all-purpose sealer, and allow it to dry. Using the base-coat brush, apply one or two coats of oyster pearl inside the pot and out.

2 Allow the paint to dry before using the tape measure and chalk pencil to draw the check design on to the pot. To accommodate the shape of the pot, the checks will need to taper upwards: the width should vary from about 4cm (1½in) at the base to about 7cm (2½in) at the rim, and the height of each row should be adjusted so that the squares look even (that is, they should be taller towards the top). Use the masking tape to mask around the outside of the checks that are going to be painted purple.

3 Make the deep blue paint mix using one part amethyst and one part dioxazine purple. With a 2cm (½in) flat brush, paint each blue square. You may need several coats to create a solid colour. When the paint is completely dry, remove the tape. Use the 2cm (½in) flat brush and oyster pearl paint to touch up any marks left by the removal of the tape.

4 Let the pot dry for 24 hours. Apply two or three coats of satin varnish with the varnish brush, letting each one dry completely.

Stamped Bees

❖ YOU WILL NEED ❖

24cm (9in) terracotta pot

All-purpose sealer (water-based)

2.5cm (1in) bristle base-coat brush

Acrylic artists' gouache paint in yellow oxide

Chalk pencil

Stamp (bee)

Waterproof ink stamp (black)

Good quality varnish brush

Satin varnish (water-based)

1 Seal the pot inside and out with all-purpose sealer, and allow it to dry. Then using the base-coat brush, apply one or two coats of yellow oxide paint to the inside and outside of the pot. Allow each one to dry.

2 Use the chalk pencil to mark the positions on the pot where you would like the bees to be placed. (Chalk pencil can be erased afterwards without marking your work.) It is best to use a fairly small stamp, as a larger one is difficult to apply accurately to a curved surface. The bees can be stamped in regular rows, as here, or for a less busy effect, stamp only a few at random over the surface of the pot or just one or two lines around the rim.

3 Then, using a waterproof ink pad, stamp the bees on the marked positions.

4 Let the pot dry for 24 hours. Wipe off any remaining chalk marks. Apply two or three coats of satin varnish with the varnish brush, allowing each one to dry completely. (If you haven't used a waterproof ink pad, apply two or three coats of spray varnish instead.)

Cord Trim

24cm (9in) terracotta pot

All-purpose sealer (water-based)

2.5cm (1in) bristle base-coat brush

Artists' acrylic gouache paint in

iridescent copper

Cotton cord

Rubber gloves

Plastic cloth or placemat

PVA glue

Good quality varnish brush

Satin varnish (water-based)

1 Seal the pot inside and out with all-purpose sealer and allow it to dry completely. Using the base-coat brush, apply one or two coats of iridescent copper paint to both the inside and outside of the pot.

2 Wrap the cord around the rim of the pot in order to determine the length required. Cut this and then measure and cut off enough cord to make half a bow with a trailing tail. Then cut off enough cord to make the centre of the bow.

3 Wearing rubber gloves and working on the plastic cloth, use the PVA glue to cover all the lengths of cord. As the glue begins to dry, wrap the first length around the rim of the pot, pressing it down firmly.

4 Start to shape the bow from the other two lengths of cord with your fingers. When the bow can hold its own shape, apply it to the pot. Once dry, coat the cord and bow with iridescent copper paint. Finally, leave the pot to dry for at least 24 hours before applying a coat of varnish.

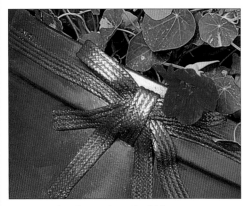

▲ Paint the decorative trim iridescent copper

Stencilled Dots

24cm (9in) terracotta pot

All-purpose sealer (water-based)

2.5cm (1in) bristle base-coat brush

Acrylic gouache paints in the following colours:

teal, naphthol red light

Felt-tip pen

Stencil blanks

Craft knife and cutting mat

Masking tape

Stencil brush

Kitchen paper

Good quality varnish brush

Satin varnish (water-based)

1 Seal the pot before applying one or two coats of teal paint to both the inside and outside of the pot.

2 Using the felt-tip pen, draw around one small circular object, such as a coin, and one larger circular object, such as a small cup, on the stencil blanks to create the dot stencil. Carefully cut this out using the craft knife and cutting mat.

3 Position the stencil on the side of the pot, and secure it in place with a small piece of masking tape. Dip the stencil brush into the naphthol red light paint. Dab the brush onto the kitchen paper to eliminate excess paint. Apply paint over the stencil, working in a circular motion to build up the depth of colour. Let it dry, move the stencil and repeat until the pot is covered. Leave to dry for 24 hours before applying two or three coats of satin varnish, allowing each application to dry.

HINTS & TIPS

• Always dab off excess paint on to kitchen paper. The bristles of the stencil brush should be almost dry, otherwise paint can seep under the edges of the stencil and spoil the design. Achieve depth of colour by repeated painting on the surface.

• Decorated pots for outdoor use will be better protected if they are varnished with an oil-based or weatherproof varnish. However, check that the varnish is compatible with the paint beneath.

▲ Contrasting colours create a lively look

Glossary

THE RANGE OF DIFFERENT materials that can be used for basic repairs and decorative techniques is vast. Whatever equipment, tool or product you plan to use, be sure to follow manufacturer's guidelines. Always wear appropriate safety equipment and work in ventilated areas.

ABRASIVE PAPER
Available in a range of fine, medium or coarse varieties, this paper is used to prepare a surface for decoration, to distress paint, and to smooth paints and varnishes. See also, silicone carbide finishing papers.

ACETATE
Used in stencilling as an alternative to oiled manila card. Designs must be traced on to acetate using a permanent marker pen.

ACRYLIC GOLDSIZE
A water-based size often used for gilding and metal leaf application. It appears milky on first application but dries to a transparent finish.

ACRYLIC PRIMER
A quick-drying primer that can be used to seal wood. Some brands may also be used on metal and masonry.

ACRYLIC SCUMBLE
A slow-drying, water-based glaze medium, which can be mixed with colour and used for stippling and sponging techniques.

ANTIQUING
The act of making an object look older than it really is. There are various techniques, including the use of colour and stains, craquelure and distressing.

ARTISTS' ACRYLIC PAINT
Quick-drying and durable, these paints are suitable for many types of surface decoration, and can be used to colour acrylic glazes.

ARTISTS' BRUSHES
Finer tipped than house decorating brushes, artists' brushes can be used for intricate painting and are available in a variety of sizes and qualities.

ARTISTS' OIL COLOURS
More slow-drying than acrylics, these paints can be mixed to a range of subtle colours and are suitable for most techniques, providing the surface is oil-based. The paints can also be used to colour oil-based glazes.

BASE COAT
The initial, base application of paint to a surface.

BLACK BISON WAX
A blend of several waxes with good resistance to water and fingermarks, suitable for applying to painted furniture. It creates a seal for crackled and peeled-paint techniques, and also enhances the ageing effect.

CHINA FILLER
Used to fill missing edges, cracks and chips on china, this filler dries to a fine, hard finish on most types of chinaware.

CRACKLE GLAZE
A water-soluble glaze that is applied as a sandwich between two layers of paint or between wood and paint. It dries clear but causes the paint applied over the top to crack, giving the appearance of peeling paint.

CRAQUELURE
The French name for the fine cracks that often cover old oil paintings. The cracks are formed by the layers of paint beneath the varnish surface gradually shrinking. The effect can be imitated by using two part crackle glaze.

DECOUPAGE
The French art of cutting, pasting and varnishing paper or fabric images to form a decorated finish.

DISTRESSING
The action of rubbing down and battering a surface to imitate age and wear and tear.

EMULSION PAINT
Available in matt or satin finishes, this paint has a tough, plastic waterproof finish when dry. It can be used as a paint, thinned with water to make a wash or tinted with acrylic paints, universal stainers or powder pigments to make a range of decorative colours.

ENAMEL PAINTS
Very smooth and fairly quick drying, these paints are suitable for projects such as barge painting. They have their own cellulose thinners to act as a solvent, but white spirit can be used as an alternative.

GESSO
Made from rabbit skin size and gilders' whiting, gesso is used as a preparation before water gilding. It can also be used to fill the grain on unpainted wood, before being rubbed down to a fine, smooth finish.

GILDING
A decorative technique involving transfer leaf, gilding cream or gilding powder to imitate a metallic finish such as gold.

GILDING POWDER
Painted on to tacky size, gilding powder creates a gold, silver, bronze or copper finish. It can also be mixed with medium to make a metallic paint.

GILT CREAM
This cream can be used as a highlighting agent, or to touch up gilding on frames and furniture. It is applied either by brush or finger and then buffed to a shine, once dry.

GLASS PAINTS
Made with resins that give a brilliant, transparent and durable finish to most glass, plastic or acetate surfaces. However, test plastic surfaces to ensure they are compatible with the paint.

HOG-FITCHES
Good all-purpose brushes, hog-fitches can be used for applying paint, glue, waxes and gilt creams. They are also effective for tamping down metal leaf and painting narrow bands of colour.

HOUSEHOLD BRUSHES
Broader and coarser than artists' brushes, these brushes are suitable for painting fairly large surfaces and come in a variety of sizes.

KEY
Rubbing a surface down to make another coat of paint or varnish adhere properly is known as 'keying'. Use fine grade abrasive paper and a tack rag.

LACQUER
Available in spray or liquid form, lacquer provides a protective varnished surface. Always apply several fine coats, rather than one heavy coat, to avoid runs and a build-up of varnish.

LIMING WAX
A rich paste of clear wax and white pigment used to give a pickled-lime effect to wood. It can also be used as a finishing wax. After opening the grain of the wood with a wire brush, apply the paste with fine wire wool or a cloth. Remove the excess with a cloth and then buff up with a neutral wax to obtain a sheen.

MDF
Medium density fibreboard (often known as MDF) is made from wood fibres that have been highly compressed to create a smooth finish. It comes in different thicknesses, can be bought in various-sized sheets and is easy to cut. Always use a protective mask when cutting or sanding MDF.

MEDIUM
A liquid in which pigment is suspended.

METHYLATED SPIRIT
Used as a solvent for emulsion paint when creating a distressed effect, methylated spirit can also be used as a thinner and a brush cleaner for shellac and french enamel varnish. It can also be used with fine wire wool for de-greasing surfaces.

MUTTON CLOTH OR STOCKINET
Ideal for polishing and mopping up, these cloths can also be used to create texture on a painted surface and for eliminating brush marks.

OIL-BASED HOUSEHOLD PAINTS
Available in flat, eggshell and gloss finishes, oil-based paints give a much tougher finish than emulsion paints and are particularly useful in light-coloured, oil-based glazes. They can be tinted with artists' oil paints or universal stainers to create an even more diverse range of colours.

OIL-BASED PRIMER
A slow-drying, durable primer which is useful for surfaces that do not easily accept or grip acrylic primers, such as some metal and plastic surfaces.

OIL-BASED VARNISH
A slow-drying varnish, available in a polyurethane or alkyd formula. It comes in matt, satin and gloss finishes and is generally more durable and heat-proof than water-based varnish, although it does yellow with time. Water-soluble crackle varnish finishes should always be sealed with a protective coat of oil-based varnish.

PAINT STRIPPERS
Use these for varnished or painted surfaces that need to be taken right back to the original wood. Always work with plenty of ventilation and follow the manufacturer's guidelines.

PALETTE KNIFE
Useful for applying filler, mixing paints, or even applying paint, these knives are very flexible and available from most art shops.

PERMANENT INK PENS
Essential for marking designs on stencil film, these pens are permanent, do not smudge, and create clear outlines.

POWDERED PIGMENTS
Natural earth and mineral pigments in powder form can be mixed with other paint colours, acrylic and PVA mediums, and wax.

PRIMER
Usually oil-based but sometimes available as acrylic, primer should be applied to all raw wood or metal surfaces before painting.

PVA & ACRYLIC MEDIUMS
These water-based mediums are coloured white but dry transparent. PVA can be used as a glue or varnish and, when thinned with water, as a paint medium or binder. It can also be mixed with acrylic, gouache, universal stainers or powder pigments to make paints and washes. Artists' acrylic mediums are very useful for extending acrylic paints and for mixing with pure powder pigment to make concentrated colour.

RABBIT SKIN GLUE
This is used as a preparation for gesso, a base for gilding, and as a sealant to stop varnish and water penetrating the paper.

RAGGING
This refers to a range of decorative finishes in which a scrunched cloth (ragging) or plastic bag (bagging) are used to make patterns in wet glaze.

ROTTENSTONE
A finely ground, greyish-brown limestone powder. It is usually used for polishing but can also be used as a powder pigment, especially for antiquing stains.

RUST-INHIBITING PRIMER
An essential base for any piece of metal that is to be coated in a water-based paint, or that has been cleaned and rubbed down of existing rust.

SANDING SEALER
Spirit-based, sanding sealer is useful for sealing new, stripped, dark or heavily knotted wood, before paint is applied. It is an excellent sealing base for decoupage projects and can be used before waxing to give a good base for the final wax sheen.

SCALPEL KNIFE
Needed for cutting stencils, cardboard templates and decoupage cut-outs. Replace blades regularly and use in conjunction with a self-healing cutting mat.

SCUMBLE GLAZE
A medium to which paint is added to suspend the colour and delay drying time. Various decorative effects can be achieved while this glaze is wet.

SEA SPONGES
These sponges have a better absorbency and more natural structure than synthetic sponges, so are ideal for creating attractive decorative patterns.

SHELLAC
The naturally occurring resin of the lac beetle, shellac is mixed with methylated spirit to form a quick-drying varnish. It is traditionally used in furniture restoration and french polishing. Shellac is available in a variety of grades and colours and may be sold under a number of different names. Use clear shellac sanding sealer, white french polish and white button polish for sealing wood, paper and paint. Use brown french polish or garnet polish for staining, ageing and sealing. French enamel varnish is transparent shellac with added dye, and is good for ageing and sealing wood.

SILICON CARBIDE FINISHING PAPERS
Sometimes known as wet-and-dry papers, these papers are obtainable in much finer grades than normal abrasive sheets. They are used to give a smooth finish to varnish, or distress a painted surface without causing scratches.

SOFTENING
A term used to refer to the 'blurring' of paint, colour or glaze edges. Soft brushes or cloths are used to blend the colours and soften the division.

SOFT-HAIRED MOP BRUSHES
These round brushes are often used in gilding because they are ideal for dusting gilding powder on to goldsize. A soft squirrel paintbrush can be used as a cheap alternative.

SPONGING
A simple decorative technique involving the application of paint with a sponge. Sponges can also be used to lift off wet paint from a surface, creating an attractive, textured effect.

SPRAY PAINT
Ideal for stencilling projects, acrylic spray paints can be used on most surface types, including wood, plaster and plastic. Spray enamels for metals and glass, including pearlized finishes and polyurethane varnishes, are also available. Apply the paint in several thin coats, rather than one heavy one, to avoid paint build-up and runs.

STENCILLING
The technique of applying a design to a surface using thin film or card. The design is cut into the stencil card, and then paint is applied through the incisions, on to the surface.

STENCIL BRUSHES
Usually made from hog's hair, stencil brushes are round and firm-bristled, and come in a wide range of sizes for both small

and large stencil work. When stencilling with acrylic paint, choose brushes that have a little 'give' in the bristles, rather than the very firm variety. A double-ended stencil brush is particularly useful when using two colours. Special stencil brushes for use on fabrics are also available; these have softer, longer bristles but are not suitable for hard surfaces.

STENCIL FILM
Made from transparent polyester sheeting, stencil film is very flexible and durable.

STENCIL PAINT AND STICKS
Water-based acrylic or oil-based stencil paint can be obtained in small pots. Stencil sticks are oil-based and wrapped in a sealed film. They are very versatile and can be blended to make different shades and colours.

STIPPLING
The term used for finely lifting on or off very fine speckles of paint.

STIPPLING BRUSHES
Stippling brushes have stiff, dense bristles in a squared-off shape. They are useful for merging paints and removing hard lines and edges.

SWORD LINERS
These long-haired, soft brushes are tapered and angled, and are capable of producing many widths of line simply by varying the pressure applied to the brush stroke.

TACK RAGS
These are small, versatile, long-lasting oily cloths that are ideal for cleaning wood, metal, plaster or any other surface (except glass). They pick up and hold dust and dirt, leaving a completely clean surface, ready to work on.

TRADITIONAL PAINT
Containing natural pigments and chalk, traditional paints dry to a completely matt finish that appears considerably lighter than the colour in the pot. They can be easily marked, however, and so should be protected with a coat of varnish or wax. The paints can be thinned with water and tinted in the same way as emulsion paint.

TRANSFER METAL LEAF
Bronze, aluminium and copper leaf are inexpensive and a good substitute for real gold and silver leaf, when adding decorative touches to furniture. Transfer leaf, which is sold in packs of 25 sheets, is available from specialist art shops. Each sheet consists of very finely beaten metal backed with waxed paper. The metal is transferred from the paper on to tacky size. Metal leaf tarnishes in time, so it needs to be sealed with shellac or varnish.

TRANSFER PAPER
Coated with a chalky film, transfer paper is coloured red, blue, black and white. It is placed between the design to be transferred and the surface to be decorated. The outline is then transferred by tracing over it with a pen or pencil.

TWO-PART CRACKLE VARNISH
This consists of a slow-drying, oil-based varnish and a quick-drying, water-soluble varnish. The water-soluble varnish is brushed over a layer of very slightly tacky oil-based varnish. A short time later, a cracked porcelain effect appears due to the difference in drying times. This becomes clearly visible when artists' oil colour is rubbed into the surface and gets caught in the cracks.

UNDERCOAT
A layer of protective paint applied between primer and final surface paint.

UNIVERSAL STAINERS
Although universal stainers lack the range of subtle colours of oil and emulsion paints, they will mix with virtually anything, including both water-based and oil-based mediums. They come in liquid form, are extremely strong and are cheap to obtain.

VARNISH REMOVERS
A number of varnish removers are available although most paint strippers can also be used on varnished surfaces.

VERDIGRIS
A bluish-green patina which forms on copper, bronze or brass with age. The effect is associated with historic spires and domes, but can be imitated with paint and gilding cream.

WATER-BASED VARNISH
Water-based acrylic varnishes are now widely available in gloss, satin, matt and occasionally flat finishes. Although they are milky in appearance, these varnishes dry to a clear finish and are non-yellowing. However, the matt and flat versions contain chalk which gives them a cloudy appearance when a number of coats are applied. This means they are unsuitable to use for the many layers that are required in decoupage. These finishes are also softer and less durable than satin or gloss varnish.

WAXES
Clear furniture wax is an effective resist (that is, it creates a block, preventing paint from reaching a surface), when creating an aged appearance to furniture. It can be used over paint or wood to prevent a new layer of paint from adhering to the surface. Clear liquid wax is particularly good for this and is obtainable from specialist suppliers. Clear wax is also used as a protective finishing wax over paint or matt varnish; it can be coloured with rottenstone and other pigments.

There is also a large variety of brown or antiquing furniture waxes that can be used for staining wood. Walnut shades are good for ageing all colours of paint, but the antiquing waxes are generally yellowing and are not suitable on blue paint. However, they give a wonderful glow to many shades of yellow and green paint.

WET-AND-DRY PAPER
See silicon carbide finishing paper.

WHITE SPIRIT
This is used as a thinner for oil-based paint and transparent oil glaze, as well as for brushes, and to clean or remove splashes and spills of oil-based paint.

WIRE BRUSHES
These are used to open up the grain on wood before liming and to remove flaking paint and rust.

WIRE WOOL
There are various grades of wire wool, from very fine (0000) to coarse (00). It can be used for cleaning wood, metal and glass, for applying wax, and for distressing painted surfaces. Fine wire wool does not scratch or mark wood if it is used gently, and can help to create a very smooth finish. Soaked in white spirit or warm water, it is very useful for cleaning wooden furniture. If it is used with varnish and paint removers, wear protective gloves and always cover the surrounding area to catch the fine steel filaments that come away as the wool is rubbed.

WOOD FILLER
Specialist wood fillers tend to be better for wooden surfaces than ordinary, multipurpose fillers. Water-based varieties are particularly easy to use and come in a variety of wood colour finishes. They can be used to fill small holes, dents and cracks, as well as seal around bad joints and joins in wood.

Templates

Vine Leaf Table
pp114–117

Display Decanter and Glasses
pp124–125

Vine Leaf Table
pp114–117

Scandinavian Scroll Chair
pp147–149

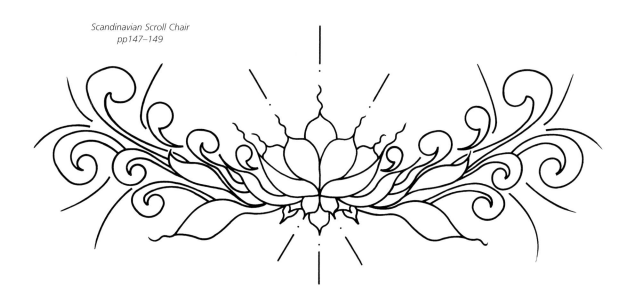

Cherub Wardrobe 1
pp182–185

Cherub Wardrobe 2

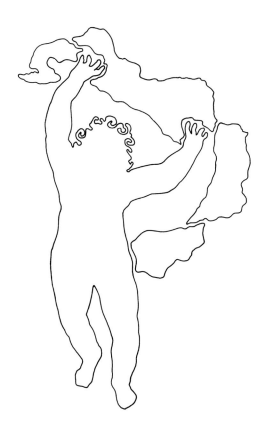

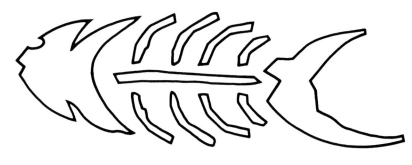

Seashore Cabinet
pp192–194

兜 术 影

Oriental Chair
pp121–123

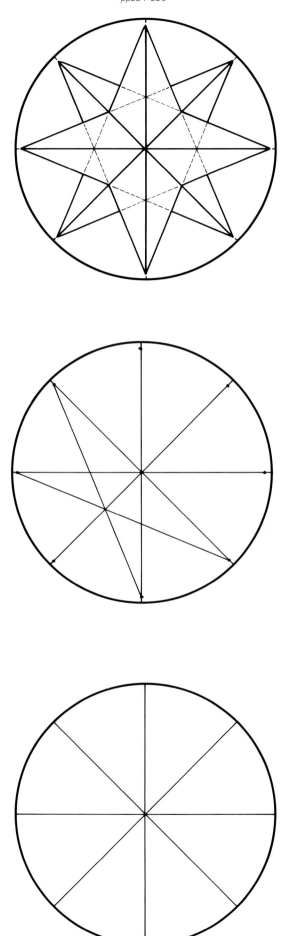

Verdigris Table
pp224–226

Bedside Chest
pp175–177

Bedside Chest
pp175–177

Laquered Butler Tray
pp129–131

The following pages contain various templates
that could be used for a range of stencilling projects.

AABBCDDEEFFGG
HHIIJJKKLLMM
NNOPPQQRRSSTT
ThUVUWXYZZ

abcdee fghijkklm
nopqrstuvwxyz

1234567890

(&$$¢¢/.,.:;?!-'""*)

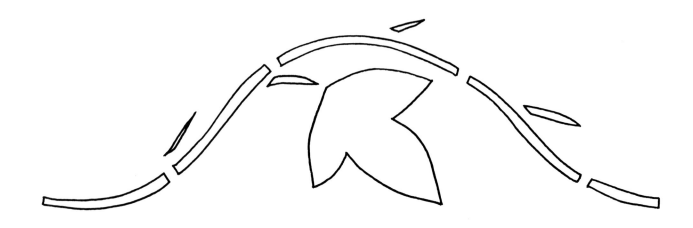

Suppliers

ARIEL PRESS
177-179 Clapham Manor Street
London
SW4 6DB
020 7720 4967/4622

THE ART & STATIONERY CENTRE
15 The Broadway
Tolworth
Surrey
KT6 7DJ
020 8390 8977

B&Q PLC
(HEAD OFFICE)
Portswood House
1 Hampshire Corporate Park
Chandlers Ford
Eastleigh
SO53 3YX
020 8877 3699

BARGAIN HUNTERS
162 High Road, East Finchley
London
N2 9AS
020 8444 2024

OLIVER BONAS
10 Kensington Church Street
London
W8
020 7368 0035

BORDERLINE FABRICS
1 Munro Terrace
London
SW10 0DL
020 7823 3567

C. BREWERS & SONS LTD
86-88 Ewell Road
Surbiton
Surrey
KT6 6EX
020 8399 1054

BRODIE & MIDDLETON
68 Drury Lane
London
WC2 5SP
020 7836 3289

**CHANCELLOR'S CHURCH
FURNISHINGS**
173 Earlsfield Road
London
SW18 3DD
020 7385 7480
(appointment only)

COLOGNE & COTTON
791 Fulham Road
London
SW6
020 7736 9261

CREATIVE INTERIORS
20 Station Parade
Chipstead
Surrey
CR5 3TE
01737 555443

DAMASK
Broxhulme House
New Kings Road
London
SW6
020 7731 3553

H.W. DAVIES & SON LTD
Decorator's Merchants
19a Monmouth Place
Bath
BA1 2AY
01225 425638

E.K.A SERVICES LTD
11 & 12 Hampton Court Parade
East Molesey
Surrey
KT8 9HB
020 8979 3466

ELEPHANT
94 Tottenham Court Road
London
W1
020 7813 2092

FOCUS DO IT ALL
(HEAD OFFICE)
Falcon House
The Minories
Dudley
West Midlands
DY2 8PG
01384 456456

FOXELL & JAMES
57 Farringdon Road
London
EC1M 3JH
020 7405 0152

GREAT MILLS RETAIL LTD
(HEAD OFFICE)
RMC House
Old Mills Trading Estate
Old Mills
Paulton
Bristol
BS18 5SX
01761 416034

GREEN & STONE
259 Kings Road
London
SW3 5ER
020 7352 0837

HALL & CO. TOOL HIRE
Wolseley Centres Ltd
P.O. Box 21
Borough Bridge Road
Rippen
North Yorkshire
HG4 1SL

HOMEBASE LTD
(HEAD OFFICE)
Beddington House
Wallington
Surrey
SN6 0HB
020 8784 7200

HSS HIRE SHOPS
25 Willow Lane
Mitchum
Surrey
CR4 4TS
020 8260 3100

JALI
Apsley House
Chartham
Canterbury
Kent
CT4 7HT
01227 831710

JERRY'S HOME STORE
163-167 Fulham Road
London
SW3 6SN
020 7581 0909

MCCLOUD & CO.
269 Wandsworth Bridge Road
London
SW6
020 7371 7151

PAPER & PAINTS
4 Park Walk
London
SW10 0AD
020 7352 8626

THE PIER
200 Tottenham Court Road
London
W1
020 7637 7001

PLASTICOTE
London Road Industrial Estate
Sawston
Cambridgeshire
CB2 4TR
01223 836400

PLOTONS
273 Archway
London
N6 5AA
020 8348 0315

REDBURN CRAFTS
The Craft & Needlecraft Centre
Squires Garden Centre
Halliford Road
Upper Halliford
Shepperton
Middlesex
TW17 8RU
01932 788052

RELICS
35 Bridge Street
Witney
Oxfordshire
OX8 6DA
01993 704611
(worldwide mail order service)

ROMANTIQUE MOSAICS
12–13 Pulteney Bridge
Bath
BA2 4AY
01225 463073

ROMO FABRICS
Lowmoor Road
Kirkby-in-Ashfield
Nottinghamshire
NG17 7DE
01623 750005

ARTHUR SANDERSON & SONS LTD
6 Cavendish Square
London
W1M 9HA
020 7636 7800

STUART STEVENSON, ARTISTS' & GILDERS' SUPPLIERS
68 Clerkenwell Road
London
EC1M 5QA
020 7253 1693

SOUTHSIDE STRIPPERS
Unit 9
Glenville Mews
Kimber Road
Wandsworth
London
SW18 4NJ
020 8875 0866

TRADITIONS
259 Ewell Road
Surbiton
Surrey
KT6 7AA
020 8390 4472

WINSOR & NEWTON
Whitefriars Avenue
Wealdstone
Harrow
Middlesex
HA3 5RH
020 8427 4343

AUSTRALIA

ECKERSLEY'S
93 York Street
Sydney
NSW 2000
(02) 9299 4151

GEELONG ST ANTIQUE CENTRE
2 Geelong Street
Fyshwick
ACT 2609
(02) 6280 7005

HAYMES PAINTS
25 Scott Parade
Ballarat Vic. 3350
(03) 5332 1234

LANGRIDGE ARTIST'S COLOURS
120 Langridge Street
Collingwood Vic. 3066
(03) 9419 4453

OXFORD ART SUPPLIES
221-223 Oxford Street
Darlinghurst
NSW 2011
(02) 9360 4066

PADDINGHURST GALLERY
32 Oxford Street
Paddington NSW 2021
(02) 9331 7818

PORTER'S ORIGINAL PAINTS
592 Willoughby Road
Willoughby NSW 2068
(02) 9958 0753

WARDLAW PTY LTD
(suppliers of Designers Guild)
NSW (02) 9660 6266
Vic. (03) 9819 4233
Qld. (07) 3257 1642
SA (08) 8332 2111
WA (08) 9283 4833

USA

ARTCRAFT ETC
(Cottage Furniture & Accessories)
802 Bittersweet
Joplin MO 64801
(417) 782 7063

BARBARA ISRAEL
21 East 79th Street
New York NY 10021
(212) 744 6281

CALICO CORNERS
203 Gale Lane
Kennett Square
PA 19348
(800) 213 6366

CRATE & BARREL
P.O. Box 9059
Wheeling
IL 60090–9059
(800) 451 8217

GAIL GRISI STENCILLING, INC.
P.O. Box 1263
Haddonfield
NJ 08033
(856) 354 1757

HOUSE PARTS
479 Whitehall Street SW
Atlanta GA 30303
(404) 577 5584

CANADA

ADELE BISHOP STENCIL INC.
3430 South Service Road
Burlington ON L7N 3T9
Canada
(905) 681 2055

Credits

*Some of the contents and projects in this book
have been previously published in the following titles:*

New Style For Old Junk by Julie Collins
(photography by Graeme Ainscough)

Decorative Decoupage by Joanna Jones
(photography by Jon Bouchier)

Doing Up Old Junk by Joanna Jones
(photography by Jon Bouchier)

Decorative Painted Furniture by Maggie Philo
(photography by Jon Bouchier & Anna Hodgson)

Decorative Stencilling by Katrina Hall &
Lawrence Llewelyn Bowen (photography by Jon Bouchier)

Furniture Makeovers in a Weekend by Alice Hamilton
(photography by William Douglas)

The Nursery in a Weekend by Roo Ryde
(photography by Dominic Blackmore)

Making Beautiful Trims, Edges & Finishing Touches
projects by Sabina Robba (p105 bottom), Frances Robinson
(pp103, 105 top, 139, 237) and Tony Robinson (p213)

Illustrations on pp16–29 by Stephen Pollitt

Text on pp32–41, 72–73, 129–131, 158–160, 192–194,
204–206, 224–226 by Maggie Philo

Text on pp 90–97, 114–128, 136–137, 144–149, 161–163,
168–169, 182–185, 195–199, 207–209, 227–229 by Julie Collins

Text on pp42–47, 98–99, 134–135, 154–157, 164–165, 170–171,
175–177, 186–189, 210–211, 220–221, 230–235 by Joanna Jones

Text on pp58–59, 60–65, 106–107, 110–111, 140–141,
200–201 by Salli Brand

Text on pp48–56 by Katrina Hall and Laurence Llewelyn Bowen

Text on pp108–109,150–153, 178–181, 218–219 by Alice Hamilton

Text on pp214–217 by Roo Ryde

Index